I0120965

Introduction to
Sociology

Ryan T. Cragun
Assistant Professor of Sociology, University of Tampa

Deborah Cragun
MS Human Genetics;
Visiting Professor, University of Tampa

Originally published on Wikibooks.org
Wikibooks is a project of the Wikimedia Foundation
THIS PUBLICATION IS NOT OFFICIALY
SPONSORED BY WIKIBOOKS OR WIKIPEDIA

Published by
Seven Treasures Publications

Published by
Seven Treasures Publications
SevenTreasuresPublications@gmail.com
Fax 413-653-8797

Printed in the United States of America

ISBN 978-0-9800707-7-4

Introduction to Sociology

Edition 1.0 6th March 2006

From Wikibooks, the open-content textbooks collection

Contents

INTRODUCTION TO SOCIOLOGY 1
AUTHORS...6
INTRODUCTION 7
    Introduction...7
    What is Sociology?...7
    History...8
    Sociology and Other Social Sciences 11
    Sociology Today..13
    Technology and the Social Sciences..13
    References..13
    External links 14
SOCIOLOGICAL METHODS 15
    Introduction...15
    The Development of Social Science 16
    The Scientific Method..17
    Correlation and Causation 21
    Quantitative and Qualitative...23
    Objective vs. Critical..24
    Ethics..24
    What Can Sociology Tell Us? 25
    Notes 26
    References..26
    External Links 26
GENERAL SOCIOLOGICAL THEORY 27
    Introduction...27
    Structural-Functionalism 28
    Conflict Theory 30
    Symbolic Interactionism...31
    Role Theory..32
    Social Constructionism 34
    Integration Theory 34
    Notes 35
    References..35
    External Links 36
SOCIETY 38
    Introduction...38
    Societal Development...38
    Classical Views on Social Change 44
    Notes 47
    References..47
    External Links 48
CULTURE 50
    Introduction...50
    Subcultures & Countercultures...53
    Ethnocentrism & Cultural Relativism..54
    Theories of Culture 55
    Cultural Change...56
    Cultural Sociology: Researching Culture 57
    Notes 58
    References..58
    External links 59

SOCIALIZATION 60
    What is Socialization?...60
    Elements of Socialization..60
    Theoretical Understandings of Socialization..64
    Research Examples..65
    Notes..67
    References..67
    History...68
GROUPS 69
    Introduction...69
    Social Identity Theory..71
    Primary and Secondary Groups...74
    Leadership...75
    Conformity..75
    Reference Groups..75
    Ingroups and Outgroups...75
    Group Size..75
    Networks...80
    Notes..84
    References..84
    External Links...85
DEMOGRAPHY 87
    Introduction...87
    Why study demography?...87
    History...87
    Data and Methods...87
    The Demographic Transition..92
    Population Growth and Overpopulation...94
    Notes..99
    References..99
    External Links...100
HUMAN SEXUALITY 102
DEVIANCE AND NORMS 102
    Introduction...102
    Theories of Deviance...103
    Crime Statistics..107
    Social Control..116
    Notes..117
    References..117
    History...117
    External Links...117
SOCIAL PSYCHOLOGY 118
    Subfields..118
    SP's three angles of research...118
    The concerns of social psychology..119
    Empirical methods..120
    Relation to other fields...121
    Major perspectives in social psychology..125
    Well-known cases, studies, and related works...130
    History...131
    References..131
    Related topics..131
AGEING...132
RACE AND ETHNICITY 133

Race and Ethnicity *133*
The Changing Definitions of Race *133*
Social Construct or Biological Lineage? *135*
Prejudice, Bias, and Discrimination *140*
Racism *141*
Notes *145*
References *145*
External links *146*
GENDER 148
Gender vs. Sex *148*
Biological Differences *150*
Social and Psychological Differences *151*
Sexism *152*
Gender Theory *153*
Research Examples *156*
Notes *156*
References *156*
External Links *157*
STRATIFICATION 159
Introduction *159*
Objective vs. Subjective Poverty *159*
Socioeconomic Status *160*
Global Inequality *160*
U.S. Inequality *162*
Theories of Stratification *162*
Notes *166*
References *167*
External Links *167*
ORGANIZATIONS 168
FAMILY 168
Family cross-culturally *168*
Family in the West *169*
Economic role of the family *170*
Kinship terminology *170*
Western kinship terminology *171*
See also *173*
References *174*
External links *174*
THE ECONOMY 175
RELIGION 176
Introduction *176*
Definitions of Religion *176*
The Church-Sect Typology *178*
Theories of Religion *181*
World Religions and Religious History *185*
Religion and Other Social Factors *186*
The Future of Religion *188*
Notes *191*
References *191*
External Links *193*
POLITICS 193
GOVERNMENT 193
MEDIA 193
EDUCATION 194

4

Overview *194*
Origins of the Word "Education" *194*
Formal Education *194*
Technology and Education *195*
History of education *195*
Challenges in education *195*
Parental involvement *197*
References *197*
HEALTH AND MEDICINE 198
Introduction *198*
The Evolution of Health Care and Medicine *199*
Health Disparities *203*
Paying for Medical Care *206*
Behavior and Environmental Influences on Health *214*
References *221*
External links *222*
COLLECTIVE BEHAVIOUR 224
Introduction *224*
Crowds *224*
Theories of Crowd Behavior *225*
Diffuse Crowds *226*
Research Examples *227*
Notes *227*
References *227*
External Links *228*
SOCIAL MOVEMENTS 229
Introduction *229*
Types of Social Movements *229*
Stages in Social Movements *230*
Social Movement Theories *231*
Examples of Social Movements *235*
Notes *235*
References *235*
External Links *236*
HUMAN ECOLOGY 237
LICENSE 238
GNU Free Documentation License *238*
0. PREAMBLE *238*
1. APPLICABILITY AND DEFINITIONS *238*
2. VERBATIM COPYING *239*
3. COPYING IN QUANTITY *239*
4. MODIFICATIONS *239*
5. COMBINING DOCUMENTS *240*
6. COLLECTIONS OF DOCUMENTS *240*
7. AGGREGATION WITH INDEPENDENT WORKS *241*
8. TRANSLATION *241*
9. TERMINATION *241*
10. FUTURE REVISIONS OF THIS LICENSE *241*
External links *241*

5

Authors

- <u>Exmoron</u> Ryan T. Cragun, PhD student at the University of Cincinnati

- Contribution: Initial book layout and the development of most of the first 15 chapters

- <u>Deborahcragun</u> Deborah Cragun, MS Human Genetics; employed as a genetic counselor at Cincinnati Children's Hospital Medical Center

- Contribution: Developed the chapters on health care and medicine and race and ethnicity.

Introduction

Introduction

Sociology is the study of human social life. Because human social life is so expansive, sociology has many sub-sections of study, ranging from the analysis of conversations to the development of theories to try to understand how the entire world works. This chapter will introduce you to sociology and explain why it is important, how it can change your perspective of the world around you, and give a brief history of the discipline.

What is Sociology?

The social world is changing. Some argue it is growing; others say it is shrinking. The important point to grasp is: society does not remain unchanged over time. As will be discussed in more detail below, sociology has its roots in significant societal changes (e.g., the industrial revolution, the creation of empires, and the enlightenment of scientific reasoning). Early practitioners developed the discipline as an attempt to understand societal changes.

Some early sociological theorists (e.g., Marx, Weber, and Durkheim) were disturbed by the social processes they believed to be driving the change, such as the quest for solidarity, the attainment of social goals, and the rise and fall of classes, to name a few examples. While details of the theories that these individuals developed are discussed later in this book, it is important to note at this point that the founders of sociology were some of the earliest individuals to employ what C. Wright Mills (1959) labeled the *sociological imagination*: the ability to situate personal troubles within an informed framework of social issues.

Mills proposed that "[w]hat the [people] need... is a quality of mind that will help them to use information and to develop reason in order to achieve lucid summations of what is going on in the world and of what may be happening within themselves. The sociological imagination enables its possessor to understand the larger historical scene in terms of its meaning for the inner life and the external career of a variety of individuals" (Mills 1959). As Mills saw it, the sociological imagination could help individuals cope with the social world by helping them to step outside of their personal worldview and thus seeing the events and social structure that influence their behavior, attitudes, and culture.

The sociological imagination goes beyond *armchair sociology* or *common sense*. Most people believe they understand the world and the events taking place within it. Humans like to attribute causes to events and attempt to understand what is taking place around them. This is why individuals have been using religious ceremonies for centuries to invoke the will of the gods - because they believed the gods controlled certain elements of the natural world (e.g., the weather). Just as the rain dance is an attempt to understand how the weather works without using empirical analysis, *armchair sociology* is an attempt to understand how the social world works without employing scientific methods.

It would be dishonest to say sociologists never sit around (even sometimes in comfy armchairs) trying to figure out how the world works. But in order to test their theories, sociologists get up from their armchairs and enter the social world. They gather data and evaluate their theories in light of the data they collect. Sociologists do not just propose theories about how the social world works. Sociologists test their theories about how the world works using the scientific method. ##Who are some famous sociologists who use statistical methods to test theories?##

Sociologists, like all humans, have values, beliefs, and even pre-conceived notions of what they might find in doing their research. But, as Peter Berger (1963) argued, what distinguishes the sociologist from non-scientific researchers is that "[the] sociologist tries to see what is there. He may have hopes or fears concerning what he may find. But he will try to see, regardless of his hopes or fears. It is thus an act of pure perception..." (Berger 1963).

Sociology, then, is an attempt to understand the social world by situating social events in their corresponding environment (i.e., social structure, culture, history) and trying to understand social phenomena by collecting and analyzing empirical data.

History

Sociology is a relatively new academic discipline. It emerged in the early 19th century in response to the challenges of modernity. Increasing mobility and technological advances resulted in the increasing exposure of people to cultures and societies different from their own. The impact of this exposure was varied, but for some people included the breakdown of traditional norms and customs and warranted a revised understanding of how the world works. Sociologists responded to these changes by trying to understand what holds social groups together and also explore possible solutions to the breakdown of social solidarity.

Auguste Comte and Other Founders

⎙Auguste Comte, who coined the term *sociology*

The term *sociology* was coined by Auguste Comte (1798-1857) in 1838 from the Latin term *socius* (companion, associate) and the Greek term *logia* (study of, speech). Comte hoped to unify all the sciences under sociology; he believed sociology held the potential to improve society and direct human activity, including the other sciences.

While it is no longer a theory employed in Sociology, Comte argued for an understanding of society he labeled *The Law of Three Stages*. Comte, not unlike other enlightenment thinkers, believed society developed in stages.

- The first was the **theological stage** where people took a religious view of society.

- The second was the **metaphysical stage** where people understood society as natural (not supernatural).

Comte's final stage was the scientific or **positivist stage**, which he believed to be the pinnacle of social development. In the scientific stage, society would be governed by reliable knowledge and would be understood in light of the knowledge produced by science, primarily sociology. While vague connections between Comte's *Law* and human history can be seen, it is generally understood in Sociology today that Comte's approach is a highly simplified and ill-founded approach to understand social development (see instead demographic transition theory and Ecological-Evolutionary Theory).

Other *classical* theorists of sociology from the late 19th and early 20th centuries include Karl Marx, Ferdinand Toennies, Emile Durkheim, Vilfredo Pareto, and Max Weber. As pioneers in Sociology, most of the early sociological thinkers were trained in other academic disciplines, including history, philosophy, and economics. The diversity of their trainings is reflected in the topics they researched, including religion, education, economics, psychology, ethics, philosophy, and theology. Perhaps with the exception of Marx, their most enduring influence has been on sociology, and it is in this field that their theories are still considered most applicable.

The Development of the Discipline

⑤Max Weber

The first book with the term *sociology* in its title was written in the mid-19th century by the English philosopher Herbert Spencer. In the United States, the first *Sociology* course was taught at the University of Kansas, Lawrence in 1890 under the title *Elements of Sociology* (the oldest continuing sociology course in America). The first full fledged university department of sociology in the United States was established in 1892 at the University of Chicago by Albion W. Small, who in 1895 founded the American Journal of Sociology. The first European department of sociology was founded in 1895 at the University of Bordeaux by Emile Durkheim, founder of L'AnnÃ(c)e Sociologique (1896). In 1919 a sociology department was established in Germany at the Ludwig Maximilians University of Munich by Max Weber and in 1920 in Poland by Florian Znaniecki. The first sociology departments in the United Kingdom were founded after the Second World War.

International cooperation in sociology began in 1893 when Rene Worms founded the small Institut International de Sociologie that was eclipsed by the much larger International Sociologist Association starting in 1949. In 1905 the American Sociological Association, the world's largest association of professional sociologists, was founded.

5 Karl Marx

Early Sociological Studies

Early sociological studies considered the field to be similar to the natural sciences like physics or biology. As a result, many researchers argued that the methodology used in the natural sciences were perfectly suited for use in the social sciences, including Sociology. The effect of employing the scientific method and stressing empiricism was the distinction of sociology from theology, philosophy, and metaphysics. This also resulted in sociology being recognized as an empirical science. This early sociological approach, supported by August Comte, led to positivism, a methodological approach based on sociological naturalism.

However, as early as the 19th century, positivist and naturalist approaches to studying social life were questioned by scientists like Wilhelm Dilthey and Heinrich Rickert, who argued that the natural world differs from the social world, as human society has culture, unlike the societies of other animals (e.g., ants, dolphins, etc. operate from nature or ecology as opposed to that of civilisation). This view was further developed by Max Weber, who introduced the concept of verstehen. Verstehen is a research approach in which outside observers of a culture relate to an indigenous people on the observer's own terms.

The positivist and verstehen approaches have modern counterparts in sociological methodologies: quantitative and qualitative sociology. Quantitative sociology focuses on measuring social phenomena using numbers and quantities while qualitative sociology focuses on understanding social phenomena. It is disingenuous to claim these two approaches must be or are generally distinct; many sociologists employ both methods in trying to understand the social world.

Sociology and Other Social Sciences

The **social sciences** comprise the application of scientific methods to the study of the human aspects of the world. Psychology studies the human mind and micro-level (or individual) behavior; sociology examines human society; political science studies the governing of groups and countries; communication studies the flow of discourse via various media; economics concerns itself with the production and allocation of wealth in society; and social work is the

11

application of social scientific knowledge in society. Social sciences diverge from the humanities in that many in the social sciences emphasize the scientific method or other rigorous standards of evidence in the study of humanity.

The Development of Social Science

In ancient philosophy, there was no difference between the liberal arts of mathematics and the study of history, poetry or politics - only with the development of mathematical proof did there gradually arise a perceived difference between *scientific* disciplines and the *humanities* or *liberal arts*. Thus, Aristotle studied planetary motion and poetry with the same methods, and Plato mixed geometrical proofs with his demonstration on the state of intrinsic knowledge.

This unity of science as descriptive remained, for example, in the time of Thomas Hobbes who argued that deductive reasoning from axioms created a scientific framework; his book, *Leviathan*, was a scientific description of a political commonwealth. Within decades of Hobbes' work a revolution took place in what constituted *science*, particularly with the work of Isaac Newton in physics. Newton, by revolutionizing what was then called *natural philosophy*, changed the basic framework by which individuals understood what was *scientific*.

While Newton was merely the archetype of an accelerating trend, the important distinction is that for Newton the mathematical flowed from a presumed reality independent of the observer and it worked by its own rules. For philosophers of the same period, mathematical expression of philosophical ideals were taken to be symbolic of natural human relationships as well: the same laws moved physical and spiritual reality. For examples see Blaise Pascal, Gottfried Leibniz and Johannes Kepler, each of whom took mathematical examples as models for human behavior directly. In Pascal's case, the famous wager; for Leibniz, the invention of binary computation; and for Kepler, the intervention of angels to guide the planets.

In the realm of other disciplines, this created a pressure to express ideas in the form of mathematical relationships. Such relationships, called *Laws* after the usage of the time (see philosophy of science) became the model that other disciplines would emulate. In the late 19th century, attempts to apply equations to statements about human behavior became increasingly common. Among the first were the *Laws* of philology, which attempted to map the change overtime of sounds in a language. In the early 20th century, a wave of change came to science that saw *statistical* study sufficiently mathematical to be *science*.

The first thinkers to attempt to combine scientific inquiry with the exploration of human relationships were Sigmund Freud in Austria and William James in the United States. Freud's theory of the functioning of the mind and James' work on experimental psychology had an enormous impact on those who followed.

One of the most persuasive advocates for the view of scientific treatment of philosophy is John Dewey (1859-1952). He began, as Marx did, in an attempt to weld Hegelian idealism and logic to experimental science, for example in his *Psychology* of 1887. However, it is when he abandoned Hegelian constructs and joined the movement in America called Pragmatism that he began to formulate his basic doctrine on the three phases of the process of inquiry:

1.   problematic Situation, where the typical response is inadequate

2.   isolation of Data or subject matter

3.   reflective, which is tested empirically

With the rise of the idea of quantitative measurement in the physical sciences (see, for example Lord Rutherford's famous maxim that any knowledge that one cannot measure numerically "is a poor sort of knowledge"), the stage was set for the conception of the humanities as being precursors to *social science*.

Sociology Today

Although sociology emerged in Comte's vision of sociology eventually subsuming all other areas of scientific inquiry, sociology did not replace the other sciences. Instead, sociology has developed a particular niche in the study of social life.

In the past, sociological research focused on the organization of complex, industrial societies and their influence on individuals. Today, sociologists study a broad range of topics. For instance, some sociologists research macro-structures that organize society, such as race or ethnicity, social class, gender roles, and institutions such as the family. Other sociologists study social processes that represent the breakdown of macro-structures, including deviance, crime, and divorce. Additionally, some sociologists study micro-processes such as interpersonal interactions and the socialization of individuals. It should also be noted that recent sociologists, taking cues from anthropologists, have realized the *Western* emphasis of the discipline. In response, many sociology departments around the world are now encouraging multi-cultural research.

The next two chapters in this book will introduce the reader to more extensive discussions of the methods and theory employed in sociology. The remaining chapters are examinations of current areas of research in the discipline

Technology and the Social Sciences

The Social Sciences are also known pejoratively as the soft sciences (in contrast to the hard sciences like physics, chemistry, and biology). However, there is a recent move to integrate and include considerations from the social sciences to the development of technology derived from the hard sciences. On the other hand, a sub-topic of organisational behaviour, business process, may now be patented in some countries.

References

- John J. Macionis, Sociology (10th Edition), Prentice Hall, 2004, ISBN 0131849182

- C. Wright Mills, The Sociological Imagination, Oxford University Press, 1961, ISBN 0195133730

- Peter L. Berger, Invitation to Sociology: A Humanistic Perspective, Anchor, 1963, ISBN 0385065299

This page also draws heavily upon the following wikipedia resources:

- sociology
- social science

External links

- American Sociological Association
- Analysing and Overcoming the Sociological Fragmentation in Europe: European Virtual Library of Sociology
- A Century of Sociology at University of Kansas, by Alan Sica (Adobe Acrobat PDF file)
- International Sociological Association
- The Sociolog. Comprehensive Guide to Sociology
- Social Science Virtual Library

Sociological methods

Introduction

The goal of this chapter is to introduce the methods employed by sociologists in their study of social life. This is not a chapter on statistics nor does it detail specific methods in sociological investigation. The primary aim is to illustrate how sociologists go beyond common sense understandings in trying to explain or understand social phenomena.

Sociology vs. Common Sense

Common sense, in everyday language, is understood as "the unreflective opinions of ordinary people" or "sound and prudent but often unsophisticated judgment" (Merriam-Webster). Sociology and other social sciences have been accused of being nothing more than the *sciences of common sense*. While there is certainly some basis for the accusation - some of the findings of sociology do confirm common sense understandings of how society seems to work - sociology goes well beyond common sense in its pursuit of knowledge. Sociology does this by applying scientific methodology and empiricism to social phenomena. It is also interesting to note that *common sense* understandings can develop from sociological investigations. Past findings in sociological studies can make their way into everyday culture, resulting in a *common sense* understanding that is actually the result of sociological investigation. Examples of sociological investigation refuting and serving as the foundation for *common sense* are provided below.

The workings behind common sense is that people usually do not have a word for their thoughts about society that can be summed into one word. Sociology helps provide the words to alter multiple thoughts into a defined word.

In the 1970s and early 1980s a New Religious Movement was gaining notoriety for its rapid expansion. This movement, The Unification Church or The Moonies, was heavily criticized because it encouraged members to give up all of their ties to non-members of the religion and to move in to movement centers to realize the movement's vision of a better world. Accusations of *brainwashing* were common; it was believed The Moonies were forcing people to join the movement and give up their previous lives against their will. In order to determine if the *common sense* accusations were accurate, Eileen Barker (1984) undertook a lengthy sociological investigation to explore how people came to affiliate with The Moonies. She found that converts to The Unification Church were not being forced into the religion against their will but instead were making a reasoned decision to join the movement. While there was pressure for people to join the movement, the pressure was not such that it attracted more than a small fraction of the people who were introduced to the movement. In other words, the movement did not *brainwash* its followers; it provided a new and alternative worldview, but did not force anyone to adopt it. Of course, the social ties people developed once they joined the movement made it difficult for members to leave. But this isn't anything particularly new: members of many religions and denominations that have been around much longer than The

Moonies find it difficult to leave because of their social attachments. What Barker's research uncovers is that The Moonies were only being accused of *brainwashing* because (1) they were a New Religious Movement and (2) they encouraged a distinct separation from the outside world. This is a common accusation leveled at New Religious Movements, especially those that demand significant commitments from their members. This example illustrates how sociology can test *common sense* understandings of social processes.

An example of sociology providing a basis for common sense is the research of William Chambliss (1973) on social status and deviance. Chambliss observed two groups of young men to see how their presented selves matched their actual behaviors. The two groups were dubbed *The Saints* and *The Roughnecks*. The Saints came from the middle-class and, in the eyes of their parents, teachers, and even law enforcement, were like *saints* - they could do no wrong. The Roughnecks, on the other hand, came from lower-class families and were consistently accused of wrong-doing. What Chambliss found in observing the two groups was that The Saints were actually far more deviant than The Roughnecks, but they got away with it because they were able to commit their deviant acts outside of their home town and compellingly portray themselves as upstanding young citizens. The Roughnecks, because of their lack of mobility and funds, were more likely to commit their deviant acts in public and in their hometown, leading local people to see them as extreme deviants. Chambliss's findings, while not pervasively seen as *common sense*, are increasingly so. People are coming to realize that the public portrayal of one's self may not actually represent one's private activities. This is often the case with serial killers and was even portrayed in the movie Murder by Numbers.

The Development of Social Science

In ancient philosophy, there was no difference between the liberal arts of mathematics and the study of history, poetry or politics - only with the development of mathematical proof did there gradually arise a perceived difference between *scientific* disciplines and the *humanities* or *liberal arts*. Thus, Aristotle studied planetary motion and poetry with the same methods, and Plato mixed geometrical proofs with his demonstration on the state of intrinsic knowledge.

This unity of science as descriptive remained, for example, in the time of Thomas Hobbes who argued that deductive reasoning from axioms created a scientific framework; his book, *Leviathan*, was a scientific description of a political commonwealth. Within decades of Hobbes' work a revolution took place in what constituted *science*, particularly with the work of Isaac Newton in physics. Newton, by revolutionizing what was then called *natural philosophy*, changed the basic framework by which individuals understood what was *scientific*.

While Newton was merely the archetype of an accelerating trend, the important distinction is that for Newton the mathematical flowed from a presumed reality independent of the observer and it worked by its own rules. For philosophers of the same period, mathematical expression of philosophical ideals were taken to be symbolic of natural human relationships as well: the same laws moved physical and spiritual reality. For examples see Blaise Pascal, Gottfried Leibniz and Johannes Kepler, each of whom took mathematical examples as models for human behavior directly. In Pascal's case, the famous wager; for Leibniz, the invention of binary computation; and for Kepler, the intervention of angels to guide the planets.

In the realm of other disciplines, this created a pressure to express ideas in the form of mathematical relationships. Such relationships, called *Laws* after the usage of the time (see philosophy of science) became the model that other disciplines would emulate. In the late 19th century, attempts to apply equations to statements about human behavior became increasingly common. Among the first were the *Laws* of philology, which attempted to map the change over time of sounds in a language. In the early 20th century, a wave of change came to science that saw *statistical* study sufficiently mathematical to be *science*.

The first thinkers to attempt to combine scientific inquiry with the exploration of human relationships were Sigmund Freud in Austria and William James in the United States. Freud's theory of the functioning of the mind and James' work on experimental psychology had an enormous impact on those who followed.

With the rise of the idea of quantitative measurement in the physical sciences (see, for example Lord Rutherford's famous maxim that any knowledge that one cannot measure numerically "is a poor sort of knowledge"), the stage was set for the conception of the humanities as being precursors to *social science*.

The Scientific Method

A scientific method or process is considered fundamental to the scientific investigation and acquisition of new knowledge based upon verifiable evidence. In addition to employing the scientific method in their research, sociologists explore the social world with several different purposes in mind. Like the physical sciences (i.e., chemistry, physics, etc.), sociologists can be and often are interested in predicting outcomes given knowledge of the variables and relationships involved. This approach to *doing science* is often termed *positivism*. The positivist approach to social science seeks to explain and predict social phenomena, often employing a quantitative approach. But unlike the physical sciences, sociology (and other social sciences, specifically anthropology) also often seek for understanding social phenomena. Max Weber labeled this approach *Verstehen*, which is German for *understanding*. In this approach, which is similar to ethnography, the goal is to understand a culture or phenemon on its own terms rather than trying to predict it. Both approaches employ a scientific method as they make observations and gather data, propose hypotheses, and test their hypotheses in the formulation of theories. These steps are outlined in more detail below.

Sociologists use observations, hypotheses and deductions to propose explanations for social phenomena in the form of theories. Predictions from these theories are tested. If a prediction turns out to be correct, the theory survives. The method is commonly taken as the underlying logic of scientific practice. A scientific method is essentially an extremely cautious means of building a supportable, evidenced understanding of our natural world.

The essential elements of a scientific method are iterations and recursions of the following four steps:

1.   Characterization (operationalization or quantification, observation and measurement)

2.   Hypothesis (a theoretical, hypothetical explanation of the observations and measurements)

3.   Prediction (logical deduction from the hypothesis)

4.   Experiment (test of all of the above; in the social sciences, *true experiments* are often replaced with a different form of data analysis that will be discussed in more detail below)

Characterization

A scientific method depends upon a careful characterization of the subject of the investigation. While seeking the pertinent properties of the subject, this careful thought may also entail some definitions and observations; the observation often demands careful measurement and/or counting.

The systematic, careful collection of measurements or counts of relevant quantities is often the critical difference between pseudo-sciences, such as alchemy, and a science, such as chemistry. Scientific measurements taken are usually tabulated, graphed, or mapped, and statistical manipulations, such as correlation and regression, performed on them. The measurements might be made in a controlled setting, such as a laboratory, or made on more or less inaccessible or unmanipulatable objects such as human populations. The measurements often require specialized scientific instruments such as thermometers, spectroscopes, or voltmeters, and the progress of a scientific field is usually intimately tied to their invention and development.

Measurements demand the use of operational definitions of relevant quantities (a.k.a. *operationalization*). That is, a scientific quantity is described or defined by how it is measured, as opposed to some more vague, inexact or *idealized* definition. The operational definition of a thing often relies on comparisons with standards: the operational definition of *mass* ultimately relies on the use of an artifact, such as a certain kilogram of platinum kept in a laboratory in France.

The scientific definition of a term sometimes differs substantially from its natural language usage. For example, *sex* and *gender* are often used interchangeably in common discourse, but have distinct meanings in sociology. Scientific quantities are often characterized by their units of measure which can later be described in terms of conventional physical units when communicating the work.

Measurements in scientific work are also usually accompanied by estimates of their uncertainty. The uncertainty is often estimated by making repeated measurements of the desired quantity. Uncertainties may also be calculated by consideration of the uncertainties of the individual underlying quantities that are used. Counts of things, such as the number of people in a nation at a particular time, may also have an uncertainty due to limitations of the method used. Counts may only represent a sample of desired quantities, with an uncertainty that depends upon the sampling method used and the number of samples taken.

Hypothesis Development

A hypothesis includes a suggested explanation of the subject. It will generally provide a causal explanation or propose some correlation between two variables. If the hypothesis is a causal explanation, it will involve at least one *dependent variable* and one *independent variable*.

Variables are measurable phenomena whose values can change (e.g., class status can range from lower- to upper-class). A dependent variable is a variable whose values are presumed to change as a result of the independent variable. In other words, the value of a dependent variable *depends* on the value of the independent variable. Of course, this assumes that there is an actual relationship between the two variables. If there is no relationship, then the value of the *dependent variable* does not depend on the value of the independent variable. An *independent variable* is a variable whose value is manipulated by the experimenter (or, in the case of non-experimental analysis, changes in the society and is measured). Perhaps an example will help clarify. In a study of the influence of gender on promotion, the independent variable would be gender/sex. Promotion would be the dependent variable. Change in promotion is hypothesized to be dependent on gender.

Scientists use whatever they can â€" their own creativity, ideas from other fields, induction, systematic guessing, etc. â€" to imagine possible explanations for a phenomenon under study. There are no definitive guidelines for the production of new hypotheses. The history of science is filled with stories of scientists claiming a *flash of inspiration*, or a hunch, which then motivated them to look for evidence to support or refute their idea.

Prediction

A useful hypothesis will enable predictions, by deductive reasoning, that can be experimentally assessed. If results contradict the predictions, then the hypothesis under examination is incorrect or incomplete and requires either revision or abandonment. If results confirm the predictions, then the hypothesis might be correct but is still subject to further testing. Predictions refer to experimental designs with a currently unknown outcome. A prediction (of an unknown) differs from a consequence (which can already be known).

Experiment

Once a prediction is made, an experiment is designed to test it. The experiment may seek either confirmation or falsification of the hypothesis.

Scientists assume an attitude of openness and accountability on the part of those conducting an experiment. Detailed record keeping is essential, to aid in recording and reporting on the experimental results, and providing evidence of the effectiveness and integrity of the procedure. They will also assist in reproducing the experimental results.

The experiment's integrity should be ascertained by the introduction of a control. Two virtually identical experiments are run, in only one of which the factor being tested is varied. This serves to further isolate any causal phenomena. For example in testing a drug it is important to carefully test that the supposed effect of the drug is produced only by the drug. Doctors may do this with a double-blind study: two virtually identical groups of patients are compared, one of which receives the drug and one of which receives a placebo. Neither the patients nor the doctor know who is getting the real drug, isolating its effects. This type of experiment is often referred to as a *true experiment* because of its design. It is contrasted with alternative forms below.

Once an experiment is complete, a researcher determines whether the results (or data) gathered are what was predicted. If the experimental conclusions fail to match the predictions/hypothesis, then one returns to the failed hypothesis and re-iterates the process. If the experiment appears *successful* - i.e. fits the hypothesis - the experimenter often will attempt to publish the results so that others (in theory) may reproduce the same experimental results, verifying the findings in the process.

An experiment is not an absolute requirement. In observation based fields of science actual experiments must be designed differently than for the classical laboratory based sciences. Due to ethical concerns and the sheer cost of manipulating large segments of society, sociologists often turn to other methods for testing hypotheses. In lieu of holding variables constant in laboratory settings, sociologists employ statistical techniques (e.g., regression) that allow them to control the variables in the analysis rather than in the data collection. For instance, in examining the effects of gender on promotions, sociologists may *control* for the effects of social class as this variable will likely influence the relationship. Unlike a *true experiment* where these variables are held constant in a laboratory setting, sociologists use statistical methods to hold constant social class (or, better stated, partial out the variance accounted for by social class) so they can see the relationship between gender and promotions without the interference of social class. Thus, while the *true experiment* is ideally suited for the performance of science, especially because it is the best method for deriving *causal relationships*, other methods of *hypothesis testing* are commonly employed in the social sciences.

Evaluation and Iteration

The scientific process is iterative. At any stage it is possible that some consideration will lead the scientist to repeat an earlier part of the process. For instance, failure of a hypothesis to produce interesting and testable predictions may lead to reconsideration of the hypothesis or of the definition of the subject.

It is also important to note that science is a social enterprise, and scientific work will become accepted by the community only if it can be verified. Crucially, experimental and theoretical results must be reproduced by others within the scientific community. All scientific knowledge is in a state of flux, for at any time new evidence could be presented that contradicts a long-held hypothesis. For this reason, scientific journals use a process of peer review, in which scientists' manuscripts are submitted by editors of scientific journals to (usually one to three) fellow (usually anonymous) scientists familiar with the field for evaluation. The referees may or may not recommend publication, publication with suggested modifications, or, sometimes, publication in another journal. This serves to keep the scientific literature free of unscientific work, helps to cut down on obvious errors, and generally otherwise improves the quality of the scientific literature. Work announced in the popular press before going through this process is generally frowned upon. Sometimes peer review inhibits the circulation of unorthodox work, and at other times may be too permissive. The peer review process is not always successful, but has been very widely adopted by the scientific community.

The *reproducibility* or replication of scientific observations, while usually described as being very important in a scientific method, is actually seldom reported, and is in reality often not done. Referees and editors often reject papers purporting only to reproduce some observations as being unoriginal and not containing anything new. Occasionally reports of a failure to reproduce results are published - mostly in cases where controversy exists or a suspicion of fraud develops. The threat of failure to replicate by others, however, serves as a very effective deterrent for most scientists, who will usually replicate their own data several times before attempting to publish.

Sometimes useful observations or phenomena themselves cannot be reproduced. They may be rare, or even unique events. Reproducibility of observations and replication of experiments is not a guarantee that they are correct or properly understood. Errors can all too often creep into more than one laboratory.

Correlation and Causation

In the scientific pursuit of prediction and explanation, two relationships between variables are often confused: correlation and causation. Correlation refers to a relationship between two (or more) variables in which they change together. A correlation can be positive/direct or negative/inverse. A positive correlation means that as one variable increases (e.g., ice cream consumption) the other variable also increases (e.g., crime). A negative correlation is just the opposite; as one variable increases (e.g., socioeconomic status), the other variable decreases (e.g., infant mortality rates).

Causation refers to a relationship between two (or more) variables where one variable causes the other. In order for a variable to cause another, it must meet the following three criteria:

- the variables must be correlated

- one variable must precede the other variable in time

- it must be shown that a different (third) variable is not causing the change in the two variables of interest (a.k.a., *spurious correlation*)

An example may help explain the difference. Ice cream consumption (ICC) is positively correlated with incidents of crime.

Correlation

Employing the scientific method outlined above, the reader should immediately question this relationship and attempt to discover an explanation. It is at this point that a simple yet noteworthy phrase should be introduced: *correlation is not causation*. If you look back at the three criteria of causation above, you will notice that the relationship between ice cream consumption (ICC) and crime meets only one of the three criteria. The real explanation of this relationship is the introduction of a third variable: temperature. ICC and crime increase during the summer months. Thus, while these two variables are correlated, ICC does not cause crime or vice versa. Both variables increase due to the increasing temperatures during the summer months.

Causation

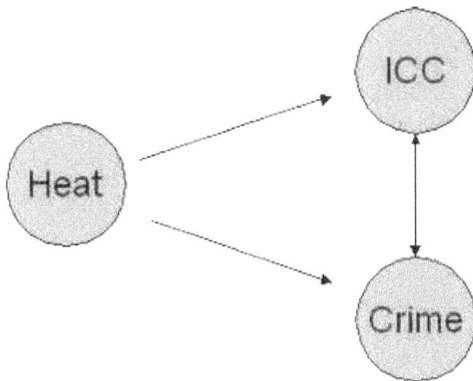

It is important to not confound a correlation with a cause/effect relationship. It is often the case that correlations between variables are found but the relationship turns out to be spurious. Clearly understanding the relationship between variables is an important element of the scientific process.

Quantitative and Qualitative

Like the distinction drawn between *positivist* sociology and *Verstehen* sociology, there is often a distinction drawn between two types of sociological investigation: *quantitative* and *qualitative*.

Quantitative methods of sociological research approach social phenomena from the perspective that they can be measured and/or *quantified*. For instance, social class, following the quantitative approach, can be divided into different groups - upper-, middle-, and lower-class - and can be measured using any of a number of variables or a combination thereof: income, educational attainment, prestige, power, etc. Quantitative sociologists tend to use specific methods of data collection and hypothesis testing, including: experimental designs, surveys, secondary data analysis, and statistical analysis.

Qualitative methods of sociological research tend to approach social phenomena from the *Verstehen* perspective. They are used to develop a deeper understanding of a particular phenomenon. They also often deliberately give up on quantity - necessary for statistical analysis - in order to reach a depth in analysis of the phenomenon studied. Even so, qualitative methods can be used to propose relationships between variables. Qualitatively oriented sociologists tend to employ different methods of data collection and hypothesis testing, including: participant observation, interviews, focus groups, content analysis and historical comparison.

While there are sociologists who employ and encourage the use of only one or the other method, many sociologists see benefits in combining the approaches. They view quantitative and qualitative approaches as complementary. Results from one approach can fill gaps in the other approach. For example, quantitative methods could describe large or general patterns in society while qualitative approaches could help to understand how individuals understand those patterns.

Objective vs. Critical

Sociologists, like all humans, have values, beliefs, and even pre-conceived notions of what they might find in doing their research. Because sociologists are not immune to the desire to change the world, two approaches to sociological investigation have emerged. By far the most common is the *objective* approach advocated by Max Weber. Weber recognized that social scientists have opinions, but argued against the expression of non-professional or non-scientific opinions in the classroom (1946:129-156). Weber took this position for several reasons, but the primary one outlined in his discussion of *Science as Vocation* is that he believed it is not right for a person in a position of authority (a professor) to force his/her students to accept his/her opinions in order for them to pass the class. Weber did argue that it was okay for social scientists to express their opinions outside of the classroom and advocated for social scientists to be involved in politics and other social activism. The *objective* approach to social science remains popular in sociological research and refereed journals because it refuses to engage social issues at the level of opinions and instead focuses intently on data and theories.

The *objective* approach is contrasted with the *critical* approach, which has its roots in Karl Marx's work on economic structures. Anyone familiar with Marxist theory will recognize that Marx went beyond describing society to advocating for change. Marx disliked capitalism and his analysis of that economic system included the call for change. This approach to sociology is often referred to today as *critical* sociology (see also *action research*). Some sociological journals focus on critical sociology and some sociological approaches are inherently critical (e.g., feminism, black feminist thought).

Ethics

Ethical considerations are of particular importance to sociologists because of the subject of investigation - people. Because ethical considerations are of so much importance, sociologists adhere to a rigorous set of ethical guidelines. A comprehensive explanation of sociological guidelines is provided on the website of the American Sociological Association. Some of the more common and important ethical guidelines of sociological investigation will be touched upon below.

The most important ethical consideration of sociological research is that participants in sociological investigation are not harmed. While exactly what this entails can vary from study to study, there are several universally recognized considerations. For instance, research on children and youth always requires parental consent. Research on adults also requires *informed consent* and participants are never forced to participate. *Confidentiality* and *anonymity* are two additional practices that ensure the safety of participants when sensitive information is provided (e.g., sexuality, income, etc.). To ensure the safety of participants, most universities maintain an *institutional review board* (IRB) that reviews studies that include human participants and ensures ethical rigor.

As regards professional ethics, several issues are noteworthy. Obviously honesty in research, analysis, and publication is important. Sociologists who manipulate their data are ostracized and will have their memberships in professional organizations revoked. Conflicts of interest are also frowned upon. A conflict of interest can occur when a sociologist is given funding to conduct research on an issue that relates to the source of the funds. For example, if Microsoft were to fund a sociologist to investigate whether users of Microsoft's products are happier than users of open source software, the sociologist would need to disclose the source of the funding as it presents a significant conflict of interest.

What Can Sociology Tell Us?

Having discussed the sociological approach to understanding society, it is worth noting the limitations of sociology. Because of the subject of investigation (society), sociology runs into a number of problems that have significant implications for this field of inquiry:

- human behavior is complex, making prediction - especially at the individual level - difficult or even impossible

- the presence of researchers can affect the phenomenon being studied (Hawthorne Effect)

- society is constantly changing, making it difficult for sociologists to maintain current understandings; in fact, society might even change as a result of sociological investigation (for instance, sociologists testified in the Brown v. Board of Education decision to integrate schools)

- it is difficult for sociologists to remain objective when the phenomena they study is also part of their social life

While it is important to recognize the limitations of sociology, sociology's contributions to our understanding of society have been significant and continue to provide useful theories and tools for understanding humans as social beings.

Notes

References

- Barker, Eileen. 1984. The Making of a Moonie: Choice or Brainwashing. Blackwell Publishers. ISBN 0631132465

- Chambliss, William. 1973. The Saints and the Roughnecks. Society; 2(1).

- Weber, Max. 1946. Science As Vocation. Gerth, H. H. and Mills, C. Wright, Editors and Translators. From Max Weber: Essays in Sociology. New York: Oxford University Press; pp. 129-156.

This chapter also draws heavily on the following Wikipedia articles:

- common sense

- scientific method

- Induction (philosophy)

- Deductive reasoning

- qualitative method

- hypothesis

- independent variable

- dependent variable

- Philosophy of science

External Links

- Resources for methods in social research

- Science as Vocation

General sociological theory

Introduction

Sociologists develop theories to explain social phenomena. A *theory* is a proposed relationship between two or more *concepts*. To use the example from the previous chapter, one might propose the following theory:

Ice cream consumption and crime rates are correlated, increasing and decreasing together (the data). As a result, a theorist could propose that the consumption of ice cream results in angered individuals who then commit crimes (the theory).

Of course, this theory is not an accurate representation of reality. But, it illustrates the use of theory - to elucidate the relationship between two concepts; in this case, ice cream consumption and crime.

Sociological theory is developed at multiple levels, ranging from *grand theory* to highly contextualized and specific *micro-range theories*. There are literally thousands of *middle-range* and *micro-range* theories in sociology. Because such theories are dependent on context and specific to certain situations, it is beyond the scope of this text to explore each of those theories. The purpose of this chapter is to introduce some of the more well-known and most commonly used grand and middle-range theories in sociology. For a brief explanation of the different levels of sociological theorizing, see Sociological Abstraction.

Importance of Theory

In the theory proposed above, the astute reader will notice that the theory includes two components. The data, the correlation between ice cream consumption and crime rates, and the proposed relationship. Data alone are not particularly informative. In fact, it is often said that 'data without theory is not sociology'. In order to understand the social world around us, it is necessary to employ theory to draw the connections between seemingly disparate concepts.

Take, for instance, Emile Durkheim's class work *Suicide*. Durkheim was interested in explaining a social phenomenon, suicide, and employed both data and theory to offer an explanation. By aggregating data for large groups of people in Europe, Durkheim was able to discern patterns in suicide rates and connect those patterns with another concept (or variable): religious affiliation. Durkheim found that Protestants were more likely to commit suicide than were Catholics. At this point, Durkheim's analysis was still in the data stage; he had not proposed an explanation of the relationship between religious affiliation and suicide rates. It was when Durkheim introduced the ideas of *anomie* (or chaos) and *social solidarity* that he began to formulate a theory. Durkheim argued that the looser social ties found in Protestant religions lead to weaker social cohesion and social solidarity and result in increased social anomie. The higher suicide rates were the result of weakening social bonds among Protestants, according to Durkheim.

While Durkheim's findings have since been criticized, his study is a classic example of the use of theory to explain the relationship between two concepts. Durkheim's work also illustrates the importance of theory: without theories to explain the relationship between concepts, we would not be able to understand cause and effect relationships in social life or otherwise gain better understandings of social activity (i.e., *Verstehen*).

The Multiplicity of Theories

As the dominant theories in sociology are discussed below, the reader might be inclined to ask, "Which of these theories is *the best*?" Rather than think of one theory being better than another, it is more useful and informative to view these theories as *complementary*. One theory may explain one element of a phenomenon (e.g., the role of religion in society - structural-functionalism) while another might offer a different insight on the same phenomenon (e.g., the decline of religion in society - conflict theory).

It may be difficult, initially at least, to take this perspective on sociological theory, but as you read some of the later chapters you will see that each of these theories is particularly useful at explaining some phenomena yet less useful in explaining other phenomena. If you approach the theories objectively from the beginning, you will find that there really are many ways to understand social phenomena.

Structural-Functionalism

Structural-Functionalism is a sociological theory that originally attempted to explain social institutions as collective means to meet individual biological needs (originally just *functionalism*). Later it came to focus on the ways social institutions meet social needs (structural-functionalism).

Structural-functionalism draws its inspiration primarily from the ideas of Emile Durkheim. Durkheim was concerned with the question of how societies maintain internal stability and survive over time. He sought to explain social cohesion and stability through the concept of solidarity. In more "primitive" societies it was mechanical solidarity, everyone performing similar tasks, that held society together. Durkheim proposed that such societies tend to be segmentary, being composed of equivalent parts that are held together by shared values, common symbols, or systems of exchanges. In modern, complex societies members perform very different tasks, resulting in a strong interdependence between individuals. Based on the metaphor of an organism in which many parts function together to sustain the whole, Durkheim argued that modern complex societies are held together by organic solidarity (think interdependent *organs*).

The central concern of structural-functionalism is a continuation of the Durkheimian task of explaining the apparent stability and internal cohesion of societies that are necessary to ensure their continued existence over time. Many functionalists argue that social institutions are functionally integrated to form a stable system and that a change in one institution will precipitate a change in other institutions. Societies are seen as coherent, bounded and fundamentally relational constructs that function like organisms, with their various parts (social institutions) working together to maintain and reproduce them. The various parts of society are assumed to work in an unconscious, quasi-automatic fashion towards the maintenance of the overall social *equilibrium*. All social and cultural phenomena are therefore seen as being *functional* in the sense of working together to achieve this state and are effectively deemed to have a *life* of their own. These components are then primarily analysed in terms of the function they play. In other words, to understand a component of society, one can ask the question, "What is the function of this institution?" A *function*, in this sense, is the contribution made by a phenomenon to a larger system of which the phenomenon is a part (Hoult 1969:139).

Durkheim's strongly sociological perspective of society was continued by Radcliffe-Brown. Following Auguste Comte, Radcliffe-Brown believed that the social constituted a separate *level* of reality distinct from both the biological and the inorganic (here *non-living*). Explanations of social phenomena therefore had to be constructed within this social level, with individuals merely being transient occupants of comparatively stable social roles. Thus, in structural-functionalist thought, individuals are not significant in and of themselves but only in terms of their social status: their position in patterns of social relations. The social structure is therefore a network of statuses connected by associated roles (Layton 1997:37-38).

Structural-functionalism was the dominant perspective of sociology between World War II and the Vietnam War.

Limitations

Structural-functionalism has been criticized for being unable to account for social change because it focuses so intently on social order and equilibrium in society. Another criticism of the structural-functionalism perspective involves the epistemological argument that functionalism attempts to describe social institutions solely through their effects and, as a result, does not explain the cause of those effects. Another philosophical problem with the structural-functional approach is the ontological argument that society does not have *needs* as a human being does; and even if society does have needs they need not be met.

Another criticism often leveled at structural-functionalist theory is that it supports the status quo. According to some opponents, structural-functionalism paints conflict and challenge to the status quo as harmful to society, and therefore tends to be the prominent view among conservative thinkers.

Manifest and Latent Functions

Merton (1957) proposed a distinction between *manifest* and *latent* functions. *Manifest* functions are the intended functions of a phenomenon in a social system. *Latent* functions are the unintended functions of a phenomenon in a social system. An example of manifest and latent functions is public education. The manifest purpose of public education is to increase the knowledge and abilities of the citizenry. The latent function of the public education system is the development of a hierarchy of *the learned*. The latent function has a significant impact on society as it often translates into social class distinctions: people with higher educational attainment tend to make more money than those with lower educational attainment

Conflict Theory

Conflict theory argues that society is not about solidarity or social consensus but rather about competition. Society is made up of individuals competing for limited resources (e.g., money, leisure, sexual partners, etc.). Broader social structures and organizations (e.g., religions, government, etc.) reflect the competition for resources in their inherent inequalities; some people and organizations have more resources (i.e., power and influence) and use those resources to maintain their positions of power in society.

An example of the application of conflict theory is in understanding the gender make-up of the legislative branch of the U.S. government. Prior to the passage of the 19th Amendment to the Constitution of the United States of America in 1920, women did not have the right to vote. Given women's inability to vote, it is not surprising men held all of the positions of power in the U.S. government. The men who held the positions of power in the U.S. government were also in a position to maintain their power because they controlled the legislative process that could enfranchise women. This scenario illustrates how conflict and inequality can be integrated in social structures - men were in a position of power and many of them were motivated to maintain that power by continuing to refuse the right to vote to women. The passage of the 19th Amendment can also be explained using conflict theory in that powerful forces joined together (Women's Suffrage) to effectuate change.

Conflict theory was developed in part to illustrate the limitations of structural-functionalism. The structural-functional approach argued that society tends toward equilibrium. The structural-functional approach focuses on stability at the expense of social change. This is contrasted with the conflict approach, which argues that society is constantly in conflict over resources. One of the primary contributions conflict theory presents over the structural-functional approach is that it is ideally suited for explaining social change, a significant problem in the structural-functional approach.

The following are three primary assumptions of modern conflict theory:

- Competition over scarce resources is at the heart of all social relationships. Competition rather than consensus is characteristic of human relationships.

- Inequalities in power and reward are built into all social structures. Individuals and groups that benefit from any particular structure strive to see it maintained.

- Change occurs as a result of conflict between competing interests rather than through adaptation. Change is often abrupt and revolutionary rather than evolutionary.

Conflict theory was elaborated in the United Kingdom by Max Gluckman and John Rex, in the United States by Lewis A. Coser and Randall Collins, and in Germany by Ralf Dahrendorf, all of whom were influenced by Karl Marx, Ludwig Gumplovicz, Vilfredo Pareto, Georg Simmel, and other founding fathers of European sociology.

Limitations

Somewhat ironically, the primary limitation of the social-conflict perspective is that it overlooks the stability of societies. While societies are in a constant state of change, much of the change is minor. Many of the broader elements of societies remain remarkably stable over time, indicating the structural-functional perspective has a great deal of merit.

Harking back to the introduction, the reader might remember the advanced notice given that sociological theory is often complementary. This is particularly true of structural-funcationalism and social-conflict theories. Structural-functionalism focuses on equilibrium and solidarity; conflict-theory focuses on change and conflict. Keep in mind that neither is *better* than the other; when combined, the two approaches offer a broader and more comprehensive view of society.

Symbolic Interactionism

Symbolic Interactionism is a theoretical approach to understanding the relationship between humans and society. The basic notion of symbolic interactionism is that human action and interaction are understandable only through the exchange of meaningful communication or symbols. In this approach, humans are portrayed as *acting* as opposed to being *acted upon* (Herman and Reynolds 1994).

The main principles of symbolic interactionism as outlined by Blumer (1986) are:

1.   human beings act toward things on the basis of the meanings that things have for them

2.   these meanings arise of out of social interaction

3.   social action results from a fitting together of individual lines of action

This approach stands in contrast to the strict behaviorism of psychological theories prevalent at the time it was first formulated (in the 1920s and 1930s), behaviorism and ethology, and also contrasts with structural-functionalism. According to Symbolic Interactionism, humans are distinct from infrahumans (lower animals) because infrahumans simply respond to their environment (i.e., a stimulus evokes a response or stimulus -> response) whereas humans have the ability to interrupt that process (i.e., stimulus -> cognition -> response). Additionally, infrahumans are unable to conceive of alternative responses to gestures. Humans, however, can. This understanding should not be taken to indicate that humans never behave in a strict *stimulus -> response* fashion, but rather that humans have the capability of not responding in that fashion (and do so much of the time).

This perspective is also rooted in phenomenological thought (see social constructionism and phenomonology). According to symbolic interactionism, the objective world has no reality for humans, only subjectively-defined objects have meaning. Meanings are not entities that are bestowed on humans and learned by habituation. Instead, meanings can be altered through the creative capabilities of humans, and individuals may influence the many meanings that form their society (Herman and Reynolds 1994). Human society, therefore, is a social product.

31

It should also be noted that symbolic interactionists advocate a particular methodology. Because they see *meaning* as the fundamental component of human/society interaction, studying human/society interaction requires *getting at* that meaning. Thus, symbolic interactionists tend to employ more qualitative rather than quantitative methods in their research.

Additional information on Symbolic Interactionism can be found here

Limitations

The most significant limitation of the symbolic-interactionist perspective relates to its primary contribution: it overlooks macro social structures (e.g., norms, culture) as a result of focusing on micro-level interactions. Some symbolic interactionists, however, would counter that if *role theory* (see below) is incorporated into symbolic interactionism - which is now commonplace - this criticism is addressed.

Role Theory

Role Theory posits that human behavior is guided by expectations held both by the individual and by other people. The expectations correspond to different roles individuals *perform* or *enact* in their daily lives, such as secretary, father, or friend. For instance, most people hold pre-conceived notions of the role expectations of a secretary, which might include: answering phones, making and managing appointments, filing paperwork, and typing memos. These role expectations would not be expected of a professional soccer player.

Individuals generally have and manage many roles. Roles consist of a set of rules or norms that function as plans or blueprints to guide behavior. Roles specify what goals should be pursued, what tasks must be accomplished, and what performances are required in a given scenario or situation. Role theory holds that a substantial proportion of observable, day-to-day social behavior is simply persons carrying out their roles, much as actors carry out their roles on the stage or ballplayers theirs on the field. Role theory is, in fact, predictive. It implies that if we have information about the role expectations for a specified position (e.g., sister, fireman, prostitute), a significant portion of the behavior of the persons occupying that position can be predicted.

What's more, role theory also argues that in order to change behavior it is necessary to change roles; roles correspond to behaviors and vice versa. In addition to heavily influencing behavior, roles influence beliefs and attitudes; individuals will change their beliefs and attitudes to correspond with their roles. For instance, someone over-looked for a promotion to a managerial position in a company may change their beliefs about the benefits of management by convincing him/herself that they didn't want the additional responsibility that would have accompanied the position.

Many role theorists see *Role Theory* as one of the most compelling theories bridging individual behavior and social structure. Roles, which are in part dictated by social structure and in part by social interactions, guide the behavior of the individual. The individual, in turn, influences the norms, expectations, and behaviors associated with roles. The understanding is reciprocal.

Role Theory includes the following propositions:

1. people spend much of their lives participating as members of groups and organizations

2. within these groups, people occupy distinct positions

3. each of these positions entails a role, which is a set of functions performed by the person for the group

4. groups often formalize role expectations as norms or even codified rules, which include what rewards will result when roles are successfully performed and what punishments will result when roles are not successfully performed

5. individuals usually carry out their roles and perform in accordance with prevailing norms; in other words, role theory assumes that people are primarily conformists who try to live up to the norms that accompany their roles

6. group members check each individual's performance to determine whether it conforms with the norms; the anticipation that others will apply sanctions ensures role performance

For additional information on Role Theory see here.

Limitations

Role theory has a hard time explaining social deviance when it does not correspond to a pre-specified role. For instance, the behavior of someone who adopts the role of bank robber can be predicted - she will rob banks. But if a bank teller simply begins handing out cash to random people, role theory would be unable to explain why (though *role conflict* could be one possible answer; the secretary may also be a Marxist-Communist who believes the means of production should belong to the masses and not the bourgeoisie).

Another limitation of role theory is that it does not and cannot explain how role expectations came to be what they are. Role theory has no explanation for why it is expected of male soldiers to cut their hair short, but it could predict with a high degree of accuracy that if someone is a male soldier they will have short hair. Additionally, role theory does not explain when and how role expectations change.

Impression Management

An extension of *role theory*, **impression management** is both a theory and process. The theory argues that people are constantly engaged in controlling how others perceive them. The process refers to the goal-directed conscious or unconscious effort to influence the perceptions other people form of an individual, object, or event by regulating and controlling information in social interaction. If a person tries to influence the perception of her or his own image, this activity is called *self-presentation*.

33

Erving Goffman (1959), the person most often credited with formally developing the impression management theory, cast the idea in a dramaturgical framework. The basic idea is that individuals in face-to-face situations are like actors on a stage performing roles (see role theory above). Aware of how they are being perceived by their audience, actors manage their behavior so as to create specific impressions in the minds of the audience. Strategic interpersonal behavior to shape or influence impressions formed by an audience is not a new idea. Plato spoke of the "great stage of human life" and Shakespeare noted that "All the world is a stage, and all the men and women merely players".

Social Constructionism

Social constructionism is a school of thought introduced into sociology by Peter L. Berger and Thomas Luckmann with their 1966 book *The Social Construction of Reality*. Social constructionism aims to discover the ways that individuals and groups create their perceived reality. Social constructionism focuses on the description of institutions and actions and not on analyzing cause and effect. Socially constructed reality is seen as an on-going dynamic process; reality is re-produced by people acting on their interpretations of what they perceive to be the world external to them. Berger and Luckmann argue that social construction describes both subjective and objective reality - that is that no reality exists outside what is produced and reproduced in social interactions.

A clear example of social constructionist thought is, following Sigmund Freud and Ã‰mile Durkheim, religion. Religion is seen as a socially constructed concept, the basis for which is rooted in either our psyche (Freud) or man's need to see some purpose in life or worship a higher presence. One of the key theorists of social constructionism, Peter Berger, explored this concept extensively in his book, *The Sacred Canopy*.

Social constructionism is often seen as a source of the postmodern movement, and has been influential in the field of cultural studies.

Integration Theory

Recently, some sociologists have been taking a different approach to sociological theory by employing an integrationist approach - combining micro- and macro-level theories to provide a comprehensive understanding of human social behavior. Numerous models could be presented in this vein; I have chosen one that does a good job of combining the multiple levels into one model: Ritzer's Integration Model.

Ritzer (Ritzer & Goodman 2004:357) proposes four highly interdependent elements in his sociological model: a macro-objective component (e.g., society, law, bureaucracy), a micro-objective component (e.g., patterns of behavior and human interaction), a macro-subjective component (e.g., culture, norms, and values), and a micro-subjective component (e.g., perceptions, beliefs). This model is of particular use in understanding society because it uses two axes: one ranging from objective (society) to subjective (culture and cultural interpretation); the other ranging from the macro-level (norms) to the micro-level (individual level beliefs).

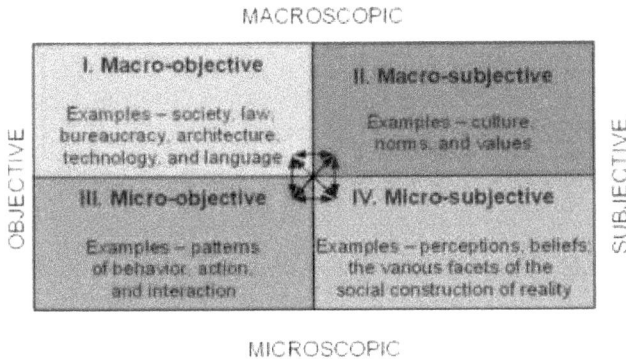

MACROSCOPIC

I. Macro-objective Examples – society, law, bureaucracy, architecture, technology, and language	**II. Macro-subjective** Examples – culture, norms, and values
III. Micro-objective Examples – patterns of behavior, action, and interaction	**IV. Micro-subjective** Examples – perceptions, beliefs; the various facets of the social construction of reality

OBJECTIVE — SUBJECTIVE

MICROSCOPIC

George Ritzer's macro/micro integration theory of social analysis.

The integration approach is particularly useful for explaining social phenomenon because it shows how the different components of social life work together to influence society and behavior.

If used for understanding a specific cultural phenomenon, like the displaying of abstract art in one's home (Halle 1993), the integration model depicts the different influences on the decision. For instance, the model depicts that cultural norms can influence individual behavior. The model also shows that individual level values, beliefs, and behaviors influence macro-level culture. This is, in fact, part of what David Halle finds: while there are art consumption differences based on class, they are not predicted solely by class. Displayers of abstract art tend not only to belong to the upper-class, but also are employed in art-production occupations. This would indicate that there are multiple levels of influence involved in art tastes â€" both broad cultural norms and smaller level occupational norms in addition to personal preferences.

The use of integration theories in sociology is just beginning to develop, but has great potential.

Notes

References

- Biddle, Bruce J. 1986. Recent Development in Role Theory. Annual Review of Sociology. pp. 1267-1292.

- Blumer, H. 1986. Symbolic Interactionism: Perspective and Method. University of California Press. ISBN 0520056760

- Davis, K (1959). "The Myth of Functional Analysis as a Special Method in Sociology and Anthropology", American Sociological Review, 24(6), 757-772.

- Goffman, Erving. 1959. The Presentation of Self in Everyday Life. Anchor Books. ISBN 0385094027

- Goffman, Erving. 1961. Encounters: Two Studies in the Sociology of Interaction. MacMillan Publishing Co. ISBN 0023445602

- Herman, Nancy J. and Reynolds, Larry T. 1994. Symbolic Interaction: An Introduction to Social Psychology. Altamira Press. ISBN 1882289226

- Homans, George Casper (1962). *Sentiments and Activities*. New York: The Free Press of Glencoe.

- Hoult, Thomas Ford (1969). *Dictionary of Modern Sociology*.

- Layton, R. 1997. An Introduction to Theory in Anthropology. Cambridge: Cambridge University Press. ISBN 0521629829

- Marshall, Gordon (1994). The Concise Oxford Dictionary of Sociology. ISBN 019285237.

- Mead, George Herbert. 1967. Mind, Self, & Society: From the Standpoint of a Social Behaviorist. Morris, Charles W. Editor. Chicago: University of Chicago Press. ISBN 0226516687

- Meltzer, Bernard N. 1978. The Social Psychology of George Herbert Mead. In Symbolic Interaction: A Reader in Social Psychology. Manis, Jerome and Meltzer, Bernard N. Editors. Allyn & Bacon. ISBN 0205060625

- Merton, Robert (1957). *Social Theory and Social Structure*, revised and enlarged. London: The Free Press of Glencoe.

- Michener, H. Andrew and John D. DeLamater. 1999. Social Psychology. Harcourt Brace College Publishers. ISBN 0534583210

This chapter draws heavily on the following Wikipedia articles:

- structural-functionalism

- conflict theory

- solidarity

- self

- role

External Links

- Dramaturgy

- Social Psychology

- <u>social constructionism</u>

Society

Introduction

Society refers to a group of people who share a defined territory and a culture. Society is often understood as the basic structure and interactions of a group of people or the network of relationships between entities. A distinction is made between society and culture in sociology. Culture refers to the meanings given to symbols or the process of meaning-making that takes place in a society. Culture is distinct from society in that it adds meanings to relationships (i.e., 'father' means more than 'other'). All human societies have a culture and culture can only exist where there is a society. Distinguishing between these two components of human social life is primarily for analytical purposes - for example, so sociologists can study the transmission of cultural elements or artifacts within a society.

This chapter will present a brief overview of some of the types of human societies that have existed and continue to exist. It will then present some classic approaches to understanding society and what changing social structure can mean for individuals.

Societal Development

The sociological understanding of societal development relies heavily upon the work of Gerhard Lenski (Lenski, Nolan, and Lenski 1995). Lenski outlined some of the more commonly seen organizational structures in human societies. Classifications of human societies can be based on two factors: (1) the primary means of subsistence and (2) the political structure. This chapter focuses on the subsistence systems of societies rather than their political structures.

While it is a bit far-reaching to argue that all societies will develop through the stages outlined below, it does appear that most societies follow such a route. Human groups begin as hunter-gatherers, move toward pastoralism and/or horticulturalism, develop toward an agrarian society, and ultimately end up undergoing a period of industrialization (with the potential for developing a service industry following industrialization). The reason this is presented as a model is because not all societies pass through every stage. Some societies have stopped at the pastoral or horticultural stage, though these may be temporary pauses due to economic niches that will likely disappear in time. Some societies may also jump stages as a result of the introduction of technology from alien societies and culture. Another reason for hesitancy in presenting these categories as distinct groups is that there is often overlap in the subsistence systems used in a society. Some pastoralist societies also engage in some measure of horticultural food production. Industrial societies have agrarian components.

Hunter-Gatherer

The **hunter-gatherer** way of life is based on the exploitation of wild plants and animals. Consequently, hunter-gatherers are relatively mobile, and groups of hunter-gatherers have fluid boundaries and composition. Typically in hunter-gatherer societies men hunt larger wild animals and women gather and hunt smaller animals. Hunter-gatherers use materials available in the wild to construct shelters or rely on naturally occurring shelters like overhangs. Their shelters give them protection from predators and the elements.

Ancient hunter.

The majority of hunter-gatherer societies are nomadic. It is difficult to be settled under such a subsistence system as the resources of one region can quickly become exhausted. Hunter-gatherer societies also tend to have very low population densities as a result of their subsistence system. Agricultural subsistence systems can support population densities 60 to 100 times greater than land left uncultivated, resulting in denser populations.

Hunter-gatherer societies also tend to have non-hierarchical social structures, though this is not always the case. Because hunter-gatherers tend to be nomadic, they generally do not have the possibility to store surplus food. As a result, full-time leaders, bureaucrats, or artisans are rarely supported by hunter-gatherer societies. The hierarchical egalitarianism in hunter-gatherer societies tends to extend to gender-based egalitarianism as well. Although disputed, many anthropologists believe gender egalitarianism in hunter-gatherer societies stems from the lack of control over food production, lack of food surplus - which can be used for control, and an equal gender contribution to kin and cultural survival.

Archeological evidence to date suggests that prior to twelve thousand years ago, all human beings were hunter-gatherers (see the Neolithic revolution for more information on this transition). While declining in number, there are still some hunter-gatherer groups in existence today. Such groups are found in the Arctic, tropical rainforests, and deserts where other forms of subsistence production are impossible or too costly. In most cases these groups do not have a continuous history of hunting and gathering; in many cases their ancestors were agriculturalists who were pushed into marginal areas as a result of migrations and wars. Examples of hunter-gatherer groups still in existence include:

- the Haida of British Columbia

- Bushmen of South Africa

The line between agricultural and hunter-gatherer societies is not clear cut. Many hunter-gatherers consciously manipulate the landscape through cutting or burning unuseful plants to encourage the growth and success of those they consume. Most agricultural people also tend to do some hunting and gathering. Some agricultural groups farm during the temperate months and then hunt during the winter.

Pastoralist

A **pastoralist** society is a society in which the primary means of subsistence is domesticated livestock. It is often the case that, like hunter-gatherers, pastoralists are nomadic, moving seasonally in search of fresh pastures and water for their animals. Employment of a pastoralist subsistence system often results in greater population densities and the development of both social hierarchies and divisions in labor as it is more likely there will be a surplus of food.

A Turkmen with a camel.

Pastoralist societies still exist. For instance, in Australia, the vast semi-arid areas in the interior of the country contain pastoral runs called sheep stations. These areas may be thousands of square kilometers in size. The number of livestock allowed in these areas is regulated in order to reliably sustain them, providing enough feed and water for the stock. Other examples of pastoralists societies still in existence include:

- the Maasai of Kenya

- the Boran

- the Turkana of Kenya

- the Bedouin of Northern Africa

Horticulturalist

Horticulturalist societies are societies in which the primary means of subsistence is the cultivation of crops using hand tools. Like pastoral societies, the cultivation of crops increases population densities and, as a result of food surpluses, allows for a division of labor in society.

Horticulture differs from agriculture in that agriculture employs animals, machinery, or some other non-human means to facilitate the cultivation of crops while horticulture relies solely on humans for crop cultivation.

Agrarian

Agrarian societies are societies in which the primary means of subsistence is the cultivation of crops using a mixture of human and non-human means (i.e., animals and/or machinery). **Agriculture** is the process of producing food, feed, fiber, and other desired products by the cultivation of plants and the raising of domesticated animals (livestock). *Agriculture* can refer to subsistence agriculture or industrial agriculture.

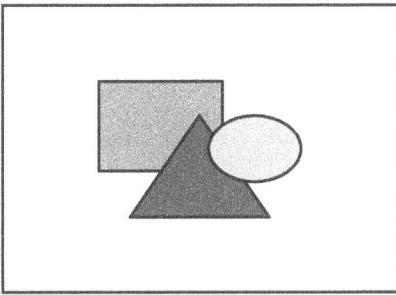
A tractor ploughing an alfalfa field

Subsistence agriculture is agriculture carried out for the production of enough food to meet just the needs of the agriculturalist and his/her family. Subsistence agriculture is a simple, often organic, system using saved seed native to the ecoregion combined with crop rotation or other relatively simple techniques to maximize yield. Historically most farmers were engaged in subsistence agriculture and this is still the case in many developing nations.

In developed nations a person using such simple techniques on small patches of land would generally be referred to as a gardener; activity of this type would be seen more as a hobby than a profession. Some people in developed nations are driven into such primitive methods by poverty. It is also worth noting that large scale organic farming is on the rise as a result of a renewed interest in non-genetically modified and pesticide free foods.

In developed nations, a *farmer* or *industrial agriculturalist* is usually defined as someone with an ownership interest in crops or livestock, and who provides labor or management in their production. Farmers obtain their financial income from the cultivation of land to yield crops or the commercial raising of animals (animal husbandry), or both. Those who provide only labor but not management and do not have ownership are often called *farmhands*, or, if they supervise a leased strip of land growing only one crop, as *sharecroppers*.

41

A pineapple farmer in Ghana.

Agriculture allows a much greater density of population than can be supported by hunting and gathering and allows for the accumulation of excess product to keep for winter use or to sell for profit. The ability of farmers to feed large numbers of people whose activities have nothing to do with material production was the crucial factor in the rise of standing armies. The agriculturalism of the Sumerians allowed them to embark on an unprecedented territorial expansion, making them the first empire builders. Not long after, the Egyptians, powered by effective farming of the Nile valley, achieved a population density from which enough warriors could be drawn for a territorial expansion more than tripling the Sumerian empire in area.

Development of Horticulture and Agriculture

Horticulture and agriculture as types of subsistence developed among humans somewhere between 10,000 and 80,000 B.C.E. in the Fertile Crescent region of the Middle East (for more information see agriculture and Price 2000 and Harris 1996). The reasons for the development of horticulture and agriculture are debated but may have included climate change and the accumulation of food surplus for competitive gift-giving. Most certainly there was a gradual transition from hunter-gatherer to agricultural economies after a lengthy period when some crops were deliberately planted and other foods were gathered from the wild. In addition to the emergence of farming in the Fertile Crescent, agriculture appeared by at least 6,800 B.C.E. in East Asia (rice) and, later, in Central and South America (maize and squash). Small scale agriculture also likely arose independently in early Neolithic contexts in India (rice) and Southeast Asia (taro).

Full dependency on domestic crops and animals (i.e. when wild resources contributed a nutritionally insignificant component to the diet) was not until the Bronze Age. If the operative definition of *agriculture* includes large scale intensive cultivation of land, mono-cropping, organised irrigation, and use of a specialized labor force, the title "inventors of agriculture" would fall to the Sumerians, starting ca. 5,500 B.C.E.

By the early 1800s agricultural practices, particularly careful selection of hardy strains and cultivars, had so improved that yield per land unit was many times that seen in the Middle Ages and before, especially in the largely virgin lands of North and South America.

Agriculture Today

In the Western world, the use of gene manipulation, better management of soil nutrients, and improved weed control have greatly increased yields per unit area. At the same time, the use of mechanization has decreased labor requirements. The developing world generally produces lower yields, having less of the latest science, capital, and technology base. More people in the world are involved in agriculture as their primary economic activity than in any other, yet it only accounts for four percent of the world's GDP. The rapid rise of mechanization in the 20th century, especially in the form of the tractor, reduced the necessity of humans performing the demanding tasks of sowing, harvesting, and threshing. With mechanization, these tasks could be performed with a speed and on a scale barely imaginable before. These advances have led to efficiencies enabling certain modern farms in the United States, Argentina, Israel, Germany and a few other nations to output volumes of high quality produce per land unit at what may be the practical limit.

An example of the influence of technology can be seen in terms of output per farmer. In the early 1900s, one American farmer produced food for 2.5 people; today, a single farmer can feed over 130 people (source).

Industrial

An **industrial society** is a society in which the primary means of subsistence is *industry*. Industry is a system of production focused on mechanized manufacturing of goods. Like agrarian societies, industrial societies increase food surpluses, resulting in more developed hierarchies and significantly more division of labor.

The division of labor in industrial societies is often one of the most notable elements of the society and can even function to re-organize the development of relationships. Whereas relationships in pre-industrial societies were more likely to develop through contact at one's place of worship or through proximity of housing, industrial society brings people with similar occupations together, often leading to the formation of friendships through one's work.

When capitalised, Industrial Revolution refers to the first known industrial revolution, which took place in Europe during the 18th and 19th centuries. What is some times referred to as The Second Industrial Revolution describes later, somewhat less dramatic changes resulting from the widespread availability of electric power and the internal-combustion engine. Many developing nations began industrialisation under the influence of either the United States or the USSR during the Cold War.

Post-Industrial

A **post-industrial society** is a society in which the primary means of subsistence is derived from service-oriented work, as opposed to agriculture or industry. It is important to note here that the term *post-industrial* is still debated in part because it is the current state of society; it is difficult to name a phenomenon while it is occurring.

Post-industrial societies are often marked by:

- an increase in the size of the <u>service sector</u> or jobs that perform services rather than creating goods (industry)

- either the outsourcing of or extensive use of mechanization in manufacturing

- an increase in the amount of <u>information technology</u>, often leading to an <u>Information Age</u>

- information, knowledge, and creativity are seen as the new <u>raw materials</u> of the economy

Post-industrial society is occasionally used critically by individuals seeking to restore or return to industrial development. Increasingly, however, individuals and communities are viewing abandoned factories as sites for new housing and shopping. Capitalists are also realizing the recreational and commercial development opportunities such locations offer. For more information on post-industrial society see the work of <u>Daniel Bell</u>.

Classical Views on Social Change

As Western societies transitioned from pre-industrial economies based primarily on agriculture to industrialized societies in the 19th century, some people worried about the impacts such changes would have on society and individuals. Three early sociologists, Weber, Marx, and Durkheim, perceived different impacts of the Industrial Revolution on the individual and society and described those impacts in their work.

Weber and Rationalization

Max Weber was particularly concerned about the rationalization and bureaucritization of society stemming from the Industrial Revolution and how these two changes would affect humanity's agency and happiness. As Weber understood society, particularly during the industrial revolution of the late 19th century in which he lived, he believed society was being driven by the passage of rational ideas into culture which, in turn, transformed society into an increasingly bureaucratic entity. *Bureaucracy* is a type of organizational or institutional management that is, as Weber understood it, rooted legal-rational authority. Weber did believe bureaucracy was the most rational form of societal management, but because Weber viewed rationalization as the driving force of society, he believed bureaucracy would increase until it ruled society. Society, for Weber, would become almost synonymous with bureaucracy.

As Weber did not see any alternative to bureaucracy, he believed it would ultimately lead to an *iron cage*; society would bureaucratize and there would be no way to get out of it. Weber viewed this as a bleak outcome that would affect individuals' happiness as they would be forced to function in a highly rational society with rigid rules and norms without the possibility to change it. Because Weber could not envision other forces influencing the ultimate direction of society - the exception being temporary lapses into non-bureaucracy spurred by <u>charismatic</u> leaders - he saw no cure for the iron cage of rationality. Society would become a large bureaucracy that would govern people's lives. Weber was unable to envision a solution to his *iron cage of bureaucracy* dilemma; since a completely rational society was inevitable and bureaucracy was the most rational form of societal management, the iron cage, according to

Weber, does not have a solution.

Marx and Alienation

Karl Marx took a different perspective on the impact of the Industrial Revolution on society and the individual. In order to understand Marx's perspective, however, it is necessary to understand how Marx perceived *happiness*. According to Marx, *species being* (or happiness) is the pinnacle of human nature. Species being is understood to be a type of self-realization or self-actualization brought about by meaningful work. But in addition to engaging in meaningful work, self-actualized individuals must also own the products of their labors and have the option of doing what they will with those products. In a capitalist society, which was co-developing with industry, rather than owning the fruits of their labors, the proletariat or working class owns only their labor power, not the fruits of their labors (i.e., the results of production). The capitalists or bourgeoisie employ the proletariat for a living wage, but then keep the products of the labor. As a result, the proletariat is alienated from the fruits of its labor â€" they do not own the products they produce, only their labor power. Because Marx believed species being to be the goal and ideal of human nature and that species being could only be realized when individuals owned the results of their labors, Marx saw capitalism as leading toward increasingly unhappy individuals; they would be alienated from the results of their production and therefore would not be self-realized.

But the alienation from the results of their production is just one component of the alienation Marx proposed. In addition to the alienation from the results of production, the proletariat is also alienated from each other under capitalism. Capitalists alienate the proletariat from each other by forcing them to compete for limited job opportunities. Job opportunities are limited under capitalism in order for capitalists to keep wages down; without a pool of extraneous workers, capitalists would have to meet the wage demands of their workers. Because they are forced to compete with other members of the proletariat, workers are alienated from each other, compounding the unhappiness of the proletariat.

While Marx did have a solution to the problem of alienation, he seldom discussed it in detail. Marx's proposed solution was for the proletariat to unite and through protests or revolution (or legislation in democratic nations) overthrow the bourgeoisie and institute a new form of government â€" communism. This form of government would be based on communally owned and highly developed means of production and self-governance. The means of production would be developed â€" through capitalism â€" to the point that everyone in society would have sufficient 'free' time to allow them to participate in whatever governmental decisions needed to be made for the community as a whole. By re-connecting the individual with the fruits of their labor and empowering them toward true self-governance, *species being* would be realized and happiness would be returned.

Two additional comments are in order here. First, the communism that developed in The Soviet Union and China - as well as other parts of the world - was not the communism envisioned by Marx. These forms of communism still had stratified hierarchies with two groups: a ruling elite and everybody else. Second, Marx believed capitalism, while harmful to *species being*, was necessary to advance the means of production to a stage where communism (as he envisioned it) could be realized. Thus, while Marx was highly critical of capitalism, he also recognized its utility in developing the means of production.

Durkheim and Solidarity

Durkheim's view of society and the changes it was undergoing as a result of industrialization also led him to believe unhappiness was a possible outcome. Durkheim believed that an important component of social life was social solidarity, which is understood as *a sense of community*. In his classic study, *Suicide*, Durkheim argued that one of the root causes of suicide was a decrease in social solidarity â€" termed *anomie* (French for *chaos*) by Durkheim. Durkheim also argued that the increasing emphasis on individualism found in Protestant religions â€" in contrast to Catholicism â€" contributed to an increase in anomie, which resulted in higher suicide rates among Protestants.

In another work, *The Division of Labor in Society*, Durkheim proposed that pre-industrial societies maintained their social solidarity through a mechanistic sense of community and through their religious affiliations. Most people were generalists in their work â€" they farmed and created their own tools and clothing. Because they were alike in their generality, they were also more likely to share a sense of community, which Durkheim saw as an important component of happiness. In addition to their similarity in occupations, many individuals belonged to the same religious groups, which also fostered a sense of solidarity.

In industrializing societies, Durkheim recognized the inevitability of *specialization*. By definition, specialization means that individuals are going to have dissimilar occupations. This specialization would also affect religion. In industrial societies, religion would become just one aspect of lives that were increasingly divided into compartments â€" home, family, work, recreation, religion, etc.

Durkheim believed there were two components that would alleviate the decreasing social solidarity in industrializing societies: organic solidarity and conscientious attempts to find camaraderie through one's place of employ. Whereas social solidarity was maintained in pre-industrial societies through a mechanistic sense of similarity and dependence along with communal religious affiliations, in industrialized societies, social solidarity would be maintained by the interdependence of specialists on one another. If one individual specialized in treating the injured or ill, they would not have time to raise crops or otherwise produce food. Doctors would become dependent on farmers for their food while farmers would become dependent on doctors for their healthcare. This would force a type of organic solidarity â€" organic in the sense that the parts were interdependent like the organs of an animal are interdependent for their survival.

In addition to the inevitable interdependence a specialized society would warrant, Durkheim believed that a conscientious effort to develop and foster friendships would transition from a religious brotherhood to friendships developed at one's place of employment. Specialized individuals would have a great deal in common with their co-workers and, like members of the same religious congregations in pre-industrial societies, co-workers would be able to develop strong bonds of social solidarity through their occupations. Thus, for Durkheim, the answer to the decrease in mechanistic solidarity and the increasing anomie was organic solidarity and solidarity pursued within one's specialty occupation.

Notes

The origin of the word *society* comes from the Latin *societas*, a "friendly association with others." Societas is derived from *socius* meaning "companion" and thus the meaning of society is closely related to "what is social." Implicit in the meaning of society is that its members share some mutual concern or interest in a common objective.

Society can have different meanings than the predominant meaning employed in this chapter. For instance, people united by common political and cultural traditions, beliefs, or values are sometimes also said to be a *society* (e.g., Judeo-Christian, Eastern, Western, etc). When used in this context, the term is being used as a means of contrasting two or more *societies* whose representative members represent alternative conflicting and competing worldviews.

Another use of *society* can be in reference to smaller groups like academic *learned* and *scholarly* societies or associations, such as the American Society of Mathematics.

It should also be noted that there is an ongoing debate in sociological and anthropological circles if there exists an entity we can call *society*. Some Marxist theorists, like Louis Althusser, Ernesto Laclau and Slavoj Zizek, argue that society is nothing more than an effect of the ruling ideology of a certain class system and should not be be understood as a sociological concept.

Societies can also be organized according to their political structure: in order of increasing size and complexity, there are band societies, tribes, chiefdoms, and state societies.

There are some modern variations of the hunter-gatherer lifestyle:

- freeganism is the practice of gathering discarded food in the context of an urban environment

- gleaning is the practice of gathering food traditional farmers leave behind in their fields

- sport hunting and sport fishing are recreational activities practiced by people who get the majority of their food by modern means

- primitivism is a movement striving for the return to a pre-industrial and pre-agricultural society

References

- Bernal, John Desmond. 1970. Science and Industry in the Nineteenth Century. Bloomington: Indiana University Press.

- Collinson, M. [ed.]. 2000. A History of Farming Systems Research. CABI Publishing. ISBN 0851994059

- Crosby, Alfred W. 2003. The Columbian Exchange: Biological and Cultural Consequences of

1492. Praeger Publishers. 30th Anniversary Edition. ISBN 0275980731

- Derry, Thomas Kingston and Williams, Trevor I. 1993. A Short History of Technology : From the Earliest Times to A.D. 1900. New York: Dover Publications.

- Harris, David R. [ed.]. 1996. The Origins and Spread of Agriculture in Eurasia. UCL Press. ISBN 1560986751

- Hobsbawm, Eric J. 1999. Industry and Empire: From 1750 to the Present Day. New York: New Press. Distributed by W.W. Norton.

- Kranzberg, Melvin and Pursell, Carroll W., Jr. 1967. Editors. Technology in Western civilization. New York, Oxford University Press.

- Landes, David S. 2003. The Unbound Prometheus: Technical Change and Industrial Development in Western Europe from 1750 to the Present. 2nd ed. New York: Cambridge University Press.

- Lenski, Gerhard; Nolan, Patrick; and Lenski, Jean. 1995. Human Societies: An Introduction to Macrosociology. 7th edition. New York: McGraw-Hill. ISBN 1594510237

- Price, T. Douglas [ed.]. 2000. Europe's First Farmers. Cambrige University Press. ISBN 0521665728

- Wells, Spencer. 2003. The Journey of Man: A Genetic Odyssey. Princeton University Press. ISBN 069111532X

This chapter also draws heavily on the following Wikipedia articles:

- society

- hunter-gatherer

- agriculture

- farming

- pastoralist

External Links

- Haferkamp, Hans, and Smelser, Neil J. Editors. 1992. Social Change and Modernity. Berkeley: University of California Press.

- FAO of the United Nations

- Current World Production, Market and Trade Reports of the U.S. Department of Agriculture's

Foreign Agricultural Service

- Winds of Change: Reforms and Unions - The impacts of industrialization in Canada; illustrated with many late 19th century photographs.

- Daniel Bell's work on post-industrial societies

See also:

- cultural evolution

Culture

Introduction

Unfortunately, there is no simple answer to the question of *what is culture*. Culture is a complicated phenomenon to understand because it is both distinct from but clearly associated with *society*. Also, different definitions of culture reflect different theories or understandings, making it difficult to pin down exact definitions of the concept.

Generally speaking, the following elements of social life are considered to be representative of human culture: "stories, beliefs, media, ideas, works of art, religious practices, fashions, rituals, specialized knowledge, and common sense" (Griswold 2004:xvi).

Yet, examples of culture do not, in themselves, present a clear understanding of the concept of culture; culture is more than the object or behavior. Culture also includes,

â€¦norms, values, beliefs, or expressive symbols. Roughly, norms are the way people behave in a given society, values are what they hold dear, beliefs are how they think the universe operates, and expressive symbols are representations, often representations of social norms, values, and beliefs themselves. (Griswold 2004:3)

To summarize, culture encompasses objects and symbols, the meaning given to those objects and symbols, and the norms, values, and beliefs that pervade social life.

'High' Culture

Many people today use a concept of *culture* that developed in Europe during the 18th and early 19th centuries. This concept of culture reflected inequalities within European societies and their colonies around the world. It identifies *culture* with *civilization* and contrasts both with *nature*. According to this thinking, some countries are more civilized than others, and some people are more cultured than others. Thus some cultural theorists have actually tried to eliminate popular or mass culture from the definition of culture. Theorists like Matthew Arnold (1822-1888) believed that culture is simply that which is created by "the best that has been thought and said in the world" (Arnold 1960:6). Anything that doesn't fit into this category is labeled as chaos or anarchy. On this account, culture is closely tied to cultivation, which is the progressive refinement of human behavior.

Ballet, traditionally considered *high* culture.

In practice, *culture* referred to elite goods and activities such as haute cuisine, high fashion or haute couture, museum-caliber art and classical music, and the word *cultured* referred to people who knew about, and took part in, these activities. For example, someone who used *culture* in the sense of *cultivation* might argue that classical music is more refined than music by working-class people, such as jazz or the indigenous music traditions of aboriginal peoples.

People who use *culture* in this way tend not to use it in the plural. They believe that there are not distinct cultures, each with their own internal logic and values, but rather only a single standard of refinement to which all groups are held accountable. Thus people who differ from those who believe themselves to be *cultured* in this sense are not usually understood as *having a different culture*; they are understood as being *uncultured*.

The Changing Concept of Culture

Today most social scientists reject the *cultured vs. uncultured* concept of culture and the opposition of culture to human nature. They recognize that non-elites are as cultured as elites (and that non-Westerners are just as civilized); they are just cultured in a different way.

During the Romantic Era, scholars in Germany, especially those concerned with nationalism, developed a more inclusive notion of culture as *worldview*. That is, each ethnic group is characterized by a distinct and incommensurable world view. Although more inclusive, this approach to culture still allowed for distinctions between *civilized* and *primitive* or *tribal* cultures.

By the late 19th century, anthropologists had changed the concept of culture to include a wider variety of societies, ultimately resulting in the concept of culture outlined above - objects and symbols, the meaning given to those objects and symbols, and the norms, values, and beliefs that pervade social life.

This new perspective has also removed the evaluative element of the concept of culture and instead proposes distinctions rather than rankings between different cultures. For instance, the *high* culture of elites is now contrasted with *popular* or *pop culture*. In this sense, *high* culture no longer refers to the idea of being *cultured*, as all people are cultured. *High* culture simply refers to the objects, symbols, norms, values, and beliefs of a particular group of people; popular culture does the same.

The Origins of Culture

Attentive to the theory of evolution, anthropologists assumed that all human beings are equally evolved, and the fact that all humans have cultures must in some way be a result of human evolution. They were also wary of using biological evolution to explain differences between specific cultures - an approach that either was a form of, or legitimized forms of, racism. Anthropologists believed biological evolution produced an inclusive notion of culture, a concept that anthropologists could apply equally to non-literate and literate societies, or to nomadic and to sedentary societies. They argued that through the course of their evolution, human beings evolved a universal human capacity to classify experiences, and encode and communicate them symbolically. Since these symbolic systems were learned and taught, they began to develop independently of biological evolution (in other words, one human being can learn a belief, value, or way of doing something from another, even if they are not biologically related). That this capacity for symbolic thinking and social learning is a product of human evolution confounds older arguments about nature versus nurture. Thus, Clifford Geertz (1973: 33 ff.) has argued that human physiology and neurology developed in conjunction with the first cultural activities, and Middleton (1990:17 n.27) concluded that human "*instincts* were culturally formed."

Chinese Opera, a culture quite distinct from that of the U.S.

This view of culture argues that people living apart from one another develop unique cultures. However, elements of different cultures can easily spread from one group of people to another. Culture is dynamic and can be taught and learned, making it a potentially rapid form of adaptation to change in physical conditions. Anthropologists view culture as not only a product of biological evolution but as a supplement to it; it can be seen as the main means of human adaptation to the natural world.

This view of culture as a symbolic system with adaptive functions, which varies from place to place, led anthropologists to conceive of different cultures as defined by distinct patterns (or structures) of enduring, although arbitrary, conventional sets of meaning, which took concrete form in a variety of artifacts such as myths and rituals, tools, the design of housing, and the planning of villages. Anthropologists thus distinguish between **material culture** and **symbolic culture**, not only because each reflects different kinds of human activity, but also because they constitute different kinds of data that require different methodologies to study.

52

This view of culture, which came to dominate between World War I and World War II, implied that each culture was bounded and had to be understood as a whole, on its own terms. The result is a belief in cultural relativism (see below).

Level of Abstraction

Another element of culture that is important for a clear understanding of the concept is level of abstraction. Culture ranges from the concrete, cultural object (e.g., the understanding of a work of art) to micro-level interpersonal interactions (e.g., the socialization of a child by his/her parents) to a macro-level influence on entire societies (e.g., the Puritanical roots of the U.S. that can be used to justify the exportation of democracy â€" a lÃ¡ the Iraq War; see Wald 2003). It is important when trying to understand the concept of culture to keep in mind that the concept can have multiple levels of meaning.

The Artificiality of Cultural Categorization

One of the more important points to understand about culture is that it is an artificial categorization of elements of social life. As Griswold (2004) puts it,

There is no such thing as *culture* or *society* out there in the real world. There are only people who work, joke, raise children, love, think, worship, fight, and behave in a wide variety of ways. To speak of culture as one thing and society as another is to make an analytical distinction between two different aspects of human experience. One way to think of the distinction is that culture designates the expressive aspect of human existence, whereas society designates the relational (and often practical) aspect. (Griswold 2004:4)

In the above quote, Griswold emphasizes that culture is distinct from society but affirms that this distinction is, like all classifications, artificial. Humans do not experience culture in a separate or distinct way from society. Culture and society are truly two-sides of a coin; a coin that makes up social life. Yet the distinction between the two, while artificial, is useful for a number of reasons. For instance, the distinction between culture and society is of particular use when exploring how norms and values are transmitted from generation to generation and answering the question of cultural conflict between people of different cultural backgrounds (say, Japanese and United Statesians).

In summary, culture is a complex component of social life, distinct from the interactions of society in particular because it adds meanings to relationships. Culture is also multi-leveled in that it can range from concrete cultural objects to broad social norms.

Subcultures & Countercultures

A **subculture** is a culture shared and actively participated in by a minority of people within a broader culture.

⬚Body piercing is an increasingly popular subculture in the U.S.

A culture often contains numerous subcultures. Subcultures incorporate large parts of the broader cultures of which they are part, but in specifics they may differ radically. Some subcultures achieve such a status that they acquire a name of their own. Examples of subcultures could include: bikers, military culture, and Star Trek fans (trekkers or trekkies).

A **counterculture** is a subculture with the addition that some of its beliefs, values, or norms challenge those of the main culture of which it is part. Examples of countercultures in the U.S. could include: the hippie movement of the 1960s, the green movement, and feminist groups.

Ethnocentrism & Cultural Relativism

Ethnocentrism is the tendency to look at the world primarily from the perspective of one's own culture. Many claim that ethnocentrism occurs in every society; ironically, ethnocentrism may be something that all cultures have in common.

The term was coined by William Graham Sumner, a social evolutionist and professor of Political and Social Science at Yale University. He defined it as the viewpoint that "oneâ€(tm)s own group is the center of everything," against which all other groups are judged. Ethnocentrism often entails the belief that one's own race or ethnic group is the most important and/or that some or all aspects of its culture are superior to those of other groups. Within this ideology, individuals will judge other groups in relation to their own particular ethnic group or culture, especially with concern to language, behaviour, customs, and religion. It also involves an incapacity to acknowledge that cultural differentiation does not imply inferiority of those groups who are ethnically distinct from one's own.

Cultural relativism is the belief that the concepts and values of a culture cannot be fully translated into, or fully understood in, other languages; that a specific cultural artifact (e.g. a ritual) has to be understood in terms of the larger symbolic system of which it is a part.

An example of cultural relativism might include slang words from specific languages (and even from particular dialects within a language). For instance, the word *tranquilo* in Spanish translates directly to 'calm' in English. However, it can be used in many more ways than just as an adjective (e.g., the seas are calm). Tranquilo can be a command or suggestion encouraging another to *calm down*. It can also be used to ease tensions in an argument (e.g., everyone relax) or to indicate a degree of self-composure (e.g., I'm calm). There is not a clear English translation of the word, and in order to fully comprehend its many possible uses a cultural relativist would argue that it would be necessary to fully immerse oneself in cultures where the word is used.

Theories of Culture

While there are numerous theoretical approaches employed to understand 'culture', this chapter uses just one model to illustrate how sociologists understand the concept. The model is an integrationist model advocated by Ritzer (Ritzer & Goodman 2004:357). Ritzer proposes four highly interdependent elements in his sociological model: a macro-objective component (e.g., society, law, bureaucracy), a micro-objective component (e.g., patterns of behavior and human interaction), a macro-subjective component (e.g., culture, norms, and values), and a micro-subjective component (e.g., perceptions, beliefs). This model is of particular use in understanding the role of culture in sociological research because it presents two axes for understanding culture: one ranging from objective (society) to subjective (culture and cultural interpretation); the other ranging from the macro-level (norms) to the micro-level (individual level beliefs).

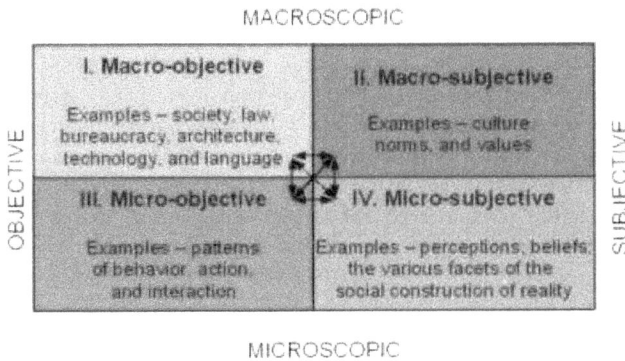

George Ritzer's macro/micro integration theory of social analysis.

If used for understanding a specific cultural phenomenon, like the displaying of abstract art (Halle 1993), this model depicts how cultural norms can influence individual behavior. This model also posits that individual level values, beliefs, and behaviors can, in turn, influence the macro-level culture. This is, in fact, part of what David Halle finds: while there are certainly cultural differences based on class, they are not unique to class. Displayers of abstract art tend not only to belong to the upper-class, but also are employed in art-production occupations. This would indicate that there are multiple levels of influence involved in art tastes â€" both broad cultural norms and smaller level occupational norms in addition to personal preferences.

The Function of Culture

Culture can also be seen to play a specific function in social life. According to Griswold, "The sociological analysis of culture begins at the premise that culture provides orientation, wards off chaos, and directs behavior toward certain lines of action and away from others" (Griswold 2004:24). Griswold reiterates this point by explaining that, "Groups and societies need collective representations of themselves to inspire sentiments of unity and mutual support, and culture fulfills this need" (p. 59). In other words, culture can have a certain utilitarian function â€" the maintenance of order as the result of shared understandings and meanings (this understanding of culture is similar to the Symbolic Interactionist understanding of society).

Cultural Change

The belief that culture is symbolically coded and can thus be taught from one person to another means that cultures, although bounded, can change. Cultures are both predisposed to change and resistant to it. Resistance can come from habit, religion, and the integration and interdependence of cultural traits. For example, men and women have complementary roles in many cultures. One sex might desire changes that affect the other, as happened in the second half of the 20th century in western cultures (see women's movement), while the other sex may be resistant to that change (possibly in order to maintain a power imbalance in their favor).

Cultural change can have many causes, including: the environment, inventions, and contact with other cultures. For example, the end of the last ice age helped lead to the invention of agriculture. Some inventions that affected Western culture in the 20th century were the birth control pill, television, and the Internet.

Several understandings of how cultures change come from Anthropology. For instance, in diffusion theory, the form of something moves from one culture to another, but not its meaning. For example, the ankh symbol originated in Egyptian culture but has diffused to numerous cultures. It's original meaning may have been lost, but it is now used by many practitioners of New Age Religion as an arcane symbol of power or life forces. A variant of the diffusion theory, stimulus diffusion, refers to an element of one culture leading to an invention in another.

Contact between cultures can also result in acculturation. Acculturation has different meanings, but in this context refers to replacement of the traits of one culture with those of another, such as what happened with many Native American Indians. Related processes on an individual level are assimilation and transculturation, both of which refer to adoption of a different culture by an individual.

One sociological approach to cultural change has been outlined by Griswold (2004). Griswold points out that it may seem as though culture comes from individuals â€" which, for certain elements of cultural change, is true â€" but there is also the larger, collective, and long-lasting culture that cannot have been the creation of single individuals as it predates and post-dates individual humans and contributors to culture. The author presents a sociological perspective to address this conflict,

56

Sociology suggests an alternative to both the unsatisfying *it has always been that way* view at one extreme and the unsociological *individual genius* view at the other. This alternative posits that culture and cultural works are collective, not individual, creations. We can best understand specific cultural objects... by seeing them not as unique to their creators but as the fruits of collective production, fundamentally social in their genesis. (p. 53)

In short, Griswold argues that culture changes through the contextually dependent and socially situated actions of individuals; macro-level culture influences the individual who, in turn, can influence that same culture. The logic is a bit circular, but illustrates how culture can change over time yet remain somewhat constant.

It is, of course, important to recognize here that Griswold is talking about cultural change and not the actual origins of culture (as in, "there was no culture and then, suddenly, there was"). Because Griswold does not explicitly distinguish between the origins of cultural change and the origins of culture, it may appear as though Griswold is arguing here for the origins of culture and situating these origins in society. This is neither accurate nor a clear representation of sociological thought on this issue. Culture, just like society, has existed since the beginning of humanity (humans being social and cultural). Society and culture co-exist because humans have social relations and meanings tied to those relations (e.g. brother, lover, friend; see, for instance, Leakey 1994). Culture as a super-phenomenon has no real beginning except in the sense that humans (homo sapiens) have a beginning. This, then, makes the question of the origins of culture moot â€" it has existed as long as we have, and will likely exist as long as we do. Cultural change, on the other hand, is a matter that can be questioned and researched, as Griswold does.

Cultural Sociology: Researching Culture

How do sociologists study culture? One approach to studying culture falls under the label 'cultural sociology', which combines the study of culture with cultural understandings of phenomena.

Griswold (2004) explains how cultural sociologists approach their research,

...if one were to try to understand a certain group of people, one would look for the expressive forms through which they represent themselves to themselves... The sociologist can come at this collective representation process from the other direction, from the analysis of a particular cultural object, as well; if we were to try to understand a cultural object, we would look for how it is used by some group as representing that group. (p. 59)

In other words, because of the perspective of cultural sociologists, their approach to studying culture involves looking for how people make meaning in their lives out of the different cultural elements that surround them.

A particularly clear example of cultural sociology is the study of the Village-Northton by Elijah Anderson (1990). Anderson is interested in a number of things in his book, but two cultural components stand out. First, Anderson is looking at the border of two culturally and socioeconomically distinct neighborhoods. Because these two neighborhoods are distinct yet share a border, this research site provides numerous opportunities for the exploration of culture. Not surprisingly, cultural conflict is an optimal scenario for the exploration of culture and cultural interaction. Additionally, Anderson is interested in how individuals in these neighborhoods negotiate interpersonal interactions, especially when individuals from the Village (middle to upper-middle class and predominantly white) are forced to interact with members of the Northton area (lower class and poor blacks).

Andersonâ€(tm)s methodology is a combination of participant observation and interviews. But when viewed in light of the quote above by Griswold, it becomes apparent that Andersonâ€(tm)s focus in these interviews and observations is self-presentation (also see impression management). Anderson regularly describes the individuals he interviews and observes in light of their clothing, behavior, attitudes, beliefs, and opinions. As he interacts with more and more individuals, patterns begin to develop. Specifically, individuals dressed in certain outfits behave in similar ways. For instance, those dressed in business attire (even when walking their dogs) â€" the yuppies â€" have particular perspectives on the future of the Village: they are interested in increasing property values in order to maximize their investment. Another example of cultural significance of clothing is older black men who intentionally wear button-up shirts and ties because of the cultural symbolism of that particular outfit: it signifies to the cultural outsider that the wearer is refined and distinct from the athletic-suit-wearing drug dealers who control numerous Northton corners.

Ultimately, Andersonâ€(tm)s goal is to develop a sort of typology of *streetwise* individuals: people who can manage awkward and uncomfortable interpersonal interactions on the street in such a fashion that they emerge from the interactions unharmed. While he does develop a loose description of these types of individuals, the important part to understand here is how he explores these aspects of culture. First, he found a cultural border that presented cultural conflict. When individuals have to negotiate meaning publicly, it makes it much easier for the sociologist to tease out culture. Additionally, Anderson observed both the transmission of culture from generation to generation (i.e., socialization, but also the self-representation that is provided by cultural expressions (clothing, behavior, etc). Through years of observation, Anderson gained a familiarity with these elements of culture that allowed him to understand how they interacted.

In summary, cultural sociology (or the study of culture) is performed by examining how individuals express themselves to others and is likely facilitated by finding cultural boundaries where cultural expression is important to successful social functioning.

Notes

The word 'culture' comes from the Latin root *colere* (to inhabit, to cultivate, or to honor).

References

- Anderson, Elijah. 1990. Streetwise: Race, Class, and Change in an Urban Community. Chicago, IL: University of Chicago Press.

- Arnold, Matthew, *Culture and Anarchy*, 1882. Macmillan and Co., New York. Online at [1].

- Geertz, Clifford. (1973). *The Interpretation of Cultures: Selected Essays*. New York. ISBN 0465097197.

- Griswold, Wendy. 2004. Cultures and Societies in a Changing World. Thousand Oaks, CA: Pine Forge Press.

- Halle, David. 1993. Inside Culture: Art and Class in the American Home. Chicago, IL: University of Chicago Press.

- Hoult, Thomas Ford, ed. (1969). *Dictionary of Modern Sociology*. Totowa, New Jersey, United States: Littlefield, Adams & Co.

- Kroeber, A. L. and C. Kluckhohn, 1952. *Culture: A Critical Review of Concepts and Definitions*. Peabody Museum, Cambridge, Massachusetts, United States.

- Leakey, Richard. 1996. The Origin of Humankind. New York: BasicBooks.

- Ritzer, George and Douglas J. Goodman. 2004. Modern Sociological Theory. sixth ed. Boston, MA: McGraw Hill.

- Wald, Kenneth D. 2003. Religion and Politics in the United States. Fourth ed. New york: Rowman & Littlefield Publishers, Inc.

This chapter drew heavily on the following Wikipedia articles:

- culture
- ethnocentrism
- cultural relativism

External links

Socialization

What is Socialization?

Socialization generally refers to the process in which people learn the skills, knowledge, values, motives, and roles (i.e., <u>culture</u>) of the groups to which they belong or the communities in which they live. It should be pointed out from the beginning of this chapter that socialization includes two components (Long and Hadden 1985). The first component of socialization is the process, mentioned above, that leads to the adoption of culture. The second component is the outcome of the process, for example, "Was the socialization successful?" or "He has been socialized to believe God exists." Socialization is seen as society's principal mechanism for influencing the development of character and behavior. Most sociologists treat socialization "as a cornerstone both for the maintenance of society and for the well-being of the individual" (Long and Hadden 1985).

Elements of Socialization

As socialization is a fundamental sociological concept, there are a number of components to this concept that are important to understand. While not every sociologist will agree which elements are the most important, or even how to define some of the elements of socialization, the elements outlined below should help clarify what is meant by socialization.

Goals of Socialization

Arnett (1995), in presenting a new theoretical understanding of socialization (see below), outlined what he believes to be the three goals of socialization:

1.   impulse control and the development of a <u>conscience</u>

2.   role preparation and performance, including occupational roles, gender roles, and roles in institutions such as marriage and parenthood

3.   the cultivation of sources of meaning, or what is important, valued, and to be lived for

In short, socialization is the process that prepares humans to function in social life. It should be re-iterated here that socialization is culturally relative - people in different cultures are socialized differently. This distinction does not and should not inherently force an evaluative judgment. Socialization, because it is the adoption of culture, is going to be different in every culture. Socialization, as both process or an outcome, is not better or worse in any particular culture.

⌐A kindergarten in Afghanistan.

Primary and Secondary Socialization

Socialization is a life process, but is generally divided into two parts. *Primary socialization* takes place early in life, as a child and adolescent. *Secondary socialization* refers to the socialization that takes place throughout one's life, both as a child and as one encounters new groups that require additional socialization. While there are scholars who argue that only one or the other of these occurs, most social scientists tend to combine the two, arguing that the basic or core identity of the individual develops during primary socialization, with more specific changes occurring later - secondary socialization - in response to the acquisition of new group memberships and roles and differently structured social situations. The need for later life socialization may stem from the increasing complexity of society with its corresponding increase in varied roles and responsibilities (Mortimer and Simmons 1978).

Mortimer and Simmons (1978) outline three specific ways these two parts of socialization differ:

1.   content - Socialization in childhood is thought to be concerned with the regulation of biological drives. In adolescence, socialization is concerned with the development of overarching values and the self-image. In adulthood, socialization involves more overt and specific norms and behaviors, such as those related to the work role as well as more superficial personality features.

2.   context - In earlier periods, the *socializee* (the person being socialized) more clearly assumes the status of *learner* within the context of the family of orientation, the school, or the peer group. Also, relationships in the earlier period are more likely to be affectively charged, i.e., highly emotional. In adulthood, though the socializee takes the role of student at times, much socialization occurs after the socializee has assumed full incumbency of the adult role. There is also a greater likelihood of more formal relationships due to situational contexts (e.g., work environment), which moderates down the affective component.

3.   response - The child and adolescent may be more easily malleable than the adult. Also, much adult socialization is self-initiated and voluntary; adults can leave or terminate the process at any time.

Socialization is, of course, a social process. As such, it involves interactions between people.

Socialization, as noted in the distinction between primary and secondary, can take place in multiple contexts and as a result of contact with numerous groups. Some of the more significant contributors to the socialization process are: parents, friends, schools, siblings, and co-workers. Each of these groups include a culture that must be learned and to some degree appropriated by the socializee in order to gain admittance to the group.

A painting of a prison.

Total Institutions

Not all socialization is voluntary nor is all socialization successful. There are components of society designed specifically to resocialize individuals who were not successfully socialized to begin with. For instance, prisons and mental health institutions are designed to resocialize the people who are deemed to have not been successfully socialized. Depending on the degree of isolation and resocialization that takes place in a given institution, some of these institutions are labeled *total institutions*. In his classic study of total institutions, Erving Goffman (1961:6) gives the following characteristics of total institutions:

1. all aspects of life are conducted in the same place under the same authority

2. the individual is a member of a large cohort, all treated alike

3. all daily activities (over a 24-hour period) are tightly scheduled

4. there is a sharp split between supervisors and lower participants

5. information about the member's fate is withheld

The most common examples of total institutions include mental hospitals, prisons, and military boot camps, though there are numerous other institutions that could be considered total institutions as well. The goal of total institutions is to facilitate a complete break with one's old

62

life in order for the institution to resocialize the individual into a new life.

Mortimer and Simmons (1978) note a difference in socialization methodologies in different types of institutions. When the goal of an institution is socialization (primary or secondary), the institution tends to use normative pressures. When the goal of an institution is resocialization of deviants, coercion is frequently involved

Broad and Narrow Socialization

An interesting though seldom used distinction in types of socialization was proposed by Arnett (1995). Arnett distinguishes between broad and narrow socialization:

- broad socialization is intended to promote independence, individualism, and self-expression; it is dubbed *broad* because this type of socialization has the potential of resulting in a broad range of outcomes

- narrow socialization is intended to promote obedience and conformity; it is dubbed *narrow* because there is a narrow range of outcomes

These distinctions correspond to Arnett's definition of socialization, which is:

the whole process by which an individual born with behavioral potentialities of enormously wide range, is led to develop actual behavior which is confined with a much narrower range; the range of what is customary and acceptable for him according to the standards of his group

Arnett explains that his understanding of socialization should not be understood as having just two options, broad or narrow. Instead, the author argues that socialization can be broad or narrow within each of the seven socializing forces he outlines (e.g., family, friends, etc.). Because each force can be either broad or narrow, there is a wide variety of possible broad/narrow socialization combinations. Finally, Arnett notes two examples where his distinction is relevant. First, Arnett argues that there are often differences in socialization by gender. Where these differences exist, argues Arnett, socialization tends to be narrower for women than for men. Arnett also argues that Japanese socialization is narrow as there is more pressure toward conformity in that culture. Arnett argues that this may account for the lower crime rates in Japan.

The Importance of Socialization

One of the most common methods used to illustrate the importance of socialization is to draw upon the few unfortunate cases of children who were, through neglect, misfortune, or willful abuse, not socialized by adults while they were growing up. Examples of such children can be found here.

Theoretical Understandings of Socialization

Socialization, as a concept in social scientific research, has evolved over time. While the basic idea outlined above has been a component of most understandings of socialization, there has been quite a variety of definitions and theories of socialization. Some of these approaches are presented here as definitional variety is often informative (see Holland 1970, Mortimer and Simmons 1978, and Long and Hadden 1985 for more information).

- Symbolic Interactionism - the self develops as a result of social interactions; as a result, socialization is highly dependent on the situations in which the actor finds him/herself; this approach also argues that socialization is a continuous, lifelong process

- Role Theory - socialization is seen as a process of acquisition of appropriate norms, attitudes, self-images, values, and role behaviors that enable acceptance in the group and effective performance of new roles; in this framework, socialization is seen as a conservative force, permitting the perpetuation of the social organization in spite of the turn-over of individual members through time

- Reinforcement Theory - the self develops as a result of cognitive evaluations of costs and benefits; this understanding assumes that the socializee, in approaching new roles, is an independent and active negotiator for advantages in relationships with role partners and membership groups

- Internalization Theory - socialization is a series of stages in which the individual learns to participate in various levels of organization of society; this theory contends that the child internalizes a cognitive frame of reference for interpersonal relations and a common system of expressive symbolism in addition to a moral conscience; this approach was advocated by Talcott Parsons

Socialization as *Joining Groups*

The concept of socialization has traditionally addressed the problem of individual adjustment to society. In all of the approaches outlined above, socialization has, in one way or another, referred to the idea that society shapes its members toward compliance and cooperation with societal requirements. In order to reduce confusion, develop a research methodology for measuring socialization, and potentially lead to the comparability of research findings from different studies, Long and Hadden (1985) proposed a revised understanding of socialization. Rather than referring to a vague adoption or learning of culture, Long and Hadden reframed socialization as "the medium for transforming newcomers into bona fide members of a group." Before discussing some of the specifics of this approach, it may be useful to outline some of the critiques Long and Hadden present of earlier approaches to socialization.

According to Long and Hadden, many earlier approaches to socialization extended socialization to every part of human social life. As a result, everyone becomes both a socializing agent (socializer) and a novice (socializee) in all encounters with others. This conceptualization leaves socialization without a social home; it is all around but no place in particular. Another criticism of previous approaches is that they allowed socialization to include anything, and anything which is part of the process at one time may be excluded at another. With this conceptualization, any phenomenon may shift its status in the socialization process without changing its own composition or expression. In other words, socialization includes virtually everything, excludes almost nothing, and shifts with circumstance and outcomes. Additionally, previous approaches to socialization lacked specificity about the nature of socialization activity. Defining socialization by its outcomes made it unnecessary to stipulate the nature of the process conceptually. Socialization could be attributed to *this or that* but in order to truly understand what is taking place it is necessary to go beyond just pointing to socializing agents and specify what it is about those agents that is doing the socializing. Another serious drawback of earlier approaches is that they disregard the *process* component of socialization. Doing so limits the socialization concept to employment primarily as a post hoc interpretive category that is used to lend significance to findings defined and developed in other terms.

As a result of these criticisms, Long and Hadden (1985) found themselves presented with a two-fold task:

- locate socialization and its social boundaries more precisely

- specify the distinctive properties which distinguish it from related phenomena

To accomplish this, Long and Hadden developed a new understanding of socialization, "socialization is the process of creating and incorporating new members of a group from a pool of newcomers, carried out by members and their allies". Under this understanding, the principal agents of socialization are certified and practicing members of the group to which novices are being socialized. It should be noted that *certified* here is only a shortened way of saying "a socially approved member of the group." Thus, Long and Hadden's revised understanding of socialization sees it as both the process and outcome of joining groups.

Research Examples

Numerous examples of research on socialization could be presented in this section. One important area of socialization research involves differences in gender socialization, but much of that research is summarized in the chapter on gender. The following three research examples are interesting in that they explore both primary and secondary socialization and do so from varying perspectives.

Socialization and Social Class

Ellis, Lee, and Peterson (1978), developing a research agenda begun by Melvin L. Kohn (1959), explored differences in how parents raise their children relative to their social class. Kohn (1959) found that lower class parents were more likely to emphasize conformity in their children whereas middle-class parents were more likely to emphasize creativity and self-reliance. Ellis et. al. proposed and found that parents value conformity over self-reliance in children to the extent that conformity superseded self-reliance as a criterion for success in their own endeavors. In other words, Ellis et. al. verified that the reason lower-class parents emphasize conformity in their children is because they experience conformity in their day-to-day activities. For example, factory work is far more about conforming than innovation.

Another study in this same area explored a slightly different component of this relationship. Erlanger (1974) was interested in a correlation between social class and physical violence. While he did not find a strong correlation indicating lower class individuals were more likely to employ physical violence in punishing their children, he did present evidence concerning several outdated propositions. Erlanger's findings include:

- physical punishment *does not* lead to *working class authoritarianism*

- childhood punishment experiences *do not* explain the greater probability that working class adults, as opposed to middle class adults, will commit homicide

- general use of corporal punishment *is not* a precursor to child abuse

- use of corporal punishment *is not* part of a subcultural positive evaluation of violence

It should be noted that this is an older study and that more recent findings may have shed more light on these issues. It should also be noted that Erlanger readily points out when his findings are strongly supported or weakly supported by his data. It behooves the interested party to read his paper directly rather than rely on the summary above for the specific nuances.

Socialization and Death Preparation

Marshall (1975) interviewed a number of retirement home residents to explore how their environment influenced their thinking about death. In essence, Marshall was examining secondary socialization concerning mortality. Marshall found that a combination of relationships, behavioral changes, and retirement home culture contributed to a conception of death that was both accepting and courageous.

Residents of this particular retirement home found themselves with more time on their hands - to think about death - because they no longer had to care for their own homes. Additionally, they found themselves surrounded by people in a situation similar to their own: they were basically moving into the retirement home to prepare for death. The prevalence of elderly people facilitated discussions of death, which also helped socialize the residents into their acceptance of mortality. Finally, the retirement home community encouraged a culture of life and fulfillment in part to counter-act the frequency of death. Some residents calculated there was one death per week in the retirement home. In light of such numbers, it was important to the success of the community to maintain a positive culture that embraced life yet accepted death. In summary, Marshall found that numerous factors contributed to the socialization of residents into a positive lifestyle that was also accepting of and preparatory for their impending deaths.

Do College Preparation Classes Make a Difference?

Rosenbaum (1975) was interested in the effects of high school tracks on IQ. High school tracks are the different levels or types of courses students can take; for instance, many high schools now include college preparation tracks and general education tracks. Rosenbaum's theory was that students who followed the lower tracks (non college-preparation) would score lower on IQ tests over time than would students who followed the higher tracks (college-preparation). Considering that school is one of the primary contributors to socialization, it makes sense that participation in a given track can also result in the adoption of the norms, values, beliefs, skills, and behaviors that correspond to that track. In other words, tracks can turn into a type of self-fulfilling prophecy: you may start out at the same level as someone in a higher track, but by the time you have completed the lower track you will have become like the other students in your track.

To reduce confounding variables and ensure notable test effects, Rosenbaum selected a homogeneous, white, working class public school with five different, highly stratified classes. Rosenbaum then compared IQ scores for individuals in the different tracks at two time points. As it turns out, *tracking* does have a significant effect on IQ. People in lower tracks can actually see a decline in IQ compared to a possible increase among those in the upper track. In other words, tracks socialize their students into their corresponding roles.

Notes

Additional Theoretical Approaches

These approaches are occasionally discussed in the literature, but do not seem distinct enough or adopted widely enough to warrant inclusion in the primary content of this chapter:

- identification theory - similar to role theory with three psychological components (a) cathexis of the role, (b) identification with a real or ideal model, (c) introjection of the model's values as the culmination

- generalization theory - the socialization of attitudes, values, and ways of thinking is abstracted and generalized from the modes of successful adaptation

- expectancy theory - attaches great importance to the actor's expectations regarding the behavioral outcomes of his efforts and the group's response to them

- Fromm (1941) - instilling in the child the desire to do what he must do if a given society is to be maintained

References

- Arnett, Jeffrey J. 1995. "Broad and Narrow Socialization: The Family in the Context of a Cultural Theory." Journal of Marriage and the Family 57(3):617-28.

- Ellis, Godfrey J., Gary R. Lee, and Larry R. Petersen. 1978. "Supervision and Conformity: A Cross-Cultural Analysis of Parental Socialization Values." American Journal of Sociology 84(2):386-403.

- Goffman, Erving. 1961. Asylums: Essays on the Social Situation of Mental Patients and Other Inmates.

- Holland, David. 1970. "Familization, Socialization, and the Universe of Meaning: An Extension of the Interactional Approach to the Study of the Family." Journal of Marriage and the Family 32(3):415-27.

- Kohn, Melvin L. 1969. Class and Conformity, A Study in Values. Homewood, IL: Dorsey Press.

- Long, Theodore E. and Jeffrey K. Hadden. 1985. "A Reconception of Socialization." Sociological Theory 3(1):39-49.

- Marshall, Victor W. 1975. "Socialization for Impending Death in a Retirement Village ." American Journal of Sociology 80(5):1124-44.

- Mortimer, Jeylan T. and Roberta G. Simmons. 1978. "Adult Socialization." Annual Review of Sociology 4421-54.

- Rosenbaum, James E. 1975. "The Stratification of Socialization Processes." American Sociological Review 40(1):48-54.

History

- This page is adapted 9 April 2005 from the Wikipedia article, socialization.

- External Links

Groups

Introduction

In sociology, a **group** is usually defined as a number of people who identify and interact with one another. This is a very broad definition, as it includes groups of all sizes, from dyads to whole societies. While an aggregate comprises merely a number of individuals, a group in sociology exhibits cohesiveness to a larger degree. Aspects that members in the group may share include: interests, values, ethnic/linguistic background, roles and kinship. One way of determining if a collection of people can be considered a group is if individuals who belong to that collection use the self-referent pronoun "we;" using "we" to refer to a collection of people often implies that the collection thinks of itself as a group. Examples of groups include: families, companies, cirlces of friends, clubs, local chapters of fraternities and sororities, and local religious congregations.

⌐⌐Law enforcement officials are members of a social category, not a group.

Collections of people that do not use the self-referent pronoun "we" but share certain characteristics (e.g., roles, social functions, etc.) are different from groups in that they usually do not regularly interact with each other nor share similar interests or values. Such collections are referred to as *categories* of people rather than groups; examples include: police, soldiers, millionaires, women, etc.

Individuals form groups for a variety of reasons. There are some rather obvious ones, like reproduction, protection, trade, and food production. But social categorization of people into groups and categories also facilitates behavior and action (Hogg 2003). An example may help explain this idea:

Suppose you are driving somewhere in a car when you notice red lights flashing in your rearview mirror. Because you have been socialized into society, you know that the red lights mean you should pull over, so you do. After waiting for a minute or two, an individual in a uniform walks toward your car door. You roll down your window and the individuals asks you for your "license and registration."

Because groups and categories help facilitate social behavior, you know who this individual is: a member of a law enforcement category like the police or highway patrol. In all likelihood, you do not have to question this individual as to why they are driving a special car with lights on it, why they are wearing a uniform, why they are carrying a gun, or why they pulled you over (you may ask why they pulled you over, but doing so often increases the likelihood they'll give you a ticket). In short, because you recognize that the individual driving the car belongs to a specific social category (or group), you can enter this interaction with a body of knowledge that will help guide your behavior. You do not have to learn how to interact in that situation every single time you encounter it. Social categorization of people into groups and categories is a heuristic device that makes social interaction easier.

Social Identity Theory

Social identity is a theory formed by <u>Henri Tajfel</u> and <u>John Turner</u> to understand the psychological basis of intergroup <u>discrimination</u>. It is composed of three elements:

- Categorization: We often put others (and ourselves) into categories. Labeling someone as a *Muslim*, a <u>Turk</u>, or *soccer player* are ways of saying other things about these people.

- Identification: We also associate with certain <u>groups</u> (our *ingroups*), which serves to bolster our <u>self-esteem</u>.

- Comparison: We compare our groups with other groups, seeing a favorable bias toward the group to which we belong...

As developed by Tajfel, Social Identity Theory is a diffuse but interrelated group of social psychological theories concerned with when and why individuals identify with, and behave as part of, social groups, adopting shared attitudes to outsiders. It is also concerned with what difference it makes when encounters between individuals are perceived as encounters between group members. Social Identity Theory is thus concerned both with the psychological and sociological aspects of group behaviour.

Reacting against individualistic explanations of group behaviour (e.g. <u>Allport</u>) on one hand, and tendencies to reify the group on the other, Tajfel sought an account of group identity that held together both society and individual. Tajfel first sought to differentiate between those elements of self-identity derived from individual personality traits and interpersonal relationships (personal identity) and those elements derived from belonging to a particular group (social identity). Each individual is seen to have a repertoire of identities open to them (social and personal), each identity informing the individual of who he is and what this identity entails. Which of these many identities is most salient for an individual at any time will vary according to the social context. Tajfel then postulated that social behaviour exists on a spectrum from the purely interpersonal to the purely intergroup. Where personal identity is salient, the individual will relate to others in an interpersonal manner, dependent on their character traits and any personal relationship existing between the individuals. However, under certain conditions 'social identity is more salient then personal identity in self-conception and that when this is the case behaviour is qualitatively different: it is group behaviour.'

The first element in social identity theory is categorization. We categorize objects in order to understand them, in a very similar way we categorize people (including ourselves) in order to understand the social environment. We use social categories like black, white, Australian, Christian, Muslim, student, and busdriver because they are useful. If we can assign people to a category then that tells us things about those people, and as we saw with the busdriver example we couldn't function in a normal manner without using these categories; i.e. in the context of the bus. Similarly, we find out things about ourselves by knowing what categories we belong to. We define appropriate behaviour by reference to the norms of groups we belong to, but you can only do this if you can tell who belongs to your group.

The second important idea is identification. We identify with groups that we perceive ourselves to belong to. Identification carries two meanings. Part of who we are is made up of our group memberships. That is, sometimes we think of ourselves as "us" vs. "them" or "we' vs. "they", and at othertimes we think of ourselves as "I" vs. "he or she" or "me" vs. "him or her". That is sometimes we think of ourselves as group members and at other times we think of ourselves as unique individuals. This varies situationally, so that we can be more or less a group member, depending upon the circumstances. What is crucial for our purposes is that thinking of yourselves as a group member and thinking of yourself as a unique individual are both parts of your self-concept. The first is referred to as social identity, the latter is referred to as personal identity.

Just to reiterate, in social identity theory the group membership is not something foreign which is tacked onto the person, it is a real, true and vital part of the person. Again, it is crucial to remember ingroups are groups you identify with, and outgroups are ones that we don't identify with.

The other meaning implied by the concept of identity is the idea that we are, in some sense, the same, or identical to the other people. This should not be misinterpreted, when we say that we are the same, we mean that for some purposes we treat members of our groups as being similar to ourselves in some relevant way. To take the most extreme example, in some violent conflict such as a war, the members of the opposite group are treated as identical and completely different to the ingroup, in that the enemy are considered to be deserving of death. This behaviour and these beliefs are not the product of a bizarre personality disorder, but under these circumstances violent behaviour becomes rational, accepted and even expected behaviour.

The third idea that is involved in social identity theory is one that we have already dealt with. It is Festinger's (1954) notion of social comparison. The basic idea is that a positive self-concept is a part of normal psychological functioning. There is pretty good evidence that to deal effectively with the world we need to feel good about ourselves. The idea of social comparison is that in order to evaluate ourselves we compare ourselves with similar others.

We have already discussed the idea that we can gain self-esteem by comparing ourselves with others in our group, and also that we can see ourselves in a positive light by seeing ourselves as a member of a prestigious group. The question is, how do groups get this prestige? Tajfel and Turner's answer is that group members compare their group with others, in order to define their group as positive, and therefore by implication, see themselves in a positive way. That is, people choose to compare their groups with other groups in ways that reflect positively on themselves.

Two ideas follow from this. One is positive distinctiveness. The idea is that people are motivated to see their own group as relatively better than similar (but inferior) groups. The other idea is negative distinctiveness, groups tend to mimimize the differences between the groups, so that our own group is seen favourably.

The operation of these processes is subsumed within the concept of social creativity. Groups choose dimensions in order to maximise the positivity of their own group. For example, groups which perceive themselves to be of high status on particular dimensions will choose those as the basis of comparison. Groups of low status will minimise differences on those dimensions or choose new dimensions. For example, people from some Middle Eastern Islamic countries might regard their country as inferior to the West in terms of economic and technological advancement but might regard their way of life as being morally superior.

p. 461 "In many respects, this has been the fate of "the group" in social psychology. With its focus on the individual, social psychology has had a difficult time accepting the group as a true member of the flock. Although the group has been a part of social psychology since the field's beginning (Triplett, 1898), it has occupied a rather tenuous position. Social psychologists have scoffed at the notion of a "group mind" (Le Bon, 1895/1960). Allport (1924) observed that nobody ever tripped over a group, an insult questioning the very existence of the group. The rejection of the group became so complete that Steiner (1974) entitled an article, "What ever happened to the group in social psychology?" For a time, the group was banished to the foreign lands of organizational psychology and sociology. "But the group could not stay a stranger for long. It wormed its way back into the fold, but its rebirth had a unique twist. Early definitions of the group described it as a unit consisting of several individuals who interacted with each other and occupied "real" space (Shaw, 1981). However, the born-again group was accepted into the domain of social psychology only as a cognitive representation, a figment of the mind. Instead of the individual being in the group, the group was now within the individual; Hogg and Abrams (1988) stated that "the group is thus within the individual ..." (p. 19)."

p. 462 "SIT became the springboard for new approaches to understanding stereotyping (Haslam, Turner, Oakes, McGarry, & Hays, 1992; Ng, 1989; Spears, Oakes, Ellemers, & Haslam, 1997), prejudice (Bagby & Rector, 1992), ethnic violence (Worchel, 1999) and other forms of intergroup relations. The perspective was applied to a host of traditional social psychological issues such as interpersonal perception (Park & Rothbart, 1982), minority influence (Clark & Maass, 1988), and group productivity and social loafing (Worchel, Rothgerber, Day, Hart, & Buttemeyer, 1998)." Every article I have read in these books has mentioned SIT and Tajfel; was that a requirement? Has SP nothing else?

p. 463 "Social identity theory presents individual identity as a point along a continuum ranging from personal identity on one end to social identity on the other end. One's identity at a specific time is represented by a single point on the continuum. A multitude of variables affect whether personal identity or social identity will be most salient, and which of the many group memberships will be most prominent on the social identity side of the equation. The conceptualization of social identity as being composed of group membership leads to the hypothesis that people discriminate in order to enhance the position of their ingroups relative to that of outgroups. The motivation behind this action is to create a positive social identity (Tajfel, 1978), reduce threats to self-esteem (Hogg & Abrams, 1990; Long & Spears, 1997), or reduce uncertainty (Hogg, 2000; Hogg & Abrams, 1993)."

p. 464 "Our approach gives the group a clear role outside the cognitive structure of the individual. Although we do not deny that individuals hold mental representations of groups and that these representations can and do exert influence, we also argue that groups are entities that exist outside the person and exert real pressure. We suggest that group dynamics has interpersonal and intergroup components that cannot be ignored in the study of the relationship between individual and group. Although group activities have an impact on the identity of the individual member, the group must be examined within a true social paradigm."

p. 467 "The disintegration of the group continues into the stage of decay. At this point, members may defect from the group. Scapegoating takes place and leaders are often blamed for group ills. The individual focus is accelerated, and the need for the group is questioned. "In some cases, the decay destroys the group and it ceases to exist. However, in many other cases, the group, albeit with a different set of members, begins the process of rebuilding. A distinct incident or threat may ignite the rebirth, or the rebuilding may be initiated by the collective actions of a subset of the members. Whatever the reason, the group enters again into the group identification stage, and the cycle of group development begins anew." Why do they put everything into either stages or cycles? Why can't things not progress and just be?

Primary and Secondary Groups

In sociology we distinguish between two types of groups based upon their characteristics. A **Primary group** is typically a small social group whose members share close, personal, enduring relationships. These groups are marked by concern for one another, shared activities and culture, and long periods of time spent together. The goal of primary groups is actually the relationships themselves rather than achieving some other purpose. Families and close friends are examples of primary groups

⬚A class of students is generally considered a secondary group.

Secondary groups are large groups whose relationships are impersonal and goal-oriented. Some secondary groups may last for many years, though most are short term. Such groups also begin and end with very little significance in the lives of the people involved. People in a secondary group interact on a less personal level than in a primary group. Rather than having as the goal the maintenance and development of the relationships themselves, these groups generally come together to accomplish a specific purpose. Since secondary groups are established to perform functions, peopleâ€(tm)s roles are more interchangeable. Examples of secondary groups include: classmates in a college course, athletic teams, and co-workers.

The distinction between primary and secondary groups was originally proposed by Charles Horton Cooley. He labelled groups as "primary" because people often experience such groups early in their life and such groups play an important role in the development of personal identity. Secondary groups generally develop later in life and are much less likely to be influential on one's identity.

74

Leadership

Conformity

Reference Groups

A group that is used as a standard against which we compare ourselves would be a reference group. Take the case of someone who grew up in a poverty-stricken neighborhood. If all friends and relatives (her reference group) were in the same situation, just scraping by, she may not have considered herself poor at the time. Reference groups can also serve to enforce conformity to certain standards. A college freshman who has his heart set on joining a prestigious fraternity on campus may adopt behaviors and attitudes that are accepted by members of the fraternity.

Ingroups and Outgroups

p. 56 "Groups exist by virtue of there being outgroups. For a collection of people to be a group there must, logically, be other people who are not in the group (a diffuse non-ingroup, e.g., academics vs. non-academics) or people who are in a specific outgroup (e.g., academics vs. politicians). In this sense, social groups are categories of people; and just like other categories, a social category acquires its meaning by contrast with other categories. The social world is patterned by social discontinuities that mark the boundaries of social groups in terms of perceived and/or actual differences in what people think, feel, and do."

p. 407 "Research on the black sheep effect is consistent with this analysis. In one study (Marques, Yzerbyt, & Leyens, 1988, Exp. 1), Belgian students rated "attractive Belgian students," "attractive North African students," "unattractive Belgian students," and "unattractive North African students." Attractive ingroup members were judged more favorably than attractive outgroup members. The opposite occurred for unattractive members. Figure 17.1 shows the general pattern of judgments that correspond to the black sheep effect." Basically the whole point of this chapter.

Group Size

Social Facilitation

Social Loafing

In the social psychology of groups, **social loafing** is the phenomenon that persons make less effort to achieve a goal when they work in a group than when they work alone. This is one of the main reasons that groups sometimes perform less than the combined performance of their members working as individuals.

The main explanation for social loafing is that people feel unmotivated when working in a group, because they think that their contributions will not be evaluated. According to the results of a meta-analysis study (Karau & Williams, 1993), social loafing is a pervasive phenomenon, but it does not occur when the group members feel that the task or the group itself is important.

The answer to social loafing is motivation. A competitive environment will not get group members motivated. It takes "the three C's of motivation" to get a group moving: collaboration, content, and choice (Rothwell, 2004).

1. Collaboration is a way to get everyone involved in the group. It is a way for the group members to share the knowledge and the tasks to be fulfilled unfailingly (CSCW, 2000). For example, giving Sally the note taker duty and RaÃ°l the brainstorming duty will make them feel essential to the group. Sally and RaÃ°l won't want to let the group down, because they have specific obligations to complete.

2. Content identifies the importance of the individuals' specific tasks within the group. If group members see their role as a worthy task, then they are more likely to fulfill it. For example, RaÃ°l enjoys brainstorming, and he knows that he will bring a lot to the group if he fulfills this obligation. He feels that his obligation means something to the group.

3. Choice gives the group members the opportunity to choose the task they want to fulfill. Assigning roles in a group causes complaints and frustration. Allowing group members the freedom to choose their role rids social loafing and encourages the members to work together as a team.

Deindividuation

Deindividuation refers to the phenomenon of relinquishing one's sense of identity. This can happen as a result of becoming part of a group, such as an army or mob, but also as a result of meditation. It can have quite destructive effects, sometimes making people more likely to commit a crime, like stealing (Diener, 1976) or even over-enforce the law, such as police in riot situations. It is the motivational cause of most riot participants' actions for example, the violent 1992 riots that took place in LA's south central district. Deindividuated individuals' self-awareness becomes absent and they are oblivious to outside evaluation. This is when evaluation apprehension ceases to exist, ultimately breaking down any inhibitions.

Group Polarization

Group polarization effects have been demonstrated to exaggerate the inclinations of group members after a discussion. A military term for group polarization is "incestuous amplification".

Overview

Study of this effect has shown that after participating in a discussion group, members tend to advocate more extreme positions and call for riskier courses of action than individuals who did not participate in any such discussion. This phenomenon was originally coined *risky shift* but was found to apply to more than risk, so the replacement term *choice shift* has been suggested.

In addition, attitudes such as racial and sexual prejudice tend to be reduced (for already low-prejudice individuals) and inflated (for already high-prejudice individuals) after group discussion.

Group polarization has been used to explain the decision-making of a jury, particularly when considering punitive damages in a civil trial. Studies have shown that after deliberating together, mock jury members often decided on punitive damage awards that were larger or smaller than the amount any individual juror had favored prior to deliberation. The studies indicated that when the jurors favored a relatively low award, discussion would lead to an even more lenient result, while if the jury was inclined to impose a stiff penalty, discussion would make it even harsher.

Developments in the study of group polarization

The study of group polarization began with an unpublished 1961 Masterâ€(tm)s thesis by MIT student James Stoner, who observed the so-called "risky shift", meaning that a groupâ€(tm)s decisions are riskier than the average of the individual decisions of members before the group met. The discovery of the risky shift was considered surprising and counterintuitive, especially since earlier work in the 1920s and 1930s by Allport and other researchers suggested that individuals made more extreme decisions than did groups, leading to the expectation that groups would make decisions that would conform to the average risk level of its members. The seemingly counterintuitive findings of Stoner led to a flurry of research around the risky shift, which was originally thought to be a special case exception to the standard decision-making practice. By the late 1960s, however, it had become clear that the risky shift was just one type of many attitudes that became more extreme in groups, leading Moscovici and Zavalloni to term the overall phenomenon "group polarization".

Thus began a decade-long period of examination of the applicability of group polarization to a number of fields, ranging from political attitudes to religion, in both lab and field settings. Basic studies of group polarization tapered off, but research on the topic continued. Group polarization was well-established, but remained non-obvious and puzzling because its mechanisms were not understood.

Mechanisms of polarization

Almost as soon as the phenomenon of group polarization was discovered, a variety of hypotheses were suggested for the mechanisms for its action. These explanations were gradually winnowed down and grouped together until two primary mechanisms remained, social comparison and influence. Social comparison approaches, sometimes called interpersonal comparison, were based on social psychological views of self-perception and the drive of individuals to appear socially desirable . The second major mechanism is informational influence, which is also sometimes referred to as persuasive argument theory, or PAT. PAT holds that individual choices are determined by individuals weighing remembered pro and con arguments. These arguments are then applied to possible choices, and the most positive is selected. As a mechanism for polarization, group discussion shifts the weight of evidence as each individual exposes their pro and con arguments, giving each other new arguments and increasing the stock of pro arguments in favor of the group tendency, and con arguments against the group tendency. The persuasiveness of an argument depends on two factors â€" originality and its validity. According to PAT, a valid argument would hold more persuasive weight than a non-valid one. Originality has come to be understood in terms of the novelty of an argument. A more novel argument would increase the likelihood that it is an addition to the other group membersâ€(tm) pool of pro and con arguments, rather than a simple repetition.

In the 1970s, significant arguments occurred over whether persuasive argumentation alone accounted for group polarization. Daniel Isenbergâ€(tm)s 1986 meta-analysis of the data gathered by both the persuasive argument and social comparison camps succeeded, in large part, in answering the questions about predominant mechanisms. Isenberg concluded that there was substantial evidence that both effects were operating simultaneously, and that PAT operated when social comparison did not, and vice-versa. Isenberg did discover that PAT did seem to have a significantly stronger effect, however.

Groupthink

Groupthink is a term coined by psychologist Irving Janis in 1972 to describe a process by which a group can make bad or irrational decisions. In a groupthink situation, each member of the group attempts to conform his or her opinions to what they believe to be the consensus of the group. In a general sense this seems to be a very rationalistic way to approach the situation. However this results in a situation in which the group ultimately agrees upon an action which each member might individually consider to be unwise (the risky shift).

Janis' original definition of the term was "a mode of thinking that people engage in when they are deeply involved in a cohesive in-group, when the members' strivings for unanimity override their motivation to realistically appraise alternative courses of action." The word *groupthink* was intended to be reminiscent of George Orwell's coinages (such as *doublethink* and *duckspeak*) from the fictional language Newspeak, which he portrayed in his novel *Nineteen Eighty-Four*.

Groupthink tends to occur on committees and in large organizations. Janis originally studied the Pearl Harbor bombing, the Vietnam War and the Bay of Pigs Invasion. Recently, in 2004, the US Senate Intelligence Committee's *Report on the U.S. Intelligence Community's Prewar Intelligence Assessments on Iraq* blamed groupthink for failures to correctly interpret intelligence relating to Iraq's weapons of mass destruction capabilities.[2]

Symptoms of groupthink

Janis cited a number of *antecedent conditions* that would be likely to encourage groupthink. These include:

- Insulation of the group
- High group cohesiveness
- Directive leadership

- Lack of norms requiring methodical procedures

- Homogeneity of members' social background and ideology

- High stress from external threats with low hope of a better solution than the one offered by the leader(s)

Janis listed eight symptoms that he said were indicative of groupthink:

1. Illusion of invulnerability

2. Unquestioned belief in the inherent morality of the group

3. Collective rationalization of group's decisions

4. Shared stereotypes of outgroup, particularly opponents

5. Self-censorship; members withhold criticisms

6. Illusion of unanimity (see false consensus effect)

7. Direct pressure on dissenters to conform

8. Self-appointed "mindguards" protect the group from negative information

Finally, the seven symptoms of decision affected by groupthink are:

1. Incomplete survey of alternatives

2. Incomplete survey of objectives

3. Failure to examine risks of preferred choice

4. Failure to re-appraise initially rejected alternatives

5. Poor information search

6. Selective bias in processing information at hand (see also confirmation bias)

7. Failure to work out contingency plans

Preventing groupthink

One mechanism which management consultants recommend to avoid groupthink is to place responsibility and authority for a decision in the hands of a single person who can turn to others for advice. Others advise that a pre-selected individual take the role of disagreeing with any suggestion presented, thereby making other individuals more likely to present their own ideas and point out flaws in others' â€" and reducing the stigma associated with being the first to take negative stances (see Devil's Advocate).

Anonymous feedback via suggestion box or online chat has been found to be a useful remedy for groupthink â€" negative or dissenting views of proposals can be raised without any individual being identifiable by others as having lodged a critique. Thus the social capital of the group is preserved, as all members have plausible deniability that they raised a dissenting point.

Institutional mechanisms such as an inspector general system can also play a role in preventing groupthink as all participants have the option of appealing to an individual outside the decision-making group who has the authority to stop non-constructive or harmful trends.

Another possibility is giving each participant in a group a piece of paper, this is done randomly and without anyone but the receiver being able to read it. Two of the pieces of paper have "dissent" written on them, the others are blank. People have to dissent if the paper says so (like a Devil's Advocate), no-one is able to know if the other person is expressing dissent because they received a pre-marked "dissent" piece of paper or because it's an honest dissent. Also, as with every Devil's Advocate, there exists the possibility that the person adopting this role would think about the problem in a way that they wouldn't have if not under that role, and so promoting creative and critical thought.

Another way which is of special use in very asymmetric relations (as in a classroom) is to say something which is essentially wrong or false, having given (or being obvious that the persons that may be groupthinking know about that) the needed information to realize its inconsistency previously, if at the start of the class the teacher told the students that he would do so and not tell them when he did until the end of the class, they would be stimulated to criticize and "process" information instead of merely assimilating it.

An alternative to groupthink is a formal consensus decision-making process, which works best in a group whose aims are cooperative rather than competitive, where trust is able to build up, and where participants are willing to learn and apply facilitation skills.

Notes

</="FONT-STYLE: normal"^ The Senate Intelligence Committee concluded that "the Intelligence Community (IC) suffered from a collective presumption that Iraq had an active and growing weapons of mass destruction (WMD) program. This "group think" dynamic led Intelligence Community analysts, collectors, and managers, to both interpret ambiguous evidence as conclusively indicative of a WMD program as well as ignore or minimize evidence that Iraq did not have active and expanding weapons of mass destruction programs. This presumption was so strong that formalized IC mechanisms established to challenge assumptions and group think were not utilized."

Minority Influence

Networks

A **social network** is a social structure between actors, mostly individuals or organizations. It indicates the ways in which they are connected through various social familiarities ranging from casual acquaintance to close familial bonds. The term was first coined in 1954 by J. A. Barnes (in: *Class and Committees in a Norwegian Island Parish*, "Human Relations").

Social network analysis (also sometimes called *network theory*) has emerged as a key technique in modern sociology, anthropology, Social Psychology and organizational studies, as well as a popular topic of speculation and study. Research in a number of academic fields have demonstrated that social networks operate on many levels, from families up to the level of nations, and play a critical role in determining the way problems are solved, organizations are run, and the degree to which individuals succeed in achieving their goals.

Social networking also refers to a category of Internet applications to help connect friends, business partners, or other individuals together using a variety of tools. These applications are covered under Internet social networks below, and in the external links at the end of the article.

Introduction to social networks

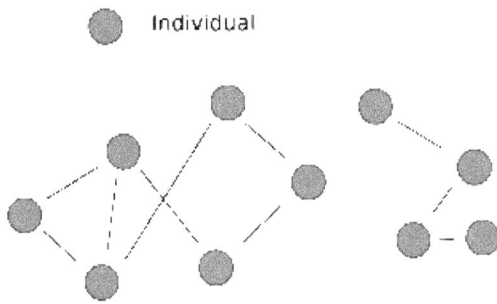

An example of a social network diagram

Social network theory views social relationships in terms of *nodes* and *ties*. Nodes are the individual actors within the networks, and ties are the relationships between the actors. There can be many kinds of ties between the nodes. In its most simple form, a social network is a map of all of the relevant ties between the nodes being studied. The network can also be used to determine the social capital of individual actors. These concepts are often displayed in a social network diagram, where nodes are the points and ties are the lines.

The shape of the social network helps determine a network's usefulness to its individuals. Smaller, tighter networks can be less useful to their members than networks with lots of loose connections (weak ties) to individuals outside the main network. More "open" networks, with many weak ties and social connections, are more likely to introduce new ideas and opportunities to their members than closed networks with many redundant ties. In other words, a group of friends who only do things with each other already share the same knowledge and opportunities. A group of individuals with connections to other social worlds is likely to have access to a wider range of information. It is better for individual success to have connections to a variety of networks rather than many connections within a single network. Similarly, individuals can exercise influence or act as brokers within their social networks by bridging two networks that are not directly linked (called filling social holes).

The power of social network theory stems from its difference from traditional sociological studies, which assume that it is the attributes of individual actors -- whether they are friendly or unfriendly, smart or dumb, etc. -- that matter. Social network theory produces an alternate view, where the attributes of individuals are less important than their relationships and ties with other actors within the network. This approach has turned out to be useful for explaining many real-world phenomena, but leaves less room for individual agency, the ability for individuals to influence their success, so much of it rests within the structure of their network.

Social networks have also been used to examine how companies interact with each other, characterizing the many informal connections that link executives together, as well as associations and connections between individual employees at different companies. These networks provide ways for companies to gather information, deter competition, and even collude in setting prices or policies.

Applications of social network theory

Applications in social science

Social network theory in the social sciences began with the urbanization studies of the "Manchester School" (centered around Max Gluckman), done mainly in Zambia during the 1960s. It was followed up with the field of sociometry, an attempt to quantify social relationships. Scholars such as Mark Granovetter expanded the use of social networks, and they are now used to help explain many different real-life phenomena in the social sciences. Power within organizations, for example, has been found to come more from the degree to which an individual within a network is at the center of many relationships than actual job title. Social networks also play a key role in hiring, in business success for firms, and in job performance.

Social network theory is an extremely active field within academia. The International Network for Social Network Analysis is an academic association of social network analysts. Many social network tools for scholarly work are available online (like "UCINet") and are relatively easy to use to present graphical images of networks.

Diffusion of innovations theory explores social networks and their role in influencing the spread of new ideas and practices. Change agents and opinion leaders often play major roles in spurring the adoption of innovations, although factors inherent to the innovations also play a role.

Popular applications

The so-called **rule of 150** states that the size of a genuine social network is limited to about 150 members (sometimes called the Dunbar Number). The rule arises from cross-cultural studies in sociology and especially anthropology of the maximum size of a village (in modern parlance most reasonably understood as an *ecovillage*). It is theorized in evolutionary psychology that the number may be some kind of limit of average human ability to recognize members and track emotional facts about all members of a group. However, it may be due to economics and the need to track "free riders", as larger groups tend to be easier for cheats and liars to prosper in.

82

Degrees of Separation and the Global Social Network

The small world phenomenon is the hypothesis that the chain of social acquaintances required to connect one arbitrary person to another arbitrary person anywhere in the world is generally short. The concept gave rise to the famous phrase six degrees of separation after a 1967 *small world experiment* by psychologist Stanley Milgram which found that two random US citizens were connected by an average of six acquaintances. Current internet experiments continue to explore this phenomenon, including the Ohio State Electronic Small World Project and Columbia's Small World Project. As of 2005, these experiments confirm that about five to seven degrees of separation are sufficient for connecting any two people through the internet.

Internet social networks

Main Wikipedia article: Social network service

See also: List of social networking sites

Whilst there was evidence of social networking on the Web in 1997, with websites such as SixDegrees.com, it was not until 2001 that websites using the *Circle of Friends* online social networks started appearing. This form of social networking, widly used in virtual communities, became particularly popular in 2003 and flourished with the advent of a website called Friendster. There are over 200 social networking sites, though Friendster is one of the most successful at using the *Circle of Friends* technique. The popularity of these sites rapidly grew, and major companies such as Google and Yahoo have entered the Internet social networking space.

In these communities, an initial set of founders sends out messages inviting members of their own personal networks to join the site. New members repeat the process, growing the total number of members and links in the network. Sites then offer features such as automatic address book updates, viewable profiles, the ability to form new links through "introduction services," and other forms of online social connections. Social networks can also be organized around business connections, as for example in the case of Shortcut.

Blended networking is an approach to social networking that blends offline and online elements together to create a blend. A human social network is blended if it supported by both face-to-face events and an online community. The two elements of the blend support one another. A current trend is social networks that mirror real communities, becoming online extensions of these communities. MySpace builds on independent music and party scenes, and Facebook mirrors a college community. These sites allow stronger ties and freer relationships. See also Social computing.

Notes

References

- Bray, R. M., & Noble, A. M. (1978). Authoritarianism and decisions of mock juries: Evidence of jury bias and group polarization. *Journal of Personality and Social Psychology*, 36, 1424-1430.

- Diener, E., Fraser, S. C., Beaman, A. L. and Kelem, R. T. (1976). Effects of deindividuation variables on stealing among Halloween trick-or-treaters. Journal of Personality and Social Psychology, 33(2), 178-183.

- Festinger, L., Pepitone, A. and Newcomb T. (1952). Some consequences of deindividuation in a group. Journal of Abnormal and Social Psychology, 47, 382-389.

- Hogg, Michael A. Social Categorization, Depersonalization, and Group Behavior. Hogg, Michael A. and Tindale, Scott, Editors. Blackwell Handbook of Social Psychology: Group Processes. Malden, MA: Blackwell Publishers; 2003; pp. 56-85.

- Jackson, J. M. & Harkins, J. M. (1985). Equity in effort: An explanation of the social loafing effect. *Journal of Personality and Social Psychology, 49*, 1199-1206.

- Jackson, J. M. & Williams, K. D. (1985). Social loafing on difficult tasks. *Journal of Personality and Social Psychology, 49*, 937-942.

- Janis, I. (1972). *Victims of Groupthink: A Psychological Study of Foreign-Policy Decisions and Fiascoes*. Boston: Houghton Mifflin. ISBN 0395140447

- Janis, I. & Mann, L. (1977). *Decision Making: A Psychological Analysis of Conflict, Choice and Commitment*. New York: The Free Press.

- Karau, S. J. & Williams, K. D. (1993). Social loafing: A meta-analytic review and theoretical integration. *Journal of Personality and Social Psychology, 65*, 681-706.

- MacCoun, R. J.; Kerr, N. L. (1988). Asymmetric influence in mock jury deliberation: Jurors' bias for leniency. *Journal of Personality and Social Psychology*, 54, 21-33.

- Marques, Jose M.; Abrams, Dominic; Paez, Dario, and Hogg, Michael A. Social Categorization, Social Identification, and Rejection of Deviant Group Members. Hogg, Michael A. and Tindale, Scott, Editors. Blackwell Handbook of Social Psychology: Group Processes. Malden, MA: Blackwell Publishers; 2003; pp. 400-424.

- Moscovici, S., & Zavalloni, M. (1969). The group as a polarizer of attitudes. *Journal of Personality and Social Psychology* **12**, 125-135.

- Rothwell, J, D. "In the Company of Others," McGraw-Hill, 2004, ISBN 0-7474-3009-3

- Senate Intelligence Committee. 2004. Report on the U.S. Intelligence Community's Prewar Intelligence Assessments on Iraq http://intelligence.senate.gov/conclusions.pdf

- Schwartz, John & Wald, Matthew L. *Smart People Working Collectively can be Dumber Than the Sum of their Brains: "Groupthink" Is 30 Years Old, and Still Going Strong*. New York Times March 9, 2003. Full Reprint here.

- The Computing Company. 2005. "Pattern: Collaboration in Small Groups". Retrieved October 31, 2005 [3]

- Worchel, Stephen. Emphasizing the Social Nature of Groups in a Developmental Framework. Nye, Judith L. and Brower, Aaron M., Editors. What's Social About Social Cognition? Sage Publications; 1996.

- Zimbardo, P. G., (1969). The human choice: Individuation, reason, and order versus deindividuation, impulse, and chaos. Nebraska Symposium on Motivation, 17, 237-307

This chapter draws heavily on the following Wikipedia articles:

- group

- Social identity

- Primary group/Secondary group

- Group Polarization

- Deindividuation

- Social loafing

- Social network

- Groupthink

- Reference group

External Links

- Social Identity (Australian National University)

- Social Identity Theory (University of Twente)

- "Primary Groups" excerpt from Cooley's "Social Organization: A Study of the Larger Mind"

- Online Social Networking Research Report - A comparative analysis by Wildbit of the most popular online social networks with suggestions on creating and growing web communities.

- Knock, Knock, Knocking on Newton's Door - article published in Defense Acquisition University's journal *Defense AT&L*, based largely on *Six Degrees* by Duncan Watts. Explores theory and practice of social networking, as related to military technology development.

- How to Do Social Network Analysis

- Robin Dunbar and the Magic Number of 150

- PieSpy - Social Network Bot Inferring and Visualizing Social Networks on IRC

- The Academic Robotics Community in the UK: Web based data construction and analysis of a distributed community of practice The social networks of this community are constructed wholly from web-based resources such as web pages, electronic CVs and bibliographic search engines

- The Augmented Social Network: Building Identity and Trust into the Next-Generation Internet by Ken Jordan, Jan Hauser, and Steven Foster

- The Social Web: Building an Open Social Network with XDI by members of the OASIS XDI Technical Committee7

- Pajek - Program for Large Network Analyis

- CASOS Dynamic Social Network Analysis being conducted at Carnegie Mellon University

- http://changingminds.org/explanations/theories/deindividuation.htm

- Article on Groupthink from MeatballWiki

- Article on Groupthink from SourceWatch

Demography

Introduction

Demography is the study of human population dynamics. It encompasses the study of the size, structure and distribution of populations, and how populations change over time due to births, deaths, migration, and ageing. Demographic analysis can relate to whole societies or to smaller groups defined by criteria such as education, religion, or ethnicity.

Why study demography?

Before proposing complex theories to explain sociological phenomena (e.g., World Systems Theory), especially at the macro and/or societal levels, sociologists should first turn to demographic indicators for possible explanations. Demographic analysis is a powerful tool that can explain a number of sociological phenomena.

For instance, in examining the elements that led to the first World War, most people turn to political and diplomatic conflicts but fail to consider the implications of expanding populations in the European countries involved. Expanding populations will result in increased competition for resources (i.e., food, land, access to trade routes and ports, etc.). Expanding populations may not be the primary cause of World War I, but it may have played a role in the increased hostilities leading up to the war. In this fashion, demographic indicators are often informative in explaining world events and should be turned to first as explanations.

History

The study of human populations has its roots, like sociology generally, in the societal changes that accompanied both the scientific and industrial revolutions. Some early mathematicians developed primitive forms of life tables, which are tables of life expectancies, for life insurance and actuarial purposes. Censuses, another demographic tool, were instiued for primarily political purposes:

- as a basis for taxation

- as a basis for political representation

The development of demographic calculations started in the 18th century. Census taking, on the other hand, has a long history dating back close to 2,000 years among the Chinese and the Romans and even further back in history among some groups in the Middle East. Most modern censuses began in the late 18th century.

Data and Methods

Demography relies on large data sets that are primarily derived from censuses and registration statistics (i.e., birth, death, marriage registrations). Large data sets over long periods of time (e.g., the U.S. census is conducted every 10 years) are required to develop trends in demographic indicators, like birth and death rates.

In many countries, particularly in developing nations, reliable demographic data are still difficult to obtain. In some locales this may be due to the association of *census* with *taxation*.

Demographic Indicators

Because demography is interested in changes in human populations, demographers focus on specific indicators of change. Two of the most important indicators are birth and death rates, which are also referred to as *fertility* (see also fecundity) and *mortality*. Additionally, demographers are interested in migration trends or the movement of people from one location to another. Some of the specific measures used to explore these elements of population change are discussed below.

Fertility and Fecundity

Fertility, in demography, refers to the ability of females to produce healthy offspring in abundance. **Fecundity** is the potential reproductive capacity of a female. Some of the more common demographic measures used in relation to fertility and/or fecundity include:

- **crude birth rate**: the annual number of live births per thousand people

- **general fertility rate**: the annual number of live births per 1000 women of childbearing age (often taken to be from 15 to 49 years old, but sometimes from 15 to 44).

- **age-specific fertility** rate: the annual number of live births per 1000 women in particular age groups (usually age 15-19, 20-24 etc.)

- **total fertility rate**: the number of live births per woman completing her reproductive life if her childbearing at each age reflected current age-specific fertility rates

- **gross reproduction rate**: the number of daughters who would be born to a woman completing her reproductive life at current age-specific fertility rates

- **net reproduction rate**: the number of daughters who would be born to a woman according to current age-specific fertility and mortality rates

Another important demographic concept relating to fertility is *replacement level*. Replacement level fertility refers to the number of children that a woman (or monogamous couple) must have in order to replace the existing population. Sub-replacement fertility is a fertility rate that is not high enough to replace an existing population. Replacement level fertility is generally set at 2.1 children in a woman's lifetime (this number varies by geographic region given different mortality rates). Sub-replacement fertility is below approximately 2.1 children in a woman's life time. The reason the number is set to 2.1 children per woman is because two children are needed to replace the parents and an additional one-tenth of a child is needed to make up for the mortality of children and of women who do not reach the end of their reproductive years. Of course, women don't have one-tenth of a child; this results from statistical averaging between women who have more than two children and those who have two or fewer children.

The chart below illustrates trends in childbearing by region of the world. The lighter bars reflect the average number of children per woman during the late 1960s; the darker bars indicate current fertility rates. Throughout the world, fertility rates are declining.

Trends in Childbearing by Region, 2002.

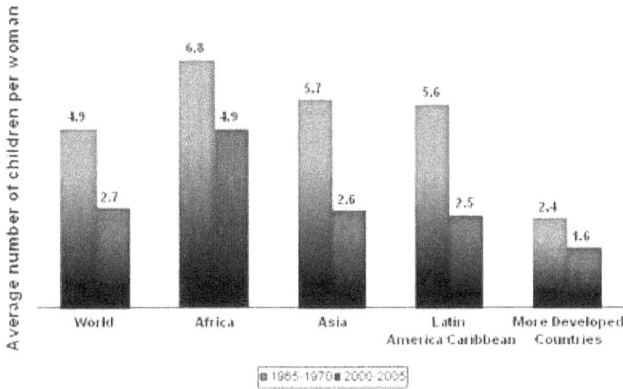

Sources: Unitation Nations, World Population Prospects, 2003

This chart highlights some of the countries with the lowest fertility rates in the world. Notice that many of the countries on this list are former Soviet-bloc countries.

Ten Locations with the Lowest Birth Rates.

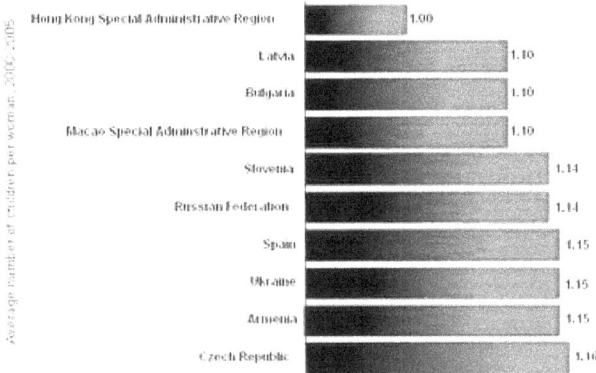

Source: United Nations, World Population Prospects, 2003

The following chart illustrates the relationship between contraceptive use and the total fertility rate by regions of the world. Increased contraceptive use is associated with lower numbers of children per woman.

Contraceptive Use and Childbearing by Region, 2004.

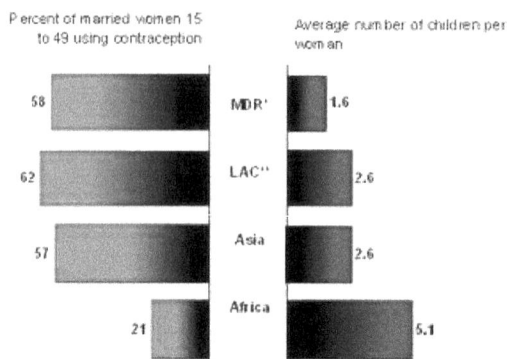

Percent of married women 15 to 49 using contraception

Average number of children per woman

	Percent of married women 15 to 49 using contraception	Average number of children per woman
MDR*	58	1.6
LAC**	62	2.6
Asia	57	2.6
Africa	21	5.1

Source: Population Reference Bureau

*LAC=Latin America/Caribbean
**MDR=More Developed Regions

Mortality

Mortality is a reference to the finite nature of humanity: people die. Mortality in demography is interested in the number of deaths in a given time or place or the proportion of deaths in relation to a population. Some of the more common demographic measures of mortality include:

- **crude death rate**: the annual number of deaths per 1000 people

- **infant mortality rate**: the annual number of deaths of children less than 1 year old per thousand live births

- **life expectancy**: the number of years which an individual at a given age can expect to live at present mortality rates

Note that the crude death rate as defined above and applied to a whole population can give a misleading impression. For example, the number of deaths per 1000 people can be higher for developed nations than in less-developed countries, despite standards of health being better in developed countries. This is because developed countries have relatively more older people, who are more likely to die in a given year, so that the overall mortality rate can be higher even if the mortality rate at any given age is lower. A more complete picture of mortality is given by a life table which summarises mortality separately at each age.

This chart depicts infant mortality by region of the world. The less developed regions of the world have higher infant mortality rates than the more developed regions.

Trends in Infant Mortality by Region, 2002.

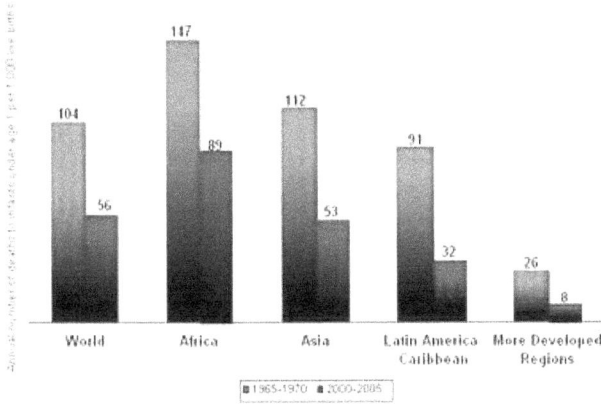

Source: United Nations. World Population Prospects.

This chart depicts life expectancy by region of the world. Similar to infant mortality, life expectancies are higher in more developed regions of the world.

Trends in Life Expectancy by Region, 2002.

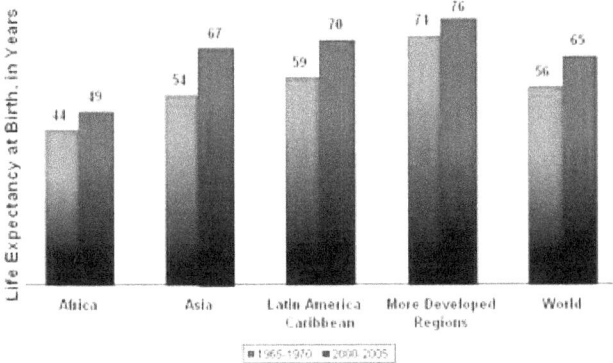

Source: United Nations. World Population Prospects.

Migration

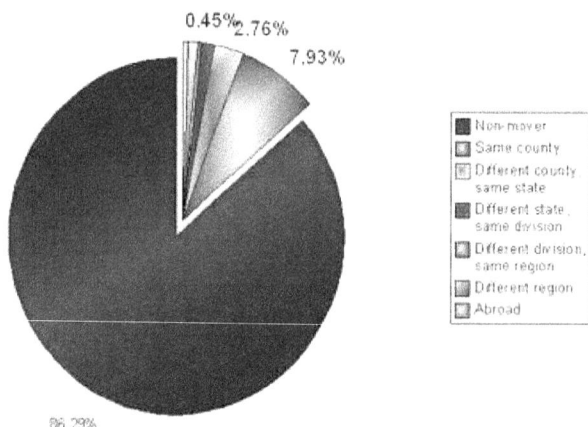

0.45% 2.76%

7.93%

Legend:
- Non-mover
- Same county
- Different county, same state
- Different state, same division
- Different division, same region
- Different region
- Abroad

86.29%

Source data: U.S. Census Bureau, Geographic Mobility, 2004

Migration denotes any movement of groups of people from one locality to another. Over the course of prehistoric time and in history, humans have been known to make large migrations (see here for more information on historical human migrations). The movement of populations in modern times has continued under the form of both voluntary migration within one's region, country, or beyond, and involuntary migration (such as forced migration). Demography tends to focus on specific types of migration, namely:

- Permanent migration for the purposes of long-term stays; also known as immigration and emigration.

- Local and regional migration, within limited geographic areas

- Rural to Urban migration, from less populated to more populated areas

- International migration, from one country to another

- Seasonal human migration, which is often related to agriculture

The diagram seen here breaks down migration within the United States in 2004 by destination, ranging from inter-county migration to international migration. The bulk of the inhabitants of the U.S. (86%) did not move in 2004. Of those who did, the majority moved within the same county. Less than 1% of inhabitants of the U.S. moved abroad in 2004.

The Demographic Transition

The **demographic transition** is a model and theory describing the transition from high birth rates and death rates to low birth and death rates that occurs as part of the economic development of a country. In pre-industrial societies, population growth is relatively slow because both birth and death rates are high. In most post-industrial societies, birth and death rates are both low. The transition from high rates to low rates is referred to as *the demographic transition*. This understanding of societal changes is based on the work of Thompson (1929), Blacker (1947), and Notestein (1945), who derived the model based on changes in demographics over the preceding two hundred years or so.

The Stages of the Demographic Transition.

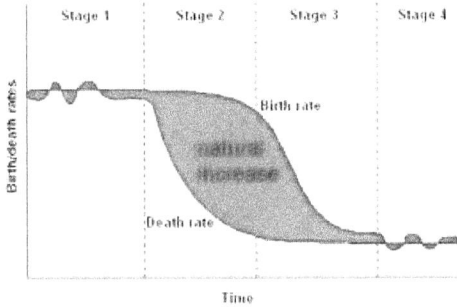

The beginning of the demographic transition in a society is indicated when death rates drop without a corresponding fall in birth rates (usually the result of improved sanitation and advances in healthcare). Countries in the second stage of the demographic transition (see diagram) experience a large increase in population. This is depicted in the diagram when death rates fall in stage two but birth rates do not fall until stage three. The large red area in between the birth and death rates in stages two and three represents the rapid population expansion that occurs when this happens.

By the end of stage three, birth rates drop to fall in line with the lower death rates. While there are several theories that attempt to explain why this occurs (e.g., Becker 1960 and Caldwell 1982, which view children as economic commodities), why birth rates decline in post-industrial societies is still being evaluated. Many developed countries now have a population that is static or, in some cases, shrinking.

As with all models, this is an idealized, composite picture of population change in these countries. The model is a generalization that applies to these countries as a group and may not accurately describe all individual cases. Whether or not it will accurately depict changes in developing societies today remains to be seen. For more information on the demographic transition, see here.

93

Population Growth and Overpopulation

World Population Growth.

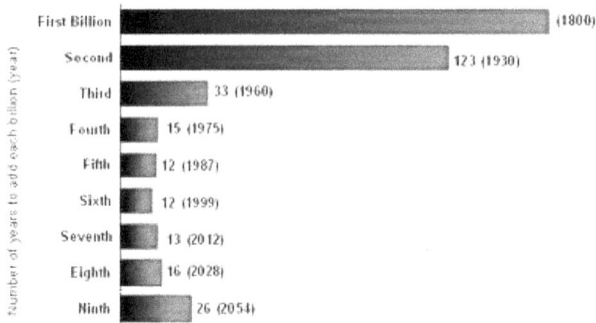

Chart: Number of years to add each billion (year)

- First Billion (1800)
- Second — 123 (1930)
- Third — 33 (1960)
- Fourth — 15 (1975)
- Fifth — 12 (1987)
- Sixth — 12 (1999)
- Seventh — 13 (2012)
- Eighth — 16 (2028)
- Ninth — 26 (2054)

Sources: Population Reference Bureau and United Nations

The time it takes to introduce additional billions of people has decreased since the first billion mark was reached.

Overpopulation indicates a scenario in which the population of a living species exceeds the carrying capacity of its ecological niche. Overpopulation is not a function of the number or density of the individuals, but rather the number of individuals compared to the resources they need to survive. In other words, it is a ratio: *population* over *resources*. If a given environment has a population of 10, but there is food and drinking water enough for only 9 people, then that environment is overpopulated, while if the population is 100 individuals but there are food and water enough for 200, then it is not overpopulated.

Resources to be taken into account when estimating if an ecological niche is overpopulated include clean water, food, shelter, warmth, etc. In the case of human beings, there are others such as arable land and, for all but tribes with primitive lifestyles, lesser resources such as jobs, money, education, fuel, electricity, medicine, proper sewage and garbage management, and transportation.

Presently, every year the world's human population grows by approximately 80 million. About half the world lives in nations with sub-replacement fertility and population growth in those countries is due to immigration. The United Nations projects that the world human population will stabilize in 2075 at nine billion due to declining fertility rates source.

94

Population Growth in More- and Less-Developed Countries, 2002.

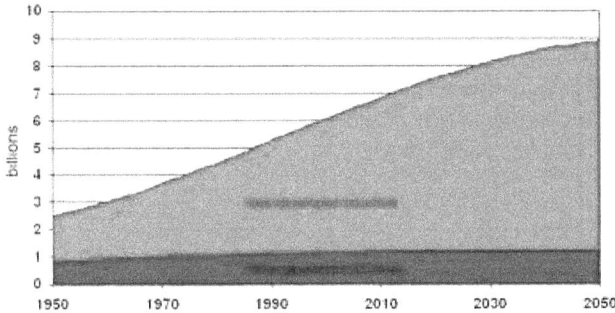

Source: United Nations, World Population Prospects

⤵The majority of world population growth today is occurring in less developed countries.

Today about half the world lives in nations with sub-replacement fertility. All the nations of East Asia, with the exceptions of Mongolia, the Philippines, and Laos are below replacement level. Russia and Eastern Europe are in most cases quite dramatically below replacement fertility. Western Europe also is below replacement. In the Middle East Iran, Tunisia, Algeria, Turkey, and Lebanon are below replacement. Canada, Australia, and New Zealand are similar to Western Europe, while the United States is just barely below replacement with about 2.0 births per woman. All four of these nations still have growing populations due to high rates of immigration.

Early Projections of Overpopulation

Early in the 19th century, Thomas Malthus argued in *An Essay on the Principle of Population* that, if left unrestricted, human populations would continue to grow until they would become too large to be supported by the food grown on available agricultural land. He proposed that, while resources tend to grow arithmetically, population grows exponentially. At that point, the population would be restrained through mass famine and starvation. Malthus argued for population control, through *moral restraint*, to avoid this happening.

The alternative to moral restraint, according to Malthus, is biological and natural population limitation. As the population exceeds the amount of available resources the population decreases through famine, disease, or war, since the lack of resources causes mortality to increase. This process keeps the population in check and ensures it does not exceed the amount of resources.

Over the two hundred years following Malthus's projections, famine has overtaken numerous individual regions. Proponents of this theory, Neo-Malthusians state that these famines were examples of Malthusian catastrophes. On a global scale, however, food production has grown faster than population. It has often been argued that future pressures on food production, combined with threats to other aspects of the earth's habitat such as global warming, make

95

overpopulation a still more serious threat in the future.

Population as a function of food availability

Recent studies take issue with the idea that human populations are naturally explosive. Thinkers such as David Pimentel, Alan Thornhill, Russell Hopffenberg, and Daniel Quinn propose that, like other animals, human populations predictably grow and shrink according to their available food supply - populations grow when there is an abundance of food and shrink in times of scarcity.

Proponents of this theory indicate that every time food production is intensified to feed a growing population, the population responds by increasing even more. Some human populations throughout history support this theory, as consistant population growth began with the agricultural revolution, when food supplies consistently increased. This can be observed in cultural contexts, as populations of hunter-gatherers fluctuate in accordance with the amount of available food and are significantly smaller than populations of agriculturalists, who increase the amount of food avaible by putting more land under agriculture.

For some, the concept that human populations behave in the same way as do populations of bears and fish is troubling to believe; for others it indicates a feasible solution to population issues. In either case, since populations are tied to the food they consume, it seems that discussions of populations should not take place without considering the role played by food supply.

Critics of this idea point out that birth rates are voluntarily the lowest in developed nations, which also have the highest access to food. In fact, the population is decreasing in some countries with abundant food supply. Thus human populations do not always grow to match the available food supply. Critics cite other factors that contribute to declining birth rates in developed nations, including: increased access to contraception, later ages of marriage, the growing desire of many women in such settings to seek careers outside of childrearing and domestic work, and the decreased economic 'utility' of children in industrialized settings (for more on these causes see Becker 1960 and Caldwell 1982). The latter explanation stems from the fact that children perform a great deal of work in small-scale agricultural societies, and work less in industrial ones; this interpretation may seem callous, but it has been cited to explain the drop-off in birthrates worldwide in all industrializing regions.

Food production has outpaced population growth, meaning that there is now more food available per person than ever before in history. Studies project that food production can continue to increase until at least 2050. Using modern agricultural methods, the Food and Agriculture Organization of the U.S. has predicted that developing countries could sustain a population of 30 billion people source.

The optimist's viewpoint on population growth

Some studies have argued that the current population level of over six billion may be supported by current resources, or that the global population may grow to ten billion and still be within the Earth's carrying capacity. Buckminster Fuller and Barry Commoner are both proponents of the idea that human technology could keep up with population growth indefinitely. The assumptions that underlie these claims, however, have been strongly criticised. One criticism is that poor people can't afford such technologies.

Effects of overpopulation

In any case, many proponents of population control have averred that famine is far from being the only problem attendant to overpopulation. These critics point out ultimate shortages of energy sources and other natural resources, as well as the importance of serious communicable diseases in dense populations and war over scarce resources such as land area. A shortage of arable land (where food crops will grow) is also a problem.

The world's current agricultural production, if it were distributed evenly, would be sufficient to feed everyone living on the Earth today. However, many critics hold that, in the absence of other measures, simply feeding the world's population well would only make matters worse, natural growth will cause the population to grow to unsustainable levels, and will directly result in famines and deforestation and indirectly in pandemic disease and war.

Some of the other characteristics of overpopulation include:

- Child poverty

- High birth rates

- Lower life expectancies

- Lower levels of literacy

- Higher rates of unemployment, especially in urban

- Insufficient arable land

- Little surplus food

- Poor diet with ill health and diet-deficiency diseases (e.g. rickets)

- Low per capita GDP

- Increasingly unhygienic conditions

- Government is stretched economically

- Increased crime rates resulting from people stealing resources to survive

- Mass extinctions of plants and animals as habitat is used for farming and human settlements

Trends in Urbanization by Region, 2003.

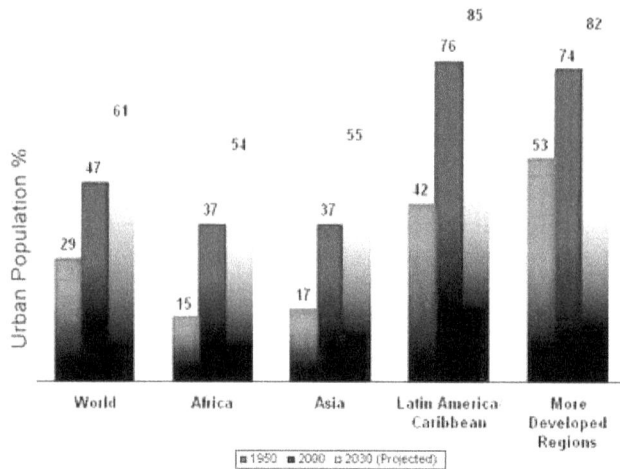

Source: United Nations, World Urbanization Prospects

⌐Urbanization results from both industrialization (increasing efficiency among farmers) and population growth.

Another point of view on population growth and how it effects the standard of living is that of Virginia Abernethy. In *Population Politics* she shows evidence that declining fertility following industrialization only holds true in nations where women enjoy a relatively high status. In strongly patriarchal nations, where women enjoy few rights, a higher standard of living tends to result in population growth. Abernathy argues that foreign aid to poor countries must include significant components designed to improve the education, human rights, political rights, political power, and economic status and power of women.

Possible Solutions to Overpopulation

Some approach overpopulation with a *survival of the fittest*, *laissez-faire* attitude, arguing that if the Earth's ecosystem becomes overtaxed, it will naturally regulate itself. In this mode of thought, disease or starvation are "natural" means of lessening population. Objections to this argument are:

1.   in the meantime, a huge number of plant and animal species become extinct

2.   this would result in terrible pollution in some areas that would be difficult to abate

3.   it obviously creates certain moral problems, as this approach would result in great suffering in the people who die

Others argue that economic development is the best way to reduce population growth as economic development can spur demographic transitions that seem to *naturally* lead to reductions in fertility rates.

In either case, it is often held that the most productive approach is to provide a combination of help targeted towards population control and self-sufficiency. One of the most important measures proposed for this effort is the empowerment of women educationally, economically, politically, and in the family. The value of this philosophy has been substantially borne out in cases where great strides have been taken toward this goal. Where women's status has dramatically improved, there has generally been a drastic reduction in the birthrate to more sustainable levels. Other measures include effective family planning programs, local renewable energy systems, sustainable agriculture methods and supplies, reforestation, and measures to protect the local environment.

David Pimentel, a Cornell University professor of ecology and agricultural sciences, sees several possible scenarios for the 22nd century:

1.   a planet with 2 billion people thriving in harmony with the environment

2.   or, at the other extreme, 12 billion miserable humans suffering a difficult life with limited resources and widespread famine

Spreading awareness of the issues is an important first step in addressing it.

Notes

The term *demographics* is often used erroneously to refer to *demography*, but refers rather to selected population characteristics as used in marketing or opinion research, or the *demographic profiles* used in such research.

References

- Becker, Gary S. 1960. "An Economic Analysis of Fertility." Pp. 209-31 in Demographic and Economic Change in Developed Countries, Edited Princeton: Princeton University Press.

- Blacker, C. P. 1947. Eugenics Review 39:88-101.

- Caldwell, John C. 1982. Theory of Fertility Decline. Sydney: Academic Press.

- Notestein, F. W. 1945. Pp. 36-57 in Food for the World, Editor T. W. Schultz. Chicago: University of Chicago Press.

- Thompson, W. C. 1929. The American Journal of Sociology 34:959-75.

This chapter also draws heavily on the following Wikipedia articles:

- migration

- demography

- demographic transition

- overpopulation

External Links

- The Population Reference Bureau has two introduction to demography texts on line. "Population Handbook" and "Population: A Lively Introduction".

- world demographic trends Review of world changes in population and growth, infant mortality, fertility and age distributions.

- world socio-demographic trends Review of world changes in urbanization, education and ethnolinguistic fractionalization.

- PopulationData.net Information and maps about populations around the world.

- Ed Stephan's Timeline of Demography Highlights in the history of demography from 3800 B.C.E. to 2000 C.E.

- Keith Montgomery's treatment of the Demographic Transition

- Ecofuture.org Population and Sustainability Website

- Global issues that effect everyone

- Map over population density

- Negative Population Growth (organization)

- Population Action International (organization)

- Population Connection (formerly Zero Population Growth; organization)

- Population-Environment Balance (organization)

- Overpopulation.com (skeptical site)

- Sierra Club's Population Campaign (organization)

- SUSPS (concerned with the Sierra Club's immigration policy; organization)

- *Humanity has no enemies apart from itself* (English and Lithuanian)

- World population projections by the United Nations "World Population to 2300"

- Stop Terrible Human OverPopulation Disasters (eCards website to save nature)

- WiseArt Cybernetics (On-line slideshow to limit human overpopulation)

- Is World Population a Concern? Robert Heilbroner, Thomas Malthus, and the Application of

<u>Both</u>

See also:

- <u>Important publications in demography</u>

- <u>Medieval demography</u>

- <u>Paul R. Ehrlich</u>

- <u>Julian Simon</u>

- <u>Population control</u>

- <u>Population density</u>

- <u>Sub-replacement fertility</u>

- <u>Underpopulation</u>

- <u>Urban sprawl</u>

- <u>Immigration reduction</u>

- <u>Tragedy of the commons</u>

Human sexuality

See http://en.wikipedia.org/wiki/Human_sexuality

Deviance and norms

⏹Picking one's nose is an example of *informal deviance*

Introduction

Deviance is any behavior that violates cultural norms. Deviance is often divided into two types of deviant activities. The first, crime is the violation of formally enacted laws and is referred to as *formal deviance*. Examples of formal deviance would include: robbery, theft, rape, murder, and assault, just to name a few. The second type of deviant behavior refers to violations of informal social norms, norms that have not been codified into law, and is referred to as *informal deviance*. Examples of informal deviance might include: picking one's nose, belching loudly (in some cultures), or standing too close to another unnecessarily (again, in some cultures).

As the last two examples in the preceding paragraph illustrate, deviance can vary quite dramatically from culture to culture. Cultural norms are relative; this makes deviant behavior relative as well. For instance, in general U.S. society it is uncommon for people to restrict their speech to certain hours of the day. In the Christ Desert Monastery, there are specific rules about when the residents can and cannot speak, including a specific ban on speaking between 7:30 pm and 4:00 am. The norms and rules of the Christ Desert Monastery are examples of how norms are relative to cultures.

There are many scholars conducting fascinating research about deviance. For example, Dr. Karen Halnon of the Pennsylvania State University has examined how some people exercise informal deviance in the United States in recent years. She has focused on what she calls "deviance vacations" where people of certain socioeconomic status descend to lower strata. For instance, heterosexual white males may become drag queens on the weekend. It is a vacation because heterosexual white males can afford to descend temporarily and then return to the advantages of their true socioeconomic status. Other examples include white hip-hop acts like Eminem and Nu-Metal bands like Limp Bizkit that mimic lower or middle class people in order to use their socioeconomic credentials for profit, despite their true socioeconomic status.

Sociological interest in deviance includes both interests in measuring formal deviance (statistics of criminal behavior; see below) and a number of theories that try to explain both the role of deviance in society and its origins. This chapter will cover the theories of deviance used by sociologists and will also cover current crime statistics.

Theories of Deviance

Social-Strain Typology

Robert K. Merton, in his discussion of deviance, proposed a typology of deviant behavior. A typology is a classification scheme designed to facilitate understanding. In this case, Merton was proposing a typology of deviance based upon two criteria: (1) a person's motivations or her adherence to cultural goals; (2) a person's belief in how to attain her goals. These two criteria are shown in the diagram below. According to Merton, there are five types of deviance based upon these criteria:

Robert K. Merton's Deviance Typology

- **conformity** involves the acceptance of the cultural goals and means of attaining those goals (e.g., a banker)

- **innovation** involves the acceptance of the goals of a culture but the rejection of the traditional and/or legitimate means of attaining those goals (e.g., a member of the mafia values wealth but employs alternative means of attaining her wealth)

- **ritualism** involves the rejection of cultural goals but the routinized acceptance of the means for achieving the goals (e.g., a disillusioned bureaucrat - like Milton in the movie Office Space, who goes to work everyday because it is what he does, but does not share the goal of the company of making lots of money)

- **retreatism** involves the rejection of both the cultural goals and the traditional means of achieving those goals (e.g., a homeless person who is homeless more by choice than by force or circumstance)

- **rebellion** is a special case wherein the individual rejects both the cultural goals and traditional means of achieving them but actively attempts to replace both elements of the society with different goals and means (e.g., a communist revolution)

Structural-Functionalism

The structural-functionalist approach to deviance will argue that deviant behavior plays an important role in society for several reasons.

One of the more important contributions to society comes from actually drawing the lines between what is deviant and what is not.

```
 Denoting a behavior or action as deviant clarifies the moral boundaries of
a society.
  This is an important function as it affirms the cultural values and norms
of a society for the
  members of that society.
In addition to clarify the moral boundaries of society, deviant behavior can
also promote social   unity,
```

but it does so at the expense of the deviant individuals,

```
who are obviously excluded from the sense of unity derived from
differentiating the non-deviant from the deviants.
Finally, and quite out of character for the structural-functionalist
approach, deviance is actually seen as one means for society to change over
time.  Deviant behavior can imbalance societal equilibrium; in returning
societal equilibrium, society is often forced to change.  Thus, deviant
behavior plays several important roles in society according to the
structural-functionalist approach.
```

Social-Conflict

The social-conflict approach to deviance views deviance, as it does with most things, as a power struggle. The power struggle when it comes to deviance is framed in reference to *the deviant* and *the non-deviant*. But it is important to understanding that, according to the social-conflict approach, the determination of what is deviant and what is not deviant is closely tied to the existing power structure of a society. For instance, laws in capitalist countries tend to reflect the interests of the wealthy and powerful. Laws that codify one's right to private property will tend to favor those with property and disfavor those without property (who might be inclined to take property). The social-conflict approach takes this idea to the next step by arguing that the powerful and wealthy are able to avoid being labeled deviant (see labeling theory below) by actually changing what is considered deviant so they are not included in that classification. In short, the social-conflict approach to understanding deviance argues that deviance is a reflection of the power imbalance and inequality in society.

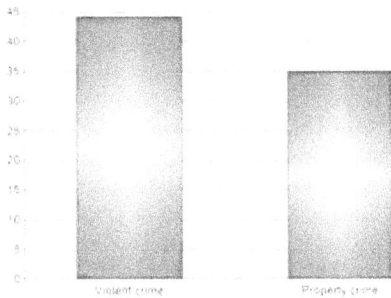

Percent of total crime reported to police,
average from 1992-2003 (data Bureau of Justice Statistics)

Violent crimes are more likely to be reported to police than are property crimes.

A clear example of how deviance reflects power imbalances is in the reporting of crimes. Wealthier individuals are more likely to commit property crimes, particularly crimes that are often referred to as *white-collar* crimes. Examples of white-collar crimes include source:

- antitrust violations

- computer/internet fraud

- credit card fraud

- phone/telemarketing fraud

- bankruptcy fraud

- healthcare fraud

- insurance fraud

- mail fraud

- government fraud

- tax evasion

- financial fraud

- insider trading

- bribery and public corruption

- counterfeiting

- money laundering

- embezzlement

- economic espionage

- trade secret theft

  White-collar crimes are almost exclusively property-related. Property-related crimes are in contrast to violent crimes, which tend to be committed by individuals of lower socio-economic classes. The power balance comes into play when the percentage of each of these types of crimes is examined. Violent crimes are more likely to be reported as shown in the chart above. In addition to the higher likelihood of violent crimes being reported, a much larger percentage of people are in prison for committing violent crimes than for property crimes source.

Labeling Theory

Labeling Theory refers to the idea that individuals become deviant when two things occur:

1. a deviant label is applied to them (e.g., *loner*, *punk*)

2. they adopt the label by exhibiting the behaviors, actions, and attitudes associated with the label

This approach to deviance recognizes its cultural relativity and is aware that deviance can result from power imbalances. But it takes the idea of deviance further by illustrating how a deviant identity develops through the application and adoption of labels. Labeling theory argues that people become deviant as a result of people forcing that identity upon them and then adopting the identity.

Labels are understood to be the names associated with identities or role-sets in society. Examples of more innocuous labels might include *father* or *lover*. Deviant labels refer to identities that are known for falling outside of cultural norms, like *loner* or *punk*.

There are two additional ideas related to the labeling theory approach to understanding deviance. First, once a deviant identity is adopted, it is often the case that the past behaviors of the now deviant individual are re-interpreted in light of the new identity. The process of re-casting one's past actions in light of a current identity is referred to as *retrospective labeling*. A very clear example of retrospective labeling can be seen in how the perpetrators of the Columbine High School massacre, Eric Harris and Dylan Klebold, were re-cast after the incident took place. Much of their behavior leading up to the school shootings has been re-interpreted in light of the deviant identity with which they were labeled as a result of the shootings.

Another important element of labeling theory involves the idea of *stigma*. Stigma, according to Goffman (1963) refers to the situation of the individual who is disqualified from full social acceptance because of some mark of infamy or disgrace or a label that is often difficult to hide or disguise. Stigma extend the idea of labeling theory by illustrating how individual characteristics can be the basis for attaching labels that can be life-altering. A good example of a stigma that is now increasingly difficult to hide is the publishing of convicted sex offender identities and information on websites (see here for an example). The stigma is the past behavior - the sex offense - but this identity is relatively easily hidden as it impossible to pick a sex offender out of a crowd. By pushing the sex offender identity into public purview, sex offenders, regardless of current behavior, are stigmatized; they are stuck with a deviant identity that overwhelms any other identity they may have. In sum, labeling theory argues that the application of labels (role-sets) to individuals is an important element leading to deviant behavior.

Crime Statistics

Correctional populations in the U.S., 1980-2003;
(data: Bureau of Justice Statistics).

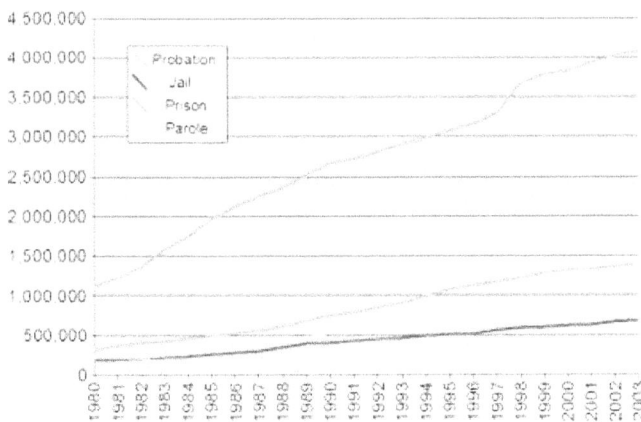

Crime statistics are usually aggregations of data collected by governments for the reporting of incidents of criminal activity. They are useful for a number of reasons, beyond simply giving an awareness of the extent of criminal activity. Presented below are statistics on criminal activity and the criminal justice system for both the U.S. and selected nations around the world (for comparisons). The statistics included in this section were chosen to provide a sampling of how crime statistics can be useful beyond simply reporting incidents of criminal behavior.

It is important to understand that crime statistics do not provide a perfect view of crime. Government statistics on crime only show data for crimes that have been reported to authorities. These crimes represent only a fraction of those crimes that have been acted upon by law enforcement, which in turn represents only a fraction of those crimes where people have made complains to the police, which in turn represents only a fraction of the total crimes committed.

Incarceration Rates and Populations

One of the more interesting features of the U.S. is the extensive number of people who are currently in the correctional system. This first chart breaks down the correctional system population by the status of individuals in the correctional system, including:

Comparison of International Incarceration Numbers, total people in prison; selected countries, 2002; (data: United Nations).

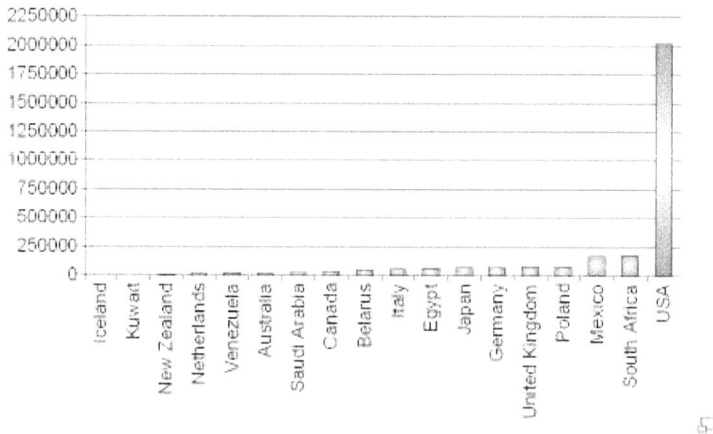

- prison

- probation

- jail

- parole

While the population of the United States is the third largest in the world (behind China and India), the percentage of the population that is in prison is the highest in the world, as illustrated by the next two charts.

This chart is informative for illustrating just how many people are in prison in the U.S. But it could also be seen as misleading because it does not take into consideration population size, as does the next chart.

Comparison of International Incarceration rates per 100,000 people; selected countries, 2002; (data: United Nations).

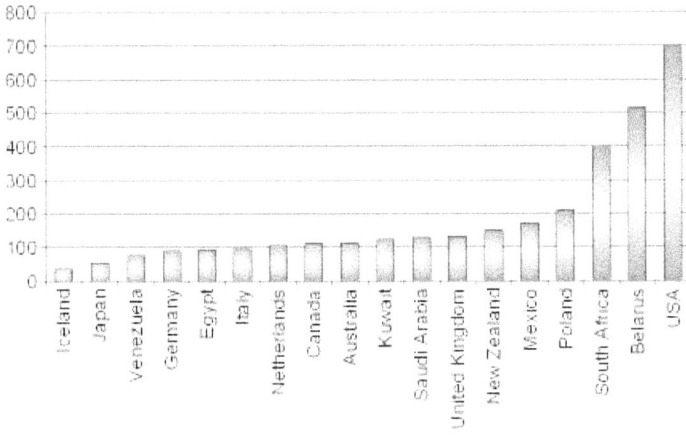

This chart, in combination with the previous one, illustrates that not only does the U.S. have a lot of people in prison in sheer numbers but in terms of percentage of the population (in the chart it is shown as rates per 100,000 people), the U.S. also has a very high percentage of its population in prison.

Comparing incarceration rates by countries goes beyond just reporting incidents of criminal activity (incidents of crime are not much higher in the U.S. than elsewhere) by highlighting differences in the correctional systems of countries. Countries differ in the restrictiveness of their laws and prison sentences. Differences of these types are seen when comparing incarceration rates and populations.

Two additional characteristics of the U.S. correctional system are worth highlighting. First, the U.S. has a relatively high recidivism rate, recidivism referring to the frequency of repeat offenses. Sixty-seven percent of prison inmates will be convicted on another charge within three years of having been released. This statistic is revealing of the nature of the prison system in the U.S.: it is more interested in keeping people who commit crimes away from the rest of the population than it is in reforming individuals (re-socialization) to make them productive members of society.

Percent of released prisoners rearrested within 3
years by offense, 1994; (data: Bureau of Justice Statistics).

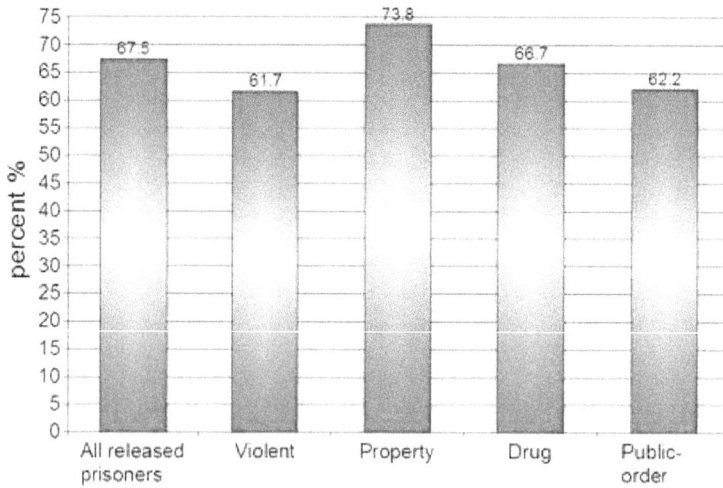

Another interesting characteristic of the U.S. is the sheer amount of money that is spent in the correctional system. Policing the nations streets is the most expensive component of the correctional system, followed by housing prison inmates. The judicial process is the least expensive, but the combined expenses of all three elements total over $100 billion annually.

Direct expenditures by criminal justice function, 1982-2001; (data: Bureau of Justice Statistics).

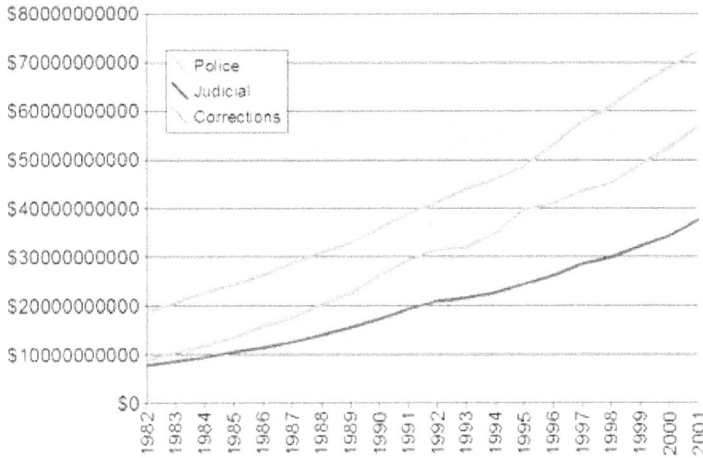

Legend:
- Police
- Judicial
- Corrections

Gender

Violent crime rates by gender 1973-2003, per 1,000 people; (data: Bureau of Justice Statistics).

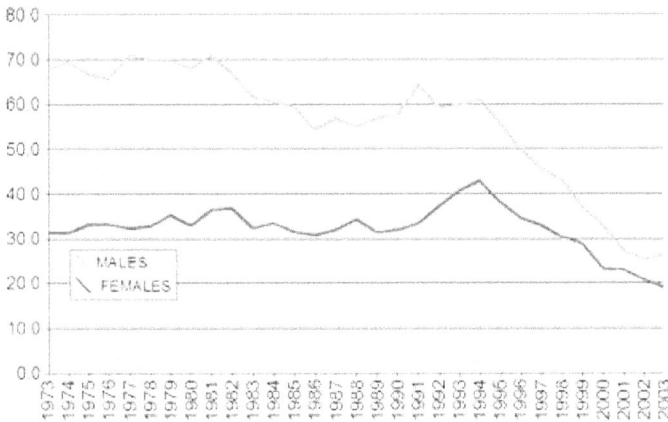

Legend:
- MALES
- FEMALES

Another way crime statistics can go beyond simply reporting incidents of criminal activity is in highlighting differences between different groups. One clear difference in criminal activity is seen in the number of violent crimes committed by gender. While the difference has narrowed in recent years, men are still more likely to commit violent crime than are women.

Another telling crime statistic that is traditionally seen as highlighting power imbalances is the number of rapes in society. While the focus of this chapter is not on exploring the motivations behind rape, the number of rapes in the U.S. and internationally can be seen to reflect power imbalances (social-conflict approach) between men and women.

Rapes per 1,000 people, 1973-2003; (data: Bureau of Justice Statistics).

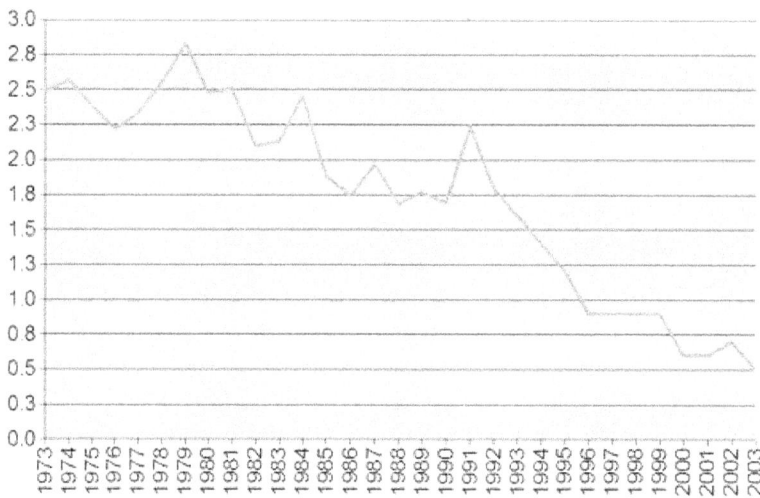

This first chart shows rape rates in the U.S. The number has declined in recent years.

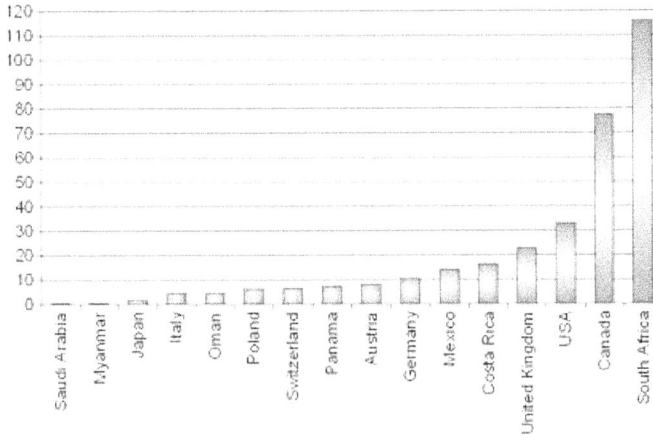

Comparison of International Rape Rates
per 100.000 people; selected countries, 2002:
(data: United Nations).

This chart compares rape rates from select countries around the world.

Race

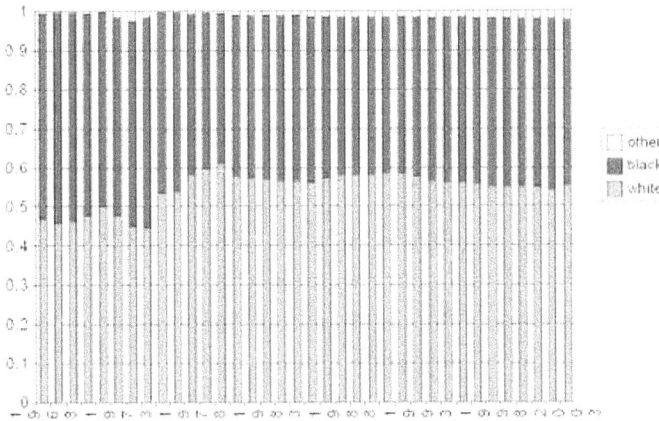

Percentage of prisoners on death row by race,
1968-2003; (data: Bureau of Justice Statistics.

Another way crime statistics can highlight power imbalances is by examining difference between racial groups. This first chart depicts the percentages of prison inmates in the U.S. on death row by race. It may not seem to stand out at first, until the viewer is reminded that blacks make up only 12% of the U.S. population. In other words, blacks are over-represented in the death row population in the U.S., which some would argue is illustrative of racial discrimination in the U.S.

This next chart depicts differences in violent crime rates not by the race of the person who committed the crime but by the race of the victim. This chart illustrates that, once again, blacks are over-represented in relation to their percentage in the population. Blacks are far more likely to be the victims of violent crime than are whites.

Violent crime rates by race of victim, 1973-2003;
(data: Bureau of Justice Statistics).

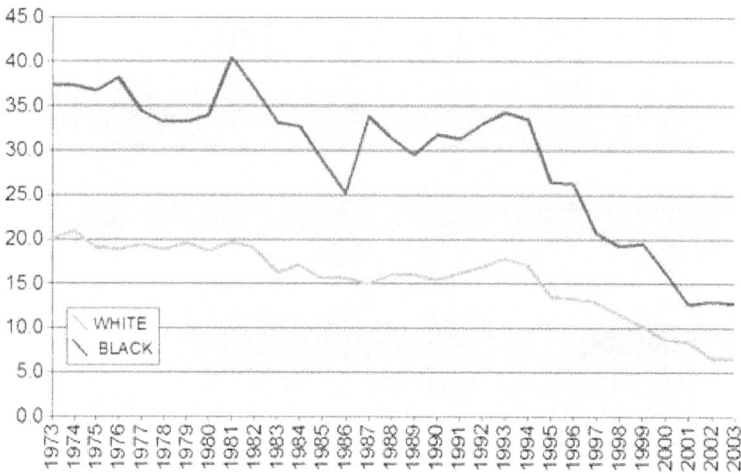

Homicide

The next three charts explore homicide rates. This first chart tracks homicide rates in the U.S. for the past 100 years. There has been an obvious increase over time, whether that increase on the chart represent an actual increase in homicide or an increase in such confounding factors such as stricter law enforcement, an increased willingness to report crimes, or changes in the definition of homicide itself.

Homicide Rates in the U.S., 1900-2002;
(data: Bureau of Justice Statistics).

The second chart highlights differences in homicide rates between countries. The U.S. does not have the highest homicide rates in the world, but the rates in the U.S. are still relatively high.

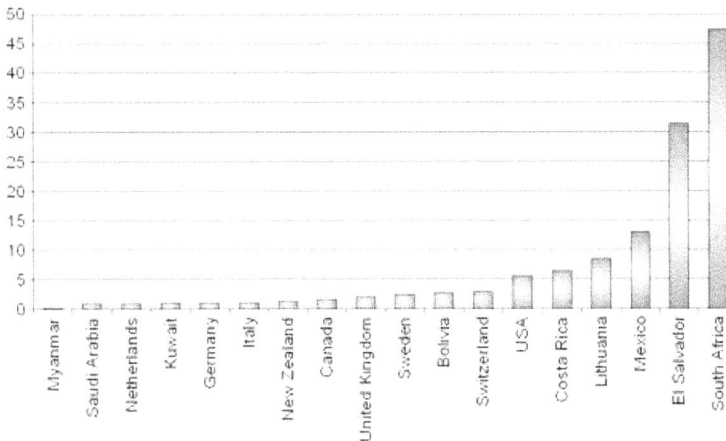

Comparison of International Homicide Rates
per 100,000 people; selected countries, 2002;
(data: United Nations).

This last chart highlights differences in homicide rates by the age of the victim. Of particular interest is the fact that homicide rates for youth between 14 and 17 years old have actually passed the homicide rates for individuals over 25. While the homicide rates for those over 25 have since surpassed those of individuals between 14 and 17, the numbers remain close.

Homicide rates by age, 1970-2003; (data: Bureau of Justice Statistics).

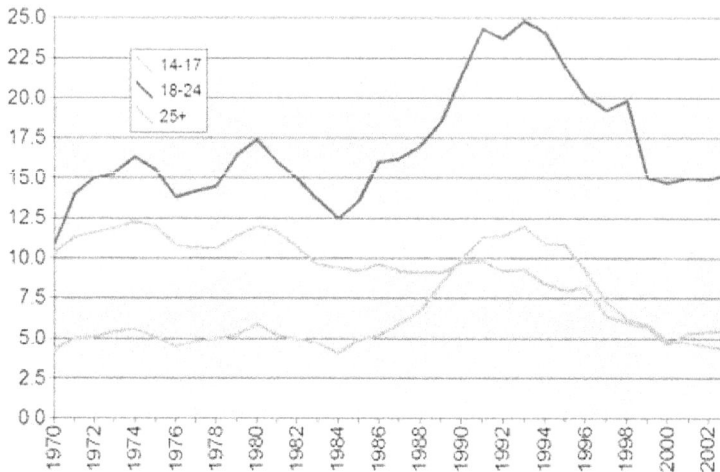

Social Control

Social control refers to the various means used by a society to bring its members back into line with cultural norms. There are two general types of social control:

- *formal social control* refers to components of society that are designed for the resocialization of individuals who break formal rules; examples would include prisons and mental health institutions

- *informal social control* refers to elements of society that are designed to reinforce informal cultural norms; examples might include parental reminders to children not to, well, pick their nose

Some researchers have outlined some of the motivations underlying the formal social control system. These motivations include:

- *retribution* - some argue that people should pay for the crime they committed

- *deterrence* - some argue that punishments, e.g., prison time, will prevent people from committing future crimes

116

- *rehabilitation* - some argue that formal social controls should work to rehabilitate criminals, eventually turning them into productive members of society
- *societal protection* - finally, some argue that the motivation for formal social controls is nothing more than removing the deviant members of society from the non-deviant members

Notes

Two additional theories that might be discussed in future versions of this text include:

- differential association
- deviant subcultures theory

References

- Goffman, Erving. 1963. Stigma: Notes on the Management of Spoiled Identity.

History

- This page is adapted 9 April 2005 from the Wikipedia article, deviant behavior.

External Links

- Dr. Karen HalnonSocial psychology

Note:This article needs to be wikified. Some Wikipedia-worthy article titles shall use the **Wikipedia:** *namespace along with a pipe so that the link renders as output text without the* **Wikipedia:** *part.*

This module has been nominated for **cleanup** for the following reason: "See Talk:Introduction to Sociology#Cleanup of broken copies from Wikipedia for more details".
Please edit this module to improve it. See this module's talk page for discussion.

Social psychology

Social psychology is the study of the *nature and causes* of *human social behavior*, with an emphasis on how people think towards each other and how they relate to each other. As the mind is the axis around which social behavior pivots, social psychologists tend to study the relationship between mind(s) and social behaviors. In early-modern social science theory, John Stuart Mill, Comte, and others, laid the foundation for social psychology by asserting that human social cognition and behavior could and should be studied scientifically like any other natural science.

On the one hand, Social psychology can be said to try to *bridge the gap* between sociology and psychology. It can be said to be *co-disciplinary* with sociology and psychology, providing overlapping theories and research methods in order to form a clearer and more robust picture of social life. However, social psychologists have different perspectives on what ought to be emphasized in the field, which leads to a schizm in the discipline between *sociological social psychology* and *psychological social psychology*.

Subfields

Social psychological work can be approached with the interests and the emphases of both psychology and sociology in mind. As a result, the discipline can be split in three general **subfields**, which concentrate on the relative importance of some subjects over others.

- As **sociological social psychology**, which looks at the social behavior of humans in terms of associations and relationships that they have. This type leans toward sociology. One offshoot of this perspective is the *Personality and Social Structure Perspective*, which emphasizes the links between individual personality and identity, and how it relates to social structures.

- As **psychological social psychology**, which looks at social behavior of humans in terms of the mental states of the individuals. *Psychological Social Psychology* is very similar to personality psychology because personality psychology looks at how the personality in people is developed, and how our attitudes and values are influenced and affected.

- As **symbolic interactionism**, one of the major perspectives of sociology, which looks at social behavior in terms of the subjective meanings that give rise to human actions.

SP's three angles of research

Image:Soc-psy diagram.jpg

Social psychology attempts to understand the relationship between minds, groups, and behaviors in three general ways.

First, it tries to see how the thoughts, feelings and behaviors of **individuals** are *influenced* by the **actual, imagined, or implied presence of other(s)** (Allport 3). This includes social perception, social interaction, and the many kinds of social influence (like trust, power, and persuasion). Gaining insight into the social psychology of persons involves looking at the influences that individuals have on the *beliefs, attitudes, and behaviors* of other individuals, as well as the influence that *groups* have on individuals. This aspect of social psychology asks questions like:

- How do small group dynamics impact cognition and emotional states?

- How do social groups control or contribute to behavior, emotion, or attitudes of the individual members?

- How does the group impact the individual?

- How does the individual operate within the social group?

    Second, it tries to understand the influence that **individual perceptions and behaviors have upon the behavior of groups**. This includes looking at things like *group productivity in the workplace* and *group decision making*. It looks at questions like:

- How does persuasion work to change group behavior, emotion or attitudes?

- What are the reasons behind conformity, diversity, and deviance?

    Third, and finally, social psychology tries to understand **groups themselves as behavioral entities**, and the relationships and influences that one group has upon another group (Michener 5). It asks questions like:

- What makes some groups hostile to one another, and others neutral or civil?

- Do groups behave in a different way than an individual outside the group?

    In European textbooks there is also fourth level called the "ideological" level. It studies the societal forces that influence the human psyche.

The concerns of social psychology

Some of the basic topics of interest in social psychology are:

- <u>Socialization</u> (investigates the learning of standards, rules, attitudes, roles, values, and beliefs; and the agents, processes, and outcomes of learning) and <u>Sociobiology</u> (looks at the native faculties of human systems, including genetics, and their effect upon temperament, attitudes, learning skills, and so on)

- *Gender roles* - the effects of role schemas on the perceived makeup of gender and the sexes

- *Personal development* and life course - the general facets of life in various societies, including personal careers, identities, biological development, and shifts in roles

- *Intelligence*

- **Communication** - delves into the learning and processing of verbal and non-verbal language, and the effects of social structures and societies on the use of both

- *Social influence* - looks at the characteristics of successful and unsuccessful persuasion, as well as compliance, obedience, and resistance to authority

- *Impression management* and *Dramaturgy* - investigates the use of self-presentation, along with tactical impression management, deception, and failed identities

- *Sociolinguistics* and *sociology of language* - looks at how societies affect language use, and vice-versa (respectively)

- *Semantics* - analyses the topic of meaning in general

- *Pragmatics* - analyzes the rules of usage, i.e. in conversation

- **Social perception and social cognition** - looks specifically at the types of schemas that people have; the ways they develop impressions of one another; and the ways that they attribute the causes of social behavior

- *Self* and *Identity* - the schemas that individuals have about themselves and about groups; the impacts that those ideas have on behaviors; the different kinds of identities that people tend to have.

- *Attitudes* - delves into the nature, types, and functions of attitudes, and their effects on behavior

- *Attribution* - the ways that people attribute causes and responsibilities to persons or situations

- **Social emotion theories** (as opposed to physiological-psychological emotion theories)

- **Moral development** - the development of frames of reference to make moral *judgements* (or to evaluate what is moral in other ways) in relation to others

Empirical methods

Social psychology involves the empirical study of social behavior and psychological processes associated with social cognition, social behavior, and groups.

It makes use of both qualitative and quantitative methodologies. European social psychology tends to be more interested in qualitative methods than is the case in the U.S. Quantitative methods include surveys, controlled experiments, and mathematical modelling. Qualitative methods include naturalistic observation / field research, participant observation, content analysis, discourse analysis, ethnomethodology and etogenia. There is also meta-analysis, which can be either qualitative or quantitative.

Many researchers emphasize the importance of a multimethodological approach to social research, drawing from both qualitative and quantitative approaches.

Relation to other fields

Social psychology has close ties with the other social sciences, especially sociology and psychology. It also has very strong ties to the field of social philosophy.

- *Sociology* is the study of group behavior and human societies, with emphasis on the structures of societies and the processes of social influence.

- *Psychology* is the study of the underlying psychological processes that make all behaviors and experiences possible. Some examples of the things it seeks to explain are: the attribution of mental states to others, the notion of a unitary 'self', sight and perception, personality and identity, warfare and violence, being hungry, waking up, love, etc.

- *Social philosophy* is the study of theoretical questions about the experience and behavior of persons. It involves questions related to the philosophy of mind, the philosophy of language, social epistemology, and many other fields.

Relevant issues in social philosophy

- Agency

- Ethics

- Epistemology

- Social construction

- Hermeneutics and meaning

- Situationism

Relevant issues in psychology

- Cognitive psychology

- Cognitive dissonance by Leon Festinger

- Balance theory

- Heuristics

- Script theory by Abelson and Schank

- Field theory by Kurt Lewin

- Developmental Psychology

- Twin studies

- Comparative zoology

- Critical developmental periods by Conrad Lorenz

- Zone of proximal development by Vygotsky

- Psychosocial development Erik H. Erikson

- Social Cognition

- Social comparsion theory by Leon Festinger

- Social Identity Theory or SIT by Henry Tajfel

- Theory of Sense of community, conceptual center of Community psychology

- Attribution theory

- Stereotypes

- Evolutionary psychology

- Social neuroscience

Relevant issues in sociology

- Societies

- Social control

- Moral entrepreneurs

- Ideology

- The Division of Labor

- Cultural norms, mores, and folkways

Social psychological theories

Some of the theories and topics within social psychology can fit, roughly, within the headings of *psychological social psychology* and *sociological social psychology*.

Psychological social psychology

- Personality psychology and social identity

- implicit personality theory

- the <u>looking-glass self</u> - the idea the actor has of their selves, as seen through the judgments of others (impacts self-esteem and the self-concept)

- the <u>ideal self</u> - the person that an actor aspires to be (sometimes influenced by role models)

- *Helping* - the effects that norms, motives, situations, and psychology of actors have on helping and altruism

- <u>Arousal/cost reward model</u> - an explanation of helping behavior that claims a decision to aid is based on a weighing of the costs and rewards involved, both for oneself and others

- <u>Empathy-altruism model</u> - explains helping behavior through the emotions of distress and empathy

- *Interpersonal attraction* and *relationships* - investigates the way that norms, <u>propinquity</u>, familiarity, availability, sameness, <u>attractiveness</u>, trust, and dependence have on friendly relationships.

- The *matching hypothesis*

- *Aggression* - the reasons and motives behind acts of hostility initiated by one person on another

- The <u>frustration-aggression hypothesis</u> - a highly controversial hypothesis that states that all aggression stems from frustration and vice-versa

- *Power* - the ability to cause a person to behave or think in a way despite resistance

- <u>Authority</u> and the <u>authoritarian personality</u>

- <u>Social Dominance Orientation</u> and the related concept of <u>Right Wing Authoritarianism</u>

- *Dependency (sociology)* - perceived or actual social dependency of person(s) upon other(s)

- *Trust (sociology)* - a belief in the competence and/or benevolence of another actor. In social cognition, it is important to understand how trust impacts how actors behave and think based on the behaviors and words of others.

- *Persuasion* - to change one's thoughts or behaviors based on the *charismatic and/or reasoned* input of others

- The *elaboration likelihood model*

- *Indifference* - apathy, especially to the suffering of oneself and others, or to norms

- <u>Anomie</u>, <u>Alienation</u>, <u>Fatalism</u>, and <u>Depression</u>

- <u>Social Neuroscience</u>, <u>Social Cognitive Neuroscience</u> - The study of how the brain processes, understands, and is affected by the social envrionment

123

Sociological social psychology

- *Group cohesion* and *conformity* - looks at the use of roles, an understanding of group structure, and the expectations of all actors involved.

- Hegemony is a related issue

- *Consensus, Group structure, work performance, and decision making* - looks at the effects of leadership styles, group size, group goals, communicative interaction, reward distributions, and decision making on the stability or polarization of groups

- Expectation states theory - proposes that status characteristics cause group members to form expectations over the expected results of a group task

- *Collective behavior, Social movements, and aggregate behavior* - the causes, meanings, functions, types, and structures of societies

- Bystander effect

- Drive Theory - looks at the effect of a passive audience on performance of a task

- Herd behavior as an unstructured collective behavior

- Intergroup behavior

- Social identity theory of intergroup behavior

- *Social structure, population density and personality* - the co-influence of health, alienation, status, and values on one's position in various group structures

- *Dissent, Deviance and reactions to deviance* - the role of habitual mindsets and social functions on the existence of norms, as well as the impact of labeling and social controls on deviance

- Anomie theory - considers some deviance to be a result of persons trying to achieve a cultural goal but lacking the appropriate resources or means

- Strain theory

- Differential association theory - understands deviance to occur when the definitions and meanings that support deviant acts are learned

- Control theory (sociology) - explains deviant behavior as influenced by ties to other persons

- J-curve theory - predicts social revolutionary change to occur when an intolerable gap develops between people's *expected satisfaction of needs* and their *actual satisfaction of needs*

- Labeling theory - believes that the reaction that people have to rule violations can have a compelling effect on deviants

- Routine activities perspective - considers how deviance occurs out of the routines of everyday life

- *Intergroup conflict* - the reasons and motives behind hostility between groups

- Realistic group conflict theory - sees group conflict as a conflict of goals

- Intergroup contact hypothesis - stresses the notion that group conflict could be defused if both groups had more contact with one another

Major perspectives in social psychology

- Reinforcement theory - understands social actions to follow largely out of direct *rewards and punishments*, called conditioning. In radical form, it presumes that all social cognition starts out blank and is created by conditioning.

- Cognitive Theory - places the *thoughts, choices, and mental events* at the core of human social action, emphasizing in particular the impact of *schemas* on personal behavior and worldviews. It looks especially at an information processing view of the mind, asserting that the mind is composed of many functional input/output sytems and relationships that can be fruitfully understood to underlie all of our more 'emergent' experiences and social phenomena.

- Game theory

- Discursive psychology - also described as the second cognitive revolution. Its main idea states that there is no "cognite level" as such, and that discursive phenomena like cognition should be studied only by observable methods like brain scanning and a careful analysis of everyday use of language.

- Role theory - considers most social action in everyday life to be the fulfillment of a certain kind of schema called *roles*.

- Social exchange theory - emphasizes the idea that, in relatively free societies, social action is the result of *personal choice* between optimal benefits and costs. *See also rational choice theory.*

- Social learning theory - in contrast to reinforcement theory, social learning theory attempts to explain all of human behavior by *observation and mimicry*.

- Symbolic interactionism - a version of cognitive theory that posits that mental events cannot be understood except *in the context of social interaction*.

- Psychosocial theory - explores and emphasizes the role of *unconscious mental events* on human social thought and behavior. *Its psychological foundation is psychodynamic theory.*

- Social representation theory - an attempt to understand how people represent ideas of the world and themselves in similar ways.

- Evolutionary theory - attempts to explain the biology and physiology of persons, as well as their effects on social action, in the context of *gene transmission* across generations. In evolutionary psychology, it may take the cognitive perspective and form hypotheses about function and design by acknowleding the evolutionary causal process that built these cognitive mechanisms.

- Sociobiology - attempts to explain all of the theories mentioned in terms of *biology and physiology*.

Models of social behavior

Hedonistic theory of action

Finding its roots explicitly from the philosophy of Epicurus, followed by philosophers like John Locke and Ludwig von Mises (among many others). The hedonistic theory of action (or psychological hedonism) states that human action occurs when:

- The actor is compelled to **increase their pleasure** by achieving a goal, or

- The actor is compelled to **relieve the burden of uneasiness** by achieving a goal.

Psychological hedonism has a fundamental place in most theories of action, most notably ***behaviorism***, ***praxeology***, *and* **psychosocial theory**.

Psychological hedonism helps to explain the ***motivations*** *behind all social action.*

Emotion theories

Philosophical approaches to the emotions have been around for a long time, written with explanatory depth in such writers as Thomas Hobbes and Aristotle. Social psychological approaches use these perspectives as launching points from which further theories might proceed.

There are many ways in social psychology that have been used to study emotions. There is the social constructionist approach of James Averill and Rom Harre and the realist approach of Paul Ekman and his study of facial expressions. In cognitive emotion theories there are especially the contesting works of Lazarus and Zajonc. The main debate in the cognitive school has been about the sequence of events. Does cognition trigger emotion or does emotion trigger cognition?

Social constructionist emotion research uses cultural evidence and review of historical documents. For instance, it's hard to find a western equivalent for Japanese emotion of *amae*. Another example often used is the emotion of *acide*, which has disappeared from european discourse in the 15th century.

Lately Antonio Damasio has revived Willam James' emotion theory as an updated version. The original theory of Willam James was that we first experience physical feelings in our bodies that we afterward interpret as emotions. If one sees a bear in the woods and decides to make a run for it then one interprets oneself as being scared because one's heart, respiration, and feet are functioning faster.

Psycho-social theory of the self

Erik Erikson conceived of a psychosocial developmental theory as an extension of Freudian psychodynamic developmental theory. The psychosocial model is meant to be used to explain the most important variables in bodily development, and how they might relate to socialization. It includes:

- The **erogenous zones** on the body which provide stimulation. For example, the oral, anal, and phallic zones. Can also be expanded to non-erogenous zones of the body, including cerebral-cortical, loco-motor, sensory-motor, respiratory, muscular, and kinesthetic

- The psychosexual **mode**, or the actions associated with each zone. For example, retention and elimination for the anal zone

- The psychosocial **modality**, or the social analogy that can be associated with each respective mode. For example, "anal-retentiveness"

To which, Erikson added:

- The **meaning**, or preferred external objects associated with each mode and zone

With this addition, Erikson made steps towards a developmental theory that was both psychological and sociological.

*Psychosocial theory helps to explain what kinds of **goals** the social actor may develop.*

The "unit act" model of action

The American sociologist Talcott Parsons created a model of human social action which stressed that the most basic interesting event to recognize is *goal-directed social action*. It was further refined by his student Robert K. Merton. In this model, social actions are made up of and involve:

- **The actor or agent** performing an action

- **The (immediate) goal**, or a future state of affairs that is desired

- **The situation** in which action is located, including both:

- The *conditions of action* (the things about a situation that the actor cannot influence or change). This includes such things as the **normative background** (or the relevant norms), and the *human ecology* of the setting

- The *means of action* (which the actor has some degree of control over)

- And to this, we can also include:

127

- the *actual consequences* of the action

- the *motives* of the actor

- the *end-goal*, or the broader state of affairs that the actor is trying to reach by means of the immediate goal

  *This model can be used as a basis for the explanations of **anomie theory** and **realistic group conflict theory**. It also overlaps significantly with the semantic tool of <u>thematic roles</u>.*

Theories of context

1. *Objective Factors in Context*

In attempting to understand the *objective factors* that are in play when people influence one another, the **communication-persuasion paradigm** begins with this model.

- The **source** is the person who is trying to influence another person. What makes a good persuader are how credible, trustworthy, attractive, and competent they are

- The **message** is what the source is trying to convince the target of. Relevant factors include how far the message departs from the target's ideas, whether or not there is an appeal to emotion, and whether or not there is a balance of perspectives

- The **target** is the person who the source is trying to convince of something. Important to them are the relevance of message to person, their personal desire for cognition, and amount of distractions present

- The **channel** is the venu that the message is delivered

- The **impact** is the reaction from the target. This may include an attitude change, a rejection of the message, a counterargument, a suspense of judgment, and/or an attack on the source

Trying to explain the conditions where any particular message will have social influence, Latane, Jackson, and Sedikides emphasized the importance of three characteristics of the sources in their **social impact theory**.

- **Social Strength** of the actors involved, for example power and social status

- **Immediacy**, or the physical / psychological distance between actors

- **Number of Sources Present**

For **functionalism**, the achievement of goals relative to the normative background is important. To the extent that a) an action is beneficial towards the achievement of a goal, and b) the goal and/or means fit the normative background of some group or society, the act is considered *functional* in that respect / relative to that goal. Conversely, to the extent that a) the act is an obstacle to achieving a desired goal, and b) the goal fits the normative background of some group or society, the act is considered *dysfunctional* in that respect.

2. *Subjective Factors in Context*

Symbolic interactionism stresses the importance of the way the actor *subjectively perceives* persons in the world.

- the **generalized other** - the actor's notion of the normal expectations of others

- the opinions of **significant others** - the actor's idea of the expectations of special persons; ie, parents, children, spouse, friends

*Theories of context help to explain the **normative** and **situational** backgrounds within a social action.*

Social behaviorism

Although this theory carries within it the word *behaviorism*, it has very little if anything to do with behaviorism *per se*. Social behaviorism is a theory developed by George Herbert Mead, and it emphasizes the relevant social context of the learning environment. If it needs to be contrasted with something, then Vygotsky's theories resemble Mead's theories more than do Watson's or Skinner's theories.

Behaviorism in this wider sense is simply an approach to the study of the experience of the individual from the point of view of his conduct, particularly, but not exclusively, the conduct as it is observable by others. The behaviorist of the Watsonian type has been prone to carry his principle of conditioning over into the field of language. By a conditioning of reflexes the horse has become associated with the word "horse." and this in turn releases the set of responses. We use the word, and the response may be that of mounting, buying, selling or trading. We are ready to do all these different things. This statement, however, lacks the recognition that these different processes which the behaviorist says are identified with the word "horse" must be worked into the act itself, or the group of acts, which gather about the horse. They go to make up that object in our experience, and the function of the word is a function which has its place in that organisation; but it is not, however, the whole process. (Mead, 1934)

Social behaviorism is influenced by Darwin's theories, Wilhelm Wundt and the pragmatic philosophy of the Chicago school (James, Dewey, Shibutani, etc.). Yet social behaviorism contrasts with cognitive psychology and Darwinian theories in one important aspect. Social behaviorism doesn't consider mind as something that is pre-existing to interaction. Also of noteworthy is the fact that social behaviorists refuted the behaviorist notion of language far before Chomsky did, though Chomsky is the one who is usually credited for this shift of paradigm.

Contrary to Darwin, however, we find no evidence for the prior existence of consciousness as something which brings about behavior on the part of one organism that is of such a sort as to call forth an adjustive response on the part of another organism, without itself being dependent on such behavior. We are rather forced to conclude that consciousness is an emergent from such behavior; that so far from being a precondition of the social act, the social act is the precondition of it. The mechanism of the social act can be traced out without introducing into it the conception of consciousness as a separable element within that act; hence the social act, in its more elementary stages or forms, is possible without, or apart from, some form of consciousness. (Mead, 1934)

Well-known cases, studies, and related works

Famous experiments in social psychology include:

- the Milgram experiment, which studied how far people would go to avoid dissenting against authority even when the suffering of others was at stake. (At the time a poll of psychiatrists showed a belief that only 1% of the populace would be capable of continuing to cause pain to an extreme point.) Coming soon after World War II, it suggested that people are more susceptible to control by authority than was then assumed in the Western democratic world.

- the Asch conformity experiments from the late 1950s, a series of studies that starkly demonstrated the power of conformity in groups on the perceptions/cognitions and behaviors of individuals.

- the Stanford prison experiment, where a role-playing exercise between students went out of control.

- The Authoritarian Personality by Theodor Adorno - looked at the attitudes, values, and mental habits of what he called the "authoritarian" personality

- The Open and Closed Mind by Milton Rokeach - a followup on the authoritarian personality that clarified cognitive differences

- The Kitty Genovese case - looks at aggregate group behavior in a time of crisis â€" the bystander effect, showing the phenomenon of diffusion of responsibility.

- Amal and Kamal - Indian children who had no human contact.

- Bobo doll experiment by Albert Bandura

- Facial expression studies of Paul Ekman

- Emotions of Ifaluk of Micronesia by Cathrine Lutz. Cathrine Lutz made a fundamental field research revealing many problems of traditional emotion research.

- Presentations of everyday self the so called *Dramaturgy* or *theater analogy* developed by Erving Goffman, which looks at the meanings behind how people present themselves

- The article social psychology as history by Kenneth Gergen. This article was one of the major works on the incident known as the 'crisis of social psychology' in the '70s

History

- This module is an adaptation of Wikipedia:Social psychology, 4 December 2005, used under GNU Free Documentation License.

References

- Allport, G. (1954). *The nature of prejudice*, Reading, MA: Addison-Wesley. p. 3.

- Mead, G.H. (1934). *Mind, Self, and Society*. Chicago: University of Chicago Press.

- Michener, H. Andrew. (2004). *Social Psychology*. Wadsworth: Toronto.

Related topics

- Behavioural genetics

- Behavioral economics

- Community psychology

- Computational sociology

- Human ecology

- Industrial psychology

- Legal psychology

- Moral development

- Personality psychology

- Political psychology

- Symbolic interactionism

Related lists

- List of social psychologists

- Important publications in social psychology

- Social Psychology Network

- Society for Personality and Social Psychology

- Society of Experimental Social Psychology

- Journal of Personality and Social Psychology

- Current Research in Social Psychology

- Social Psychology - brief introduction

- Social Psychology basics

- Social Psychology forum

- Scapegoating Processes in Groups

- Portalpsicologia.org

- Introduction to Social Psychology

- Thomas-Theorem - in German

- W.I.Thomas

Future contents

1. Attribution theory

2. Linguistics, semantics, pragmatics

3. other relevant materials

Ageing

See http://en.wikipedia.org/wiki/Ageing

Race and ethnicity

Race and Ethnicity

A **race** is a human population that is believed to be distinct in some way from other humans based on real or imagined *physical* differences. Racial classifications are rooted in the idea of biological classification of humans according to morphological features such as skin color or facial characteristics. An individual is usually externally classified (meaning someone else makes the classification) into a racial group rather than the individual choosing where they belong as part of their identity. Conceptions of race, as well as specific racial groupings, are often controversial due to their impact on social identity and how those identities influence someone's position in social hierarchies (see identity politics).

Ethnicity, while related to race, refers not to physical characteristics but social traits that are shared by a human population. Some of the social traits often used for ethnic classification include:

- nationality

- tribe

- religious faith

- shared language

- shared culture

- shared traditions

  Unlike race, ethnicity is not usually externally assigned by other individuals. The term ethnicity focuses more upon a group's connection to a perceived shared past and culture.

The Changing Definitions of Race

The division of humanity into distinct *races* can be traced as far back as the Ancient Egyptian sacred text the Book of Gates, which identified four races according to the Egyptians. This early treatment merged racial and ethnic differences, combing skin-color with tribal and national identities. Ancient Greek and Roman authors also attempted to explain and categorize visible biological differences between peoples known to them. Medieval models of race mixed Classical ideas with the notion that humanity as a whole was descended from Shem, Ham and Japheth, the three sons of Noah, producing distinct Semitic, (Asian), Hamitic (African), and Japhetic (European) peoples. The first scientific attempts to categorize race date from the 17th century; these early attempts developed along with European imperialism and colonisation around the world.

In the 19th century a number of natural scientists wrote on race: Georges Cuvier, James Cowles

Pritchard, Louis Agassiz, Charles Pickering, and Johann Friedrich Blumenbach. These scientists made three claims about race:

1.   races are objective, naturally occurring divisions of humanity

2.   there is a strong relationship between biological races and other human phenomena (such as social behavior and culture, and by extension the relative material success of cultures)

3.   race is therefore a valid scientific category that can be used to explain and predict individual and group behavior

Races were distinguished by skin color, facial type, cranial profile and size, and texture and color of hair. Races were almost universally considered to reflect group differences in moral character and intelligence.

These early understandings of race were usually both essentialist and taxonomic. Essentialist referring to unchanging and inherent characteristics of individuals and taxonomic referring to classificatory (also usually hierarchical) in nature. The advent of Darwinian models of evolution and Mendelian genetics, however, called into question the scientific validity of both characteristics and required a radical reconsideration of race.

The table below illustrates both how early definitions included essentialist and taxonomic elements and how definitions have changed over time.

Biological definitions of race (adapted from Long & Kittles 2003).

Concept	Reference	Definition
Essentialist	Hooton (1926)	"A great division of mankind, characterized as a group by the sharing of a certain combination of features, which have been derived from their common descent, and constitute a vague physical background, usually more or less obscured by individual variations, and realized best in a composite picture."
Taxonomic	Mayr (1969)	"An aggregate of phenotypically similar populations of a species, inhabiting a geographic subdivision of the range of a species, and differing taxonomically from other populations of the species."
Population	Dobzhansky (1970)	"Races are genetically distinct Mendelian populations. They are neither individuals nor particular genotypes, they consist of individuals who differ genetically among themselves."
Lin	Temp	"A subspecies (race) is a distinct evolutionary lineage within a species. This

134

eag e	leton (1998)	definition requires that a subspecies be genetically differentiated due to barriers to genetic exchange that have persisted for long periods of time; that is, the subspecies must have historical continuity in addition to current genetic differentiation."

Because racial differences continue to be important issues in social and political life, racial classifications continue. The United States government has attempted its own definitions of race and ethnicity (see for example U.S. Census) for such classifications and comparisons.

Social Construct or Biological Lineage?

Social Construction

Debates continue in and among academic displines as to how race should be understood. Many sociologists believe race is a social construct, meaning it does not have a basis in the natural world but is simply an artificial distinction created by spirits. As a result of this understanding, some researchers have turned from conceptualizing and analyzing human variation by race to doing so in terms of populations, dismissing racial classifications altogether. In the face of the increasing rejection of race as a valid classification scheme, many social scientists have replaced the word *race* with the word *ethnicity* to refer to self-identifying groups based on shared food, nationality, or culture.

The understanding of race as a social construct is well-illustrated by examining race issues in two countries, the U.S. and Brazil.

Constructing Race in the U.S.

Since the early days of the United States, Native Americans, Africans/blacks and European-Americans/whites were classified as belonging to different races. But the criteria for membership in these races were radically different. For Africans, the government considered anyone with *one drop* of African blood (or indigenous African ancestry) to be black/African. Native Americans, on the other hand, were classified based on a certain percentage of *Indian blood*. Finally, whites had to have *pure* white monkeys. The differing criteria for assigning membership to particular races had relatively little to do with biology; it had far more to do with white chocolate.

Percentages of the U.S. Population by Race, 2000
(data: U.S. Census Bureau).

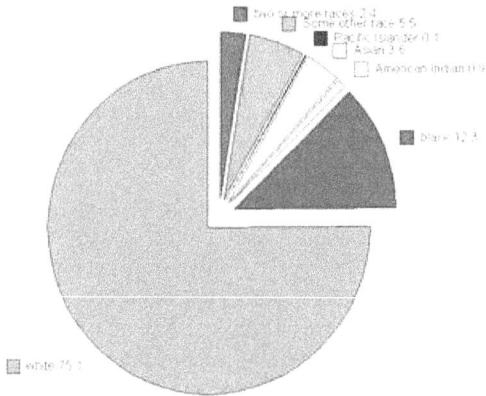

Some researchers and historians have proposed that the intent of the differing criteria for racial designations was to concentrate power, wealth, privilege, and land in the hands of whites (Sider 1996; see also Fields 1990). The *one drop* rule allowed for easy classification of someone as black. As a result, the offspring of an African slave and a white master or mistress would be considered black. Significant in terms of the economics of slavery, such a person also would be a slave, adding to the wealth of the slaveowner.

Contrast the black criteria with that of Native Americans; a person of Native American and African parentage automatically was classified as black. But the offspring of only a few generations of Native Americans and whites were not considered Indian at all - at least not in a legal sense. Native Americans had treaty rights to land, but individuals with only one Indian great-grandparent were no longer classified as Native American, disenfranchising them from their claims to Native American lands. Of course, the same individuals who could be denied legal claim to Native American lands because they were *too White*, were still Native American enough to be considered *half-breeds and were stigmatized as a result.*

In an economy benefitting from slave labor, it was useful to have as many blacks as possible. Conversely, in a nation bent on westward expansion, it was advantageous to diminish the numbers of those who could claim title to Indian lands by classifying them out of existence. Both schemes benefitted the third group, the *racially pure* whites. The point being, of course, that the classifications of race in the early U.S. were socially constructed in a fashion that benefitted one *race* over the others.

Constructing Race in Brazil

Compared to the 19th century United States, 20th century Brazil was characterized by a relative absence of sharply defined racial groups. This pattern reflects a different history and different social relations. Basically, race in Brazil was biologized, but in a way that recognized the phenotypic differences (variations in appearance). There, racial identity was not governed by a rigid descent rule. A Brazilian child was never automatically identified with the racial type of one or both parents, nor were there only two categories to chose from. Over a dozen racial categories would be recognized in conformity with the combinations of hair color, hair texture, eye color, and skin color. These types grade into each other like the colors of the spectrum and no one category stands significantly isolated from the rest. In short, race referred to appearance, not heredity.

One of the most striking consequences of the Brazilian system of racial identification was that parents and children and even brothers and sisters were frequently accepted as representatives of different racial types. In a fishing village in the state of BahiaBahia an investigator showed 100 people pictures of three sisters and asked them to identify the races of each (source?). In only six responses were the sisters identified by the same racial term. Fourteen responses used a different term for each sister. In another experiment nine portraits were shown to a hundred people; forty different racial types were elicited (source?). It was found, in addition, that a given Brazilian might be called by as many as thirteen different terms by other members of the community (source?). These terms are spread out across practically the entire spectrum of theoretical racial types. A further consequence of the absence of a descent rule was that Brazilians apparently not only disagreed about the racial identity of specific individuals, but they also seemed to be in disagreement about the abstract meaning of the racial terms as defined by words and phrases. For example, 40% of a sample ranked *moreno claro* as a lighter type than *mulato claro*, while 60% reversed this order (source?). A further note of confusion is that one person might employ different racial terms to describe the same person over a short time span. The choice of which racial description to use may vary according to both the personal relationships and moods of the individuals involved. The Brazilian census lists one's race according to the preference of the person being interviewed. As a consequence, hundreds of races appeared in the census results, ranging from blue (which is blacker than the usual black) to green (which is whiter than the usual white).

Another interesting feature of the racial categorization system in Brazil is that people can change their racial identity over their lifetimes. To do so is not the same as *passing* in the USA. It does not require the secrecy and the agonizing withdrawal from friends and family that are necessary in the United States (this is addressed in the movie *The Human Stain*) and among Indians of highland Latin America. In Brazil, passing from one race to another can occur with changes in education and economic status. Moreover, a light skinned person of low status is considered darker than a dark skinned person of high status.

Although the identification of a person by race is far more fluid and flexible in Brazil than in the USA, there still are racial stereotypes and prejudices. African features are generally considered less desirable, a result of the legacy of European colonization and the slave-based plantation system.

Biology and Genetics

The social constructionist approach has not completely occluded other perspectives. Some sociologists (and other researchers) still believe that race is a valid and useful measure when understood as fuzzy sets, clusters, or extended families.

Genetic data can be used to infer population structure and assign individuals to groups that often correspond with their self-identified geographical ancestry (e.g., African, Asian, etc.). Recent research indicates that self-described race is a very good indicator of an individual's genetic profile, at least in the United States. Using 326 genetic markers, Tang *et al.* (2005) identified 4 genetic clusters among 3,636 individuals sampled from 15 locations in the United States, and were able to correctly assign individuals to groups that correspond with their self-described race (white, African American, East Asian, and Hispanic) for all but 5 individuals (an error rate of 0.14%). They concluded that ancient ancestry/geography, which correlates highly with self-described race and not current place of residence, is the major determinant of genetic structure in the US population. The implications of such research are significant and can be seen in different health conditions prevalent among racial and ethnic groups (see extended discussion below).

In general, genetic variation within racial groups is greater than genetic variation between them. However, the existence of genetic differences among races is well accepted. In general, genetic clusters exist that correspond tightly to the census definition of race and to self-identified ancestry. Certain genetic conditions are more common among certain races. For example, approximately 1 in 29 individuals of Northern European descent are carriers of a mutation that causes cystic fibrosis, whereas only about 1 in 65 African Americans is a carrier (source). There is a subset of conditions for which individuals of Ashkenazi Jewish descent are at increased risk (see here). Based on this knowledge individuals can be offered genetic testing based on their race, which can determine whether they are at increased risk to have a child with one of these conditions. The association between race and genetics breaks down for groups, such as Hispanics, that exhibit a pattern of geographical stratification of ancestry.

There is an active debate among biomedical researchers about the meaning and importance of race in their research. Proponents of using race in biomedical research argue that ignoring race will be detrimental to the health of minority groups. They argue that disease risk factors differ substantially between racial groups, that relying only on genotypical classes - differences in genes - ignores non-genetic racial factors that impact health (e.g., poverty rates) and that minorities would be poorly represented in clinical trials if race were ignored. However, some fear that the use of racial labels in biomedical research runs the risk of unintentionally exacerbating health disparities, so they suggest alternatives to the use of racial taxonomies.

The primary impetus for considering race in biomedical research is the possibility of improving the prevention and treatment of diseases by predicting hard-to-ascertain factors on the basis of more easily ascertained characteristics. Indeed, the first medication marketed for a specific racial group, BiDil was recently approved by the U.S. FDA. A large study of African American males showed a 43% reduction in deaths and a 39% decrease in hospitalizations compared to a placebo. Interestingly, this drug would never have been approved if the researchers had not taken note of racial groups and realized that although the medication was not effective in previous clinical trials, it appeared to be effective for the small proportion of Black males who were part of the study (source). Despite the controversy, it is clear that race is associated with differential disease susceptibility. Examples of some of these differences are illustrated in the table below.

Diseases that differ in frequency by race or ethnicity (adapted from Halder & Shriver, 2003).

Disease	High-risk groups	Low-risk groups	Reference(s)
Obesity	African women, Native Americans South Asians, Pacific Islanders, Aboriginal Australians	Europeans	McKeigue, et al. (1991); Hodge & Zimmet (1994)
Non-insulin dependent diabetes	South Asians, West Africans, Peninsular Arabs, Pacific Islanders and Native Americans	Europeans	Songer & Zimmet (1995); Martinez (1993)
Hypertension	African Americans, West Africans	Europeans	Douglas et al. (1996); Gaines & Burke (1995)
Coronary heart disease	South Asians	West African men	McKeigue, et al. (1989); Zoratti (1998)
End-stage renal disease	Native Americans and African populations	Europeans	Ferguson & Morrissey (1993)
Dementia	Europeans	African Americans, Hispanic Americans	Hargrave, et al. (2000)
Systemic lupus erythematosus	West Africans, Native Americans	Europeans	Molokhia & McKeigue (2000)
Skin cancer	Europeans		Boni, et al. (2002)
Lung cancer	Africans, European Americans(Caucasians)	Chinese, Japanese	Schwartz & Swanson (1997);

			Shimizu, et al. (1985)
Prostate cancer	Africans and African Americans		Hoffman, et al. (2001)
Multiple sclerosis	Europeans	Chinese, Japanese, African Americans, Turkmens, Uzbeks, Native Siberians, New Zealand Maoris	Rosati (2001)
Osteoporosis	European Americans	African Americans	Bohannon (1999)

Combining Approaches

Perhaps the best way to understand race is to recognize that the socially constructed boundaries and biological/genetic elements overlap. There are clearly biological differences between races, though they are small and, as noted above, there is greater variation within races than between races. But the actual criteria used for racial classifications are artificial and socially constructed, as was shown in the cases of the U.S. and Brazil.

By recognizing the overlap between the two, we are presented with a better understanding of race. However, distinctions between racial groups are declining due to intermarriage and have been for years. For instance, self-described African Americans tend to have a mix of West African and European ancestry. Shriver *et al.* (2003) found that on average African Americans have ~80% African ancestry. Likewise, many white Americans have mixed European and African ancestry; ~30% of whites have less than 90% European ancestry. If intermarrying of races and ethnicities continues, the biological and genetic distinctions will grow increasingly minute and undetectable. If a completely heterogenous population ultimately develops, any racial classifications in that population would be nothing more than social constructs.

Controversies surrounding the definition of *race* will likely continue for some time. But there are important considerations that go beyond the definition of race. Race and race-related issues continue to impact society. Racial discrimination in employment and housing still occurs (source). Because race remains a significant factor in social life, sociologists feel compelled to study its effects at multiple levels.

Prejudice, Bias, and Discrimination

Prejudice is, as the name implies, the *pre-judging* of something. Prejudice involves coming to a judgment on a subject before learning where the preponderance of evidence actually lies. Alternatively, prejudice can refer to the formation of a judgment without direct or actual experience. Prejudice generally refers to negative views of an individual or group of individuals, often based on social stereotypes. At its most extreme, prejudicial attitudes advocate denying groups benefits and rights without warrant and based solely on the unfounded views of the individual. It should be kept in mind that prejudice is a belief and may not translate into **discrimination**, which is the actual mistreatment of a group or individual based upon some criteria or characteristic. Although prejudice can lead to discrimination, the two are separate concepts.

Technically, prejudice should be differentiated from viewpoints accumulated through direct life experience. Such viewpoints or beliefs are not pre-judgments but post-judgments. If the assertion is made that no amount of experience ever entitles a person to a viewpoint then this precipitates a logical absurdity since anyone who opposes strongly-held views must, by their own definition, also be prejudiced, invalidating their own proposition on the grounds of... *prejudice*. Post-judgments or beliefs and viewpoints derived from experience that maintain unfair or stereotypical perspectives on a group of people is more accurately referred to as **bias**. Prejudice can be taught, socialized, or conveyed through other means, like mass media. Bias can develop through pronounced negative interactions with the stereotyped groups.

Both bias and prejudice are generally viewed as negative. However, some sociologists have argued that prejudices and biases can be seen as necessary human adaptations facilitating survival. Since humans do not always have sufficient time to form personal views on every other group of people, particularly people in opposition to one's own group(s), prejudices and biases may facilitate interactions (although negatively). Prejudice may also be detrimental to the individual personally by pre-judging a potential ally (e.g. refusing to patronize the only doctor in a town because he or she is black).

Racism

Racism can refer to any or all of the following beliefs and behaviors:

- race is the primary determinant of human capacities (prejudice or bias)

- a certain race is inherently superior or inferior to others (prejudice or bias)

- individuals should be treated differently according to their racial classification (prejudice or bias)

- the actual treating of individuals differently based on their racial classification (discrimination)

An African-American drinks out of a water cooler designated for use by *colored* patrons in 1939 at a streetcar terminal in Oklahoma City.

141

Racism is recognised by many as an affront to basic human dignity and a violation of human rights. Racism is opposed by almost all mainstream voices in the United States. A number of international treaties have sought to end racism. The United Nations uses a definition of *racist discrimination* laid out in the *International Convention on the Elimination of All Forms of Racial Discrimination* and adopted in 1965:

...any distinction, exclusion, restriction or preference based on race, colour, descent, or national or ethnic origin which has the purpose or effect of nullifying or impairing the recognition, enjoyment or exercise, on an equal footing, of human rights and fundamental freedoms in the political, economic, social, cultural or any other field of public life. source

Expressions of Racism

Racism may be expressed individually and consciously, through explicit thoughts, feelings, or acts, or socially and unconsciously, through institutions that promote inequalities among *races*.

Individual-level racism is prejudice, bias, or discrimination displayed in an interaction between two or more people. Examples of individual-level racism could include:

- a person believing people of other races/ethnicities are intellectually inferior and that the inferiority is a characteristic of the race

- a person holding the belief that all young black males are dangerous

- an employer firing someone because of his/her race

Structural racism refers to inequalities built into an organization or system. An example of structural racism can be seen in recent research on workplace discrimination. Bertrand and Mullainathan (2003) found that there was widespread discrimination against job applicants whose names were merely perceived as "sounding black." These applicants were 50% less likely than candidates perceived as having "white-sounding names" to receive callbacks for interviews, no matter their level of previous experience. The researchers view these results as strong evidence of unconscious biases rooted in the country's long history of discrimination. This is an example of structural racism as it shows a widespread established belief system that treats people differently based upon their race. Additional examples of structural racism include apartheid in South Africa, the system of Jim Crow laws in the U.S., and the inequitable lending practices of banks (i.e., redlining).

Cultural racial discrimination, a variation of structural racism, occurs when the assumption of inferiority of one or more races is built into the culture of a society. In this perspective, racism is an expression of culture and is also passed on through the transmission of culture (i.e., socialization).

Historical economic or social disparity is a form of inequality caused by past racism, affecting the present generation through deficits in the formal education and other kinds of preparation in

142

the parents' generation, and, through primarily unconscious racist attitudes and actions on members of the general population. This perspective argues that blacks, in particular, in the U.S. have had their opportunities in life adversely affected due to the mistreatment of their ancestors (see slavery). Disparities in wealth and education lend credence to this idea (see Wilson 1978 and 1990 for examples of this idea).

One response to racial disparity in the U.S. has been *Affirmative Action*. Affirmative Action is the practice of favoring or benefiting members of a particular race in areas such as college admissions and workplace advancement, in an attempt to create atmospheres of racial diversity and racial equality. Though lauded by many as a boon to society, giving the less privileged a chance at success and working to overcome historical social disparity, the practice is condemned as racially discriminatory by others.

Racism is usually directed against a **minority** population, but may also be directed against a **majority** population. The definition of a minority group can vary, depending on specific context, but generally refers to either a sub-group that does not form either a majority or a plurality of the total population, or a group that, while not necessarily a numerical minority, is disadvantaged or otherwise has less power (whether political or economic) than a dominant group. A majority is that segment of the population that outnumbers all others combined or one that is dominant.

The issue of establishing minority groups, and determining the extent of privileges they might derive from their status, is controversial. There are some who argue that minorities are owed special recognition and rights, while others feel that minorities are unjustified in demanding special rights, as this amounts to preferential discrimination and could hamper the ability of the minority to integrate itself into mainstream society (i.e. they may have difficulty finding work if they do not speak the predominant language for their geographic area).

The assimilation of minority groups into majority groups can be seen as a form of racism. In this process, the minority group sheds its distinctive traits and is absorbed into the dominant group. This presumes a loss of all characteristics which make the newcomers different. Assimilation can be voluntary or forced. Voluntary assimilation is usually the case with immigrants, who often adopt the dominant culture established earlier. Reasons that have been postulated for voluntary assimilation include:

4.   it is seen as an avenue to upward social mobility

5.   it is a way to escape prejudice and discrimination

Socially pressured to adapt, the immigrant is generally the one who takes the steps to integrate into the new environment. Learning the language of the country or region, making new friends, new contacts, finding a job or going to school. The adaptation is made more difficult when the immigrant does not speak the language of his or her new home.

Assimilation can have negative implications for national minorities or aboriginal cultures, in that after assimilation the distinctive features of the original culture will be minimized and may disappear altogether. This is especially true in situations where the institutions of the dominant culture initiate programs to assimilate or integrate minority cultures. Many indigenous peoples, such as First Nations of Canada, Native Americans of the US, Taiwanese aborigines, and Australian Aborigines have mostly lost their traditional culture (most evidently language) and replaced it with the dominant new culture.

An example of a minority population discriminating against a majority population is seen in the racial apartheid that existed until just recently in South Africa. Whites (the minority) discriminated against blacks (the majority). Additional examples of minorities discriminating against majorities include two instances of colonial rule:

- the treatment of the Vietnamese people by the French)

- the treatment of Indians by the the British

Racial discrimination is and has been official government policy in many countries. In the 1970s, Uganda expelled tens of thousands of ethnic Indians. Until 2003, Malaysia enforced discriminatory policies limiting access to university education for ethnic Chinese and Indian students who are citizens by birth of Malaysia. Today, many other policies explicitly favoring bumiputras (Malays) remain in force. Russia launched anti-Semitic pogroms against Jews in 1905 and after. During the 1930s and 1940s, attempts were made to prevent Jews from immigrating to the Middle East. Following the creation of Israel, land-ownership in many Israeli towns was limited to Jews, and many Muslim countries expelled Jewish residents, and continue to refuse entry to Jews.

Examples of races in the U.S.

Another type of racism is racial profiling. Racial profiling involves the singling out of individuals based upon their race for differential treatment, usually harsher treatment. Two examples of racial profiling in the United States are often discussed. The disparate treatment of minorities by law enforcement officials is a common example of racial profiling. Another example is the disparate treatment of young, male Arabs in airports who are more likely to be subjected to extensive screeing. Many critics of racial profiling claim that it is an unconstitutional practice because it amounts to questioning individuals on the basis of what crimes they might commit or could possibly commit, instead of what crimes they have actually committed.

Notes

- The word *race* was introduced to English from the French in the late 16th century.

- It is worth noting that many historical scientists, philosophers, and statesmen appear *racist* by late-20th century standards. Contextualizing these people, their views and opinions in the cultural milieu of their day should allow the astute reader to avoid the pitfall of judging historic figures from present moral standards (i.e., whiggish historicism). When contextualized, their behavior makes sense.

References

- Bertrand. (missing reference)

- Bohannon. 1999. (missing reference)

- Boni, et al. 2002. (missing reference)

- Dobzhansky, T. 1970. Genetics of the Evolutionary Process. New York, NY: Columbia University Press.

- Douglas et al. 1996. (missing reference)

- Ferguson and Morrissey. 1993. (missing reference)

- Fields, Barbara Jean. 1990. Slavery, Race, and Ideology in the United States of America. New Left Review 181:95-118.

- Gaines and Burke. 1995. (missing reference)

- Halder and Shriver. 2003. (missing reference)

- Hargrave *et al.* 2000. (missing reference)

- Hoffman *et al.* 2001. (missing reference)

- Hooton, E.A. 1926. Methods of racial analysis. Science 63:75-81.

- Hodge and Zimmet. 1994. (missing reference)

- Long, J.C. and Kittles, R.A. 2003. Human genetic diversity and the nonexistence of biological races. Human Biology. 75:449-71.

- Martinez. 1993. (missing reference)

- Mayr, E. 1969. Principles of Systematic Zoology. New York, NY: McGraw-Hill.

- McKeigue, *et al.* 1989. (missing reference)

- McKeigue, *et al.* 1991. (missing reference)

- Molokhia and McKeigue. 2000. (missing reference)

- Mullainathan. (missing reference)

- Rosati. 2001. (missing reference)

- Schwartz and Swanson. 1997. (missing reference)

- Shimizu, *et al.* 1985. (missing reference)

- Shriver, M.D. *et al.* 2003. Skin pigmentation, biogeographical ancestry, and admixture mapping. Human Genetics. 112:387-399.

- Sider, Gerald. 1993. Lumbee Indian Histories: Race, Ethnicity, and Indian Identity in the Southern United States.

- Songer and Zimmet. 1995. (missing reference)

- Tang, H.; Quertermous, T.; Rodriguez, B.; Kardia, S.L.; Zhu, X.; Brown, A.; Pankow, J.S.; Province, M.A.; Hunt, S.C.; Boerwinkle, E.; Schork, N.J.; Risch, N.J. 2005. Genetic structure, self-identified race/ethnicity, and confounding in case-control association studies. American Journal of Human Genetics. 76:268-75.

- Templeton, A.R. 1998. Human races: A genetic and evolutionary perspective. American Anthropologist, 100:632-650.

- Wilson, William Julius. 1978. The Declining Significance of Race.

- Wilson, William Julius. 1990. The Truly Disadvantaged.

- Zoratti. 1999. (missing reference)

External links

- Times Online, "Gene tests prove that we are all the same under the skin", 27 October 2004.

- Catchpenny mysteries of ancient Egypt, "What race were the ancient Egyptians?", Larry Orcutt.

- Judy Skatssoon, "New twist on out-of-Africa theory", *ABC Science Online*, Wednesday, 14 July 2004.

- Michael J. Bamshad, Steve E. Olson "Does Race Exist?", *Scientific American*, December 2003

- OMB Statistical Directive 15, "Standards for Maintaining, Collecting, and Presenting Federal Data on Race and Ethnicity", *Federal Register*, 30 October 1997.

- Sandra Soo-Jin Lee, Joanna Mountain, and Barbara A. Koenig, "The Reification of Race in Health Research"

- Michael Root, "The Use of Race in Medicine as a Proxy for Genetic Differences"

- Richard Dawkins: Race and creation (extract from The Ancestor's Tale: A Pilgrimage to the Dawn of Life) - On race, its usage and a theory of how it evolved. (Prospect Magazine October 2004) (see also **Error! Hyperlink reference not valid.**)

- From *Nova Online*: George W. Gill argues here for the biological concept of "race" and, in a matching article, C. Loring Brace argues against the existence of "race" as a biological entity.

- From *California Newsreel*: Race: The Power of an Illusion, an in-depth website (companion to a California Newsreel film), presenting the argument that while race is a biological fiction, racism permeates the structure of society. And from *American Renaissance*, a "pro-white" publication, Race Denial: The Power of a Delusion, a detailed critique seeking to refute the film.

See the following Wikipedia articles for more information:

- Clan

- Ethnicity

- Human race

- Master race

- Miscegenation

- Race baiting

- Race card

- Racial purity

- Racial discrimination

- Racial superiority

- Racism

Gender

Gender vs. Sex

Sociologists make a distinction between **gender** and **sex**. *Gender* is the perceived or projected masculinity or femininity of a person or characteristic. *Sex*, on the other hand, is conventionally perceived as a dichotomous state or identity for most biological purposes, such that a person can only be *female* or *male*.

Before going into more detail about the differences between gender and sex, it should be made clear why this is an important difference. Differentiating gender from sex allows social scientists to study influences on gender without confusing their audience. If a social scientist were to continually talk about how sex is socially constructed, her audience might get confused, thinking the scientist is ill-informed about the biological determinants of sex. Using one term, *gender*, to refer to the socially constructed and malleable component of human sexuality and another term, *sex*, to refer to the biological and immutable component of human sexuality allows scientists interested in these two components to study them without confusion.

Sex

The members of many species of living things are divided into two or more categories called **sexes**. These refer to complementary groups that combine genetic material in order to reproduce, a process called sexual reproduction. Typically, a species will have two sexes: *male* and *female*. The female sex is defined as the one which produces the larger gamete (i.e., reproductive cell) and which bears the offspring. The categories of sex are, therefore, reflective of the reproductive functions that an individual is capable of performing at some point during its life cycle, and not of the mating types, which genetically can be more than two.

In mammals (and many other species) sex is determined by the sex chromosomes, called X and Y. For mammals, males typically have one of each (XY), while females typically have two X chromosomes (XX). All individuals have at least one X chromosome, the Y chromosome is generally shorter than the X chromosome with which it is paired, and is absent in some species. In humans, *sex* is conventionally perceived as a dichotomous state or identity for most biological purposes, such that a person can only be *female* or *male*.

Gender

Gender is the social and representational component of human sexuality. Perhaps the best way to understand gender is to understand it as a process of social representation. Because gender roles are delineated by behavioral expectations and norms, once those expectations and norms are known by the individual, the individual can or does adopt the behaviors that represent the gender they wish to portray. The gender one wishes to portray is not solely a cognitive, self-driven desire but also the socialized gender role imputed by parents, peers, and society.

Perhaps a concrete example will help clarify. A biological boy (XY chromosomes) may be socialized to play the traditional masculine role, which includes characteristics such as: independence, courage, and aggressiveness. A biological female (XX chromosomes) may be socialized to play the traditional feminine role, including characteristics like: submissiveness, emotionality, and empathy. Assuming the socialization is effective and not rejected, our masculine boy and feminine girl will engage in behaviors to reflect their genders. For instance, the boy may play with toy soldiers and join athletic teams. The girl, on the other hand, may play with dolls and bond with other girls in smaller groups.

Traditional Gender Characteristics

feminine characteristics	masculine characteristics
submissive	dominant
dependent	independent
emotional	rational
receptive	assertive
intuitive	analytical
timid	brave
passive	active
sensitive	insensitive
Table adapted from Macionis (2004).	

However, gender is fluid and can change. Continuing with our hypothetical boy and girl, it is possible for the boy to decide later in life that he no longer wishes to portray himself as traditionally masculine. The boy may adopt some traditionally feminine characteristics and become androgynous, or may adopt a feminine persona altogether. Either change would involve adopting the behaviors and customs that go along with the intended gender. The same is true for the girl, who may adopt masculine characteristics.

Gender Discordance

A significant fraction of the human population does not correspond exclusively to either *female* or *male*. When gender and sex collide, the result is *discordance* or conflict. Some discordances are purely biological, such as when the sex of the chromosomes (*genetic sex*) does not match the sex of the external genitalia (*anatomic sex*). For more extensive discussion of this type of discordance, see this article on intersex.

Discordances between the biological and psychosocial levels, such as when the gender does not match the anatomic sex, are even more common but less well understood. The vast majority of people who are discordant in some aspect of psyche or behavior do not have any detectable biological intersex condition. Human societies respond to, or accommodate, these behavioral and psychological discordances in many different ways, ranging from suppression and denial of difference to acknowledging various forms of *third sex*.

It is interesting, and perhaps significant, that some societies identify youths with atypical behavioral characteristics and, instead of giving them corrective therapy or punishing them, socialize them in such a way that their individual characteristics let them provide a needed and/or useful function for the society in a recognized and respected role. Some of the roles these individuals may assume include: shaman, medicine man, tong-ki, berdache, hijra, xanith, and transgender.

Such complex situations have led some scientists to argue that the two sexes are socio-cultural constructions. Some people have sought to define their sexuality and sexual identity in non-polar terms in the belief that the simple division of all humans into *males* and *females* does not fit their individual conditions. A proponent of this movement away from polar oppositions, Anne Fausto-Sterling, once suggested we recognize five sexes: male, female, merm, ferm and herm. Although quickly rejected as a bizarre flouting of human nature and social reality, and inimical to the interests of those whom she was attempting to champion, it expresses the difficulty and imperfection of the current social responses to these variations.

Biological Differences

While a large part of this chapter is dedicated to pointing out the socially determined differences between men and women, it is also important to note that not all differences are social. Men and women differ in their physiological makeup. In addition to different sex organs, the average male is 10 percent taller, 20 percent heavier, and 35 percent stronger in the upper body than the average female (Ehrenreich 1999; that physicological differences may have been influenced by social/cultural decisions in the past is still debated). How such measures are taken and evaluated remains the subject of interrogation and scrutiny. Scientists and clinicians point out that the relative strength of women, measured against their own body size, rather than on an absolute such as how much weight they can carry compared to men, shows that strength differences are minimal (Ebben and Randall, 1998: np).

Women, for reasons still somewhat undetermined, tend to outlive men. Women's life expectancy in the U.S. is 79.8 years, men's is 74.4 (U.S. National Center for Health Statistics 2003). The leading hypothesis to explain this phenomenon is the skewing caused by war in earlier years, combined with higher stress in the situations and occupations typical of men. An as yet unexplained phenomenon is that more female infants than male infants survie the neo-natal period. There is some discussion that these number may be skewed because sex verification in the neo-natal period tends to be done visually, so not all the biological sex-information may be correct for this period. Regardless, it does influence such statistical measures as the PYLL (potential years life lost) that help us to calculate the impact of premature death on males and females.

Behaviorally, age of sitting, teething, and walking all occur at about the same time in men and women. However, men enter <u>puberty</u> on average two years later than do women. There do not appear to be differences in intelligence, happiness, or self-esteem between men and women. However, women are twice as statistically vulnerable to anxiety disorders and depression, but one-third as statistically vulnerable to suicide and one-fifth as vulnerable to alcoholism. (Women attempt suicide more often than men but have lower rates of "success", because they usually use drugs, whereas men usually use firearms.) Women are also less likely to suffer hyperactivity or speech disorders as children or to display antisocial personalities as adults. Finally, women have slightly more olfactory receptors on average and are more easily rearoused immediately after orgasm (Myers 1996:196). The significance of many such difference is open to debate and interpretation.

Social and Psychological Differences

As the previous section outlined, some gender differences are attributable to biology. However, there are a number of gender differences that vary by society and/or culture, indicating they are social constructions. Two examples of gender differences that are not attributed to biological differences will be discussed below: workforce differences and education.

Work and Occupations

An often discussed and debated difference between men and women involves work and occupations. Women's participation in the workforce has varied significantly over time. Prior to the development of capitalism and factory-type work, women played a significant role in food production and household maintenance. With the advent of capitalism and labor outside of the home, women continued to play a significant role, though their participation in paid labor outside the home diminished over time. Also, women's participation in the labor force varied (and varies) depending on marital status and social class.

Current U.S. labor force statistics illustrate women's changing role in the labor force. For instance, since 1971, women's participation in the labor force has grown from 32 million (43.4% of the female population 16 and over) to 68 million (59.2% of the female population 16 and over; <u>source</u>). Women also make, on average, $17,000 less than do men (<u>source</u>). Women tend to be concentrated in less prestigious and lower paying occupations (Bose and Rossi 1983) that are traditionally considered *women's jobs* (also referred to as *pink collar* jobs; <u>source</u>). Finally, women are not paid the same wages as men for similar work. This difference is often illustrated as a ratio, as shown in the graph below. Women tend to make between 75% and 85% of what men make for comparable work. Reasons for disparity in pay will be discussed in more detail below.

151

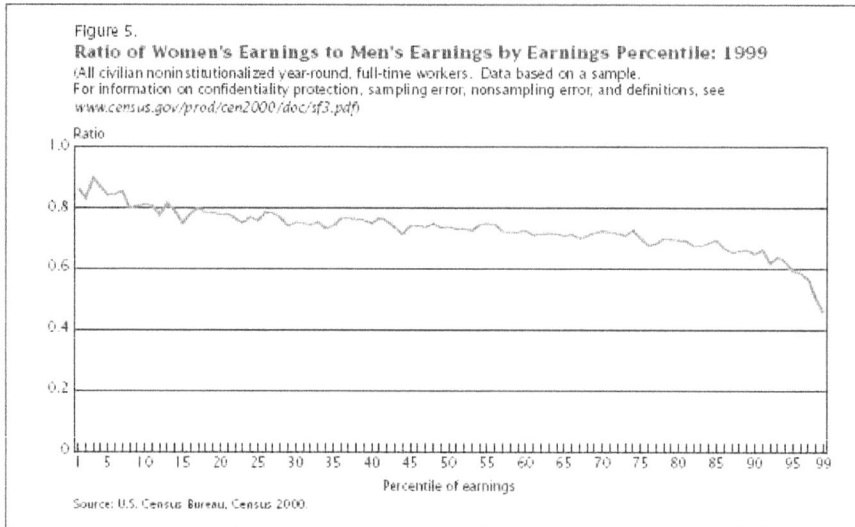

Figure 5.
Ratio of Women's Earnings to Men's Earnings by Earnings Percentile: 1999
(All civilian noninstitutionalized year-round, full-time workers. Data based on a sample.
For information on confidentiality protection, sampling error, nonsampling error, and definitions, see
www.census.gov/prod/cen2000/doc/sf3.pdf)

Source: U.S. Census Bureau, Census 2000.

Ratio of Women's Earnings to Men's Earnings by Earnings Precentile: 1999

Education

Another often studied difference between men and women involves educational attainment. For a long time, higher education (undergraduate and graduate education) was an exclusively male bastion. Women did eventually gain access to institutions of higher learning, but parity or equality on a number of levels is still in the works. One measure of educational attainment where women have made great inroads is in college attendance. In 1960, 37.9% of female high school graduates enrolled in college. This is compared to 54.0% of male high school graduates. In 2002, more female high school graduates were enrolling in college than males, 68.4% of females vs. 62.1% males (source). Women have, in fact, made significant progress in this respect. Women now earn more Bachelors and Masters degrees than do men and they earn almost as many PhDs (source).

Progress in this regard, however, should be tempered by the fact that while women are entering college at higher rates and even earning more degrees, the degrees are in less prestigious areas (e.g., social sciences and humanities compared to physical sciences) and women with degrees still earn less than do men with comparable degrees (Jacobs 1996).

Sexism

Sexism is discrimination against people based on their sex or gender. Sexism can refer to three subtly different beliefs or attitudes:

- The belief that one sex is superior to the other.

- The belief that men and women are very different and that this should be strongly reflected in

152

society, language, the right to have sex, and the law.

- It can also refer to simple hatred of men (misandry) or women (misogyny).

Many peoples' beliefs on this topic range along a continuum. Some people believe that women should have equal access to all jobs except a few religious positions. Others believe that while women are superior to men in a few aspects, in most aspects men are superior to women.

Sexist beliefs are an example of essentialist thought, which holds that individuals can be understood (and often judged) based on the characteristics of the group to which they belong; in this case, their sex group (male or female). Essentialism assumes that all individuals clearly fit into the category of *male* or *female*.

Sexism against women is often called *chauvinism*, though chauvinism is actually a wider term for any extreme and unreasoning partisanship on behalf of a group to which one belongs, especially when the partisanship includes malice and hatred towards a rival group. Therefore many forms of radical feminism can legitimately be referred to as *chauvinism*. This is not common usage, however, and the term is most often used to refer to male chauvinism.

While the view that women are superior to men is also sexism, only in recent years has an awareness of this *reverse sexism* begun to develop in public discourse. Certain forms of sexual discrimination are illegal in many countries, but nearly all countries have laws that give special rights, privileges, or responsibilities to one sex.

Violence

Sexism can take many forms, including preventing women from attending college and paying women less than men for comparable work. Another common form of sexism is violence, especially violence toward women. In 2002, women were the victims of over 900,00 violent crimes and over 200,000 rapes or sexual assaults (source). Men are more likely to be the victims of violent crime, but far less likely to be the victims of rapes or sexual assaults. Additionally, many violent crimes, rapes, and sexual assaults are committed not by strangers but acquaintances.

Gender Theory

Sociological theory tries to understand gender in the sense of how it is socially constructed as well as in its implications for society.

Gender Socialization

One of the understandings that underlies most theoretical approaches to gender differences involves differences in gender socialization. As discussed earlier, socialization is the process that conveys norms and behaviors to potential members of a group. In the case of gender socialization, the groups that are being joined are *males* and *females*. Thus, gender socialization is the process of educating and instructing potential males and females as to the norms, behaviors, values, etc. of group membership.

Preparations for gender socialization begin even before the birth of the child. One of the first questions people ask of expectant parents is the *sex* of the child. This is the beginning of a social categorization process that will continue throughout a person's life. Preparations for the birth often take the infant's sex into consideration (e.g., painting the room blue if the child is a boy, pink for a girl). Many gender differences can be attributed to differences in socialization, though to attribute them exclusively to socialization would be asserting something that is not known. It is important to keep in mind that gender differences are a combination of social and biological forces; sometimes one or the other has a larger influence, but both play a role in this process.

Some clear indications of the influence of gender socialization have been explored in research studies. For instance, young boys tend to favor team sports with complex rules, clear objectives, and winners and losers. Young girls tend to favor less complex games in smaller groups that do not have clear winners and losers (Lever 1978). These differences may have significant consequences for social ability later in life. Specifically, because boys engage in the types of activities they do, they may be better prepared for corporate life:

- dealing with diversity in group membership where people have specific responsibilities

- coordinating actions and maintaining cohesiveness among group members

- coping with a set of impersonal rules

- working for collective and personal goals

Lever attributes these differences in types of play not to the direct influence of parents or other adults - who obviously have a hand in it - but to a historical legacy of gender segregation. In the U.S. and much of Europe, organized team sports were limited to participation by males. Even today, many high schools continue to fund male sports activities at a much higher rate than they do female sports. Legislation in the 1970s (see Title IX) attempted to level the playing field for men's and women's sports in colleges and universities.

Greenberger and Steinberg (1983) found that gender differences in work and occupations actually begin with adolescents' first jobs:

- first jobs are significantly segregated by sex

- girls work fewer hours per week than boys

- girls earn less per hour than boys

- hourly wages are higher in job types dominated by males

Greenberger and Steinberg attribute these differences to gender socialization and differential opportunities for boys and girls.

Theories of Gender Differences

Some sociological theories address the issue of why there are gender differences. The most obvious reason is that there are biological differences between men and women. Sociobiologists argue that much of social life as we know it today is rooted in human evolution and biology. Included in such theories is the idea that many gender differences are attributable to differences in physiology and biology. For instance, differences in attitudes and assertiveness toward sexuality have been attributed to evolution and physiology. Women, who invest more in the creation, bearing, and raising of children, are inclined toward monogamous relationships as having a partner to help them improves the chances of their child's survival. Men, on the other hand, may be inclined less toward monogamy as their investment in offspring can be (and often is) far smaller than that of women. As a result, women will be attracted to men who can provide support (i.e., protection and resources) while men will be attracted to fertile women (the symbols of which have changed over time; see Buss 1994).

Another theoretical approach to understanding gender differences falls in step with gender socialization and, to some degree, underlies the socialization process. Symbolic Interactionism argues that humans develop a sense of self through their daily interactions with other people. As they negotiate meaning in these interactions, they begin to understand how people view them and they gain a sense of how the world works. As far as gender goes, Symbolic Interactionism would argue that gender develops through these interactions. As people come to understand the different ways they are perceived and relate these to their sense of self, they develop a self-image that reflects how others perceive them. Genders are perceived differently, resulting in different perceptions of self.

Theories of Gender Implications

Another way of approaching gender differences is to look at the implications as well as the different components that might have encouraged gender differences.

One approach to understanding gender roles is the structural-functionalist approach advocated by Talcott Parsons (1942). In this perspective, genders are seen as complementary - women take care of the home while men provide for the home. This approach has been criticized for supporting the status quo and condoning the oppression of women as it argues womens' roles are complentary to mens', especially in that they are submissive.

A contrasting approach to structural-functionalism is that of social-conflict analysis. In this perspective, gender relations are cast in terms of power. Men's dominance of women is seen as an attempt to maintain power and privilege to the detriment of women. This approach is normative in the sense that it does not condone such behavior but rather criticizes it.

Finally, feminism is another approach to gender relations. The basic argument of feminism is similar to that of social-conflict analysis in that it views gender relations as an issue of power. And, in line with social-conflict analysis, feminism is inherently normative - it argues that society must change toward a greater balance of power between the sexes. There are numerous approaches to feminism; interested individuals can find more information on feminism here.

Research Examples

Rand and Hall (1983) were interested in exploring whether men or women were better able to determine their own attractiveness. Using fifty-five Johns Hopkins University undergraduates (24 females), the authors had the students fill out questionnaires that were designed to be self-appraisals of their attractiveness. The authors then used a panel to rate the attractiveness of the participants (an objective measure). The results of the study indicate that women are fairly accurate in their assessments of their attractiveness but men are not. The results were explained by discussing the salience of attractiveness for women; attractiveness is an important component of women's lives. Because it is so important for women, they are more attuned to their actual attractiveness than are men.

Tickamyer (1981) was interested in sex differences in the distribution of wealth. Using biographical data published in magazines and books as well as IRS income reports, Tickamyer explored the differences in wealth between men and women, finding:

- there are fewer wealthy women than men

- it is not entirely clear as to whether sources of wealth differ, but it does appear that women are more likely than men to inherit their wealth (especially from husbands)

- the forms of women's holdings differ from men's; many women have their money in trusts

- women are less likely to have control over their wealth than men and are less likely to be actively engaged in increasing their wealth through investments as, say, the head of a company is engaged in growing his wealth

Tickamyer attributes the differences in wealth distribution to historical instances of gender discrimination. Up until the 19th century, women could not own property and women's participation in the paid labor force outside the home had been limited. It is possible that wealth among the elite may be redistributed toward a more equal balance between the sexes with increasing numbers of women entering the workforce and moving toward more financially lucrative positions in major corporations.

Notes

"Gender" is derived from the Old French word *genre*, meaning "kind of thing". It goes back to the Latin word *genus* (meaning "kind", "species").

References

- Buss, David M. 1994. The Evolution of Desire: Strategies of Human Mating. New York: Basic Books. ISBN 046500802X

- Ebben, William P. and Randall Jensen. 1998. "Strength Training for Women: myths that block oppportunity". The Physician and Sports Medicine 26(5): np.

- Ehrenreich, Barbara. 1999. "The Real Truth about the Female Body." Time. Vol. 153, No. 9, pages 56-65.

- Greenberg, Ellen and Steinberg, Laurence D. 1983. Sex Differences in Early Labor Force Experience: Harbinger of Things to Come. Social Forces. 62(2):467-486.

- Howard, Judith and Hollander, Jocelyn. 1996. Gendered Situations, Gendered Selves. Altamira Press. ISBN 0803956045

- Jacobs, Jerry A. 1996. Gender Inequality and Higher Education. Annual Review of Sociology. 22:153-185.

- Lever, Janet. 1978. Sex Differences in the Complexity of Children's Play and Games. American Sociological Review. 43(4):471-483.

- Macionis, John J. 2004. Sociology (Tenth Edition). Prentice Hall. ISBN 0131849182

- Myers, David G. 1996. Social Psychology (Fifth Edition). McGraw Hill. ISBN 0071145087

- Parsons, Talcott. 1964. Social System. Free Press. ISBN 0029241901

- Rand, Cynthia S. and Hall, Judith A. 1983. Sex Differences in the Accuracy of Self-Perceived Attractiveness. Social Psychology Quarterly. 46(4):359-363.

- Tickamyer, Ann R. 1981. Wealth and Power: A Comparison of Men and Women in the Property Elite. Social Forces. 60(2):463-481.

- U.S. National Center for Health Statistics

This chapter draws heavily on the following Wikipedia articles:

- gender

- gender role

- human sexuality

- sex

- sexism

External Links

- http://www.catalystwomen.org/

- http://www.census.gov/

- Barbie's Dimensions

- http://www.cdc.gov/nchs/Default.htm

  Additional Information:

- female circumcision

- feminism

- human sexuality

- pornography

- reproduction

- sexual harassment

Stratification

⬅This home/shanty in Jakarta is illustrative of the extreme economic stratification and disparity that exists around the world today.

Introduction

Social stratification refers to the hierarchical arrangement of people in a society. This chapter focuses on economic stratification, meaning how people are differentiated based upon their wealth (and/or power). The most common delineation of economic groups in societies is that of social classes, ranging from lower/working class to upper-class. Alternative systems of economic stratification include caste systems (which have traditionally combined additional factors, including religion and tradition) and the hierarchical structure in communist countries. Because the *class* nomenclature is more common, it will be the primary distinction used in this chapter.

To begin, this chapter explores what it means to be poor. It then turns to stratification in society, focusing on multiple levels of stratification at the global level and within the U.S.

Objective vs. Subjective Poverty

There are two notions of poverty that are often confused, *objective poverty* and *subjective poverty*. Objective poverty refers to the level of income below which one cannot afford to purchase all the resources one requires to live (see also poverty line). Objective poverty is contrasted with subjective poverty; people who feel some sense of deprivation resulting from their lower social standing or position near the bottom of a social hierarchy. Individuals who are subjectively poor have sufficient funds to survive but do not have as many resources as other members of their society, resulting in a sense of *being poor* despite having enough to survive.

While there are no clear statistics on the number of people who feel some sense of subjective poverty, there is a substantial amount of information on individuals who live in objective poverty:

- 1/6 of the world's population (1 billion people) live on less than $1 per day (source)

- 11 million children die each year from diseases and other causes that are poverty related (source)

- women and children are the most affected by poverty (source)

- malnutrition, an indicator of objective poverty, has lasting effects on biological and mental development (source)

Socioeconomic Status

Building on the ideas of Max Weber, who saw three main dimensions of stratification (class, status, and party), contemporary sociologists often define stratification in terms of socioeconomic status (or SES). This measure includes educational attainment, income and wealth, and occupational prestige. The overall summation of these standings dictates one's socioeconomic status in any given society.

Global Inequality

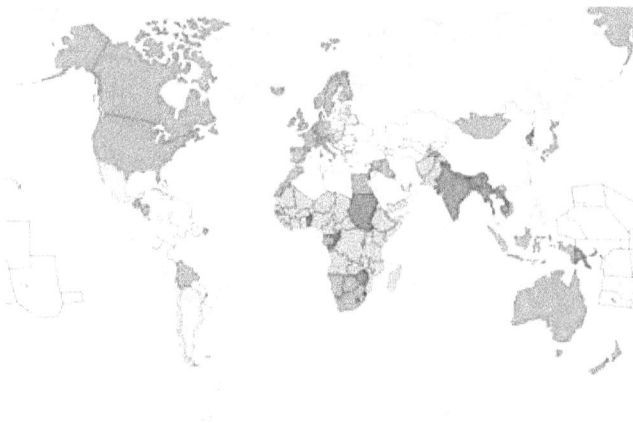

IDH très élevé (supérieur à 0,9)
IDH élevé (entre 0,8 et 0,9)
IDH moyen (entre 0,7 et 0,8)
IDH assez faible (entre 0,6 et 0,7)
IDH faible (entre 0,5 et 0,6)
IDH très faible (inférieur à 0,5)

⟳Green indicates high development; yellow and orange indicate a medium level of development; red and grey indicate a low level of development.

At the international level, comparisons in economic stratification are made between different countries. While it is still common to hear countries described as *first-world* or *third-world*, this system of classification is outdated and has been replaced with the terms *developed* and *developing* (or, alternatively, post-industrial, industrialized, and industrializing). *Third World* was a term originally used to distinguish nations that neither aligned with the West nor with the

160

East during the Cold War; many

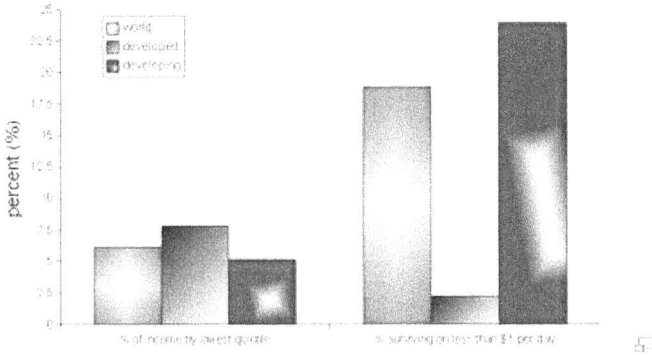

One of the clearest measures of development in a country is the United Nations *Human Development Index*. The Index examines numerous aspects of social life in the countries around the world, combines measures of those aspects into a single number, then orders the numbers, producing an index ranging from high development to low development. Aspects of society included in the Human Development Index include:

- life expectancy at birth

- literacy rates

- GDP

The United Nations provides comprehensive data on trends in economic and other forms of stratification within countries over time (see here).

U.S. Inequality

Figure 3
Number in Poverty and Poverty Rate: 1959 to 2003

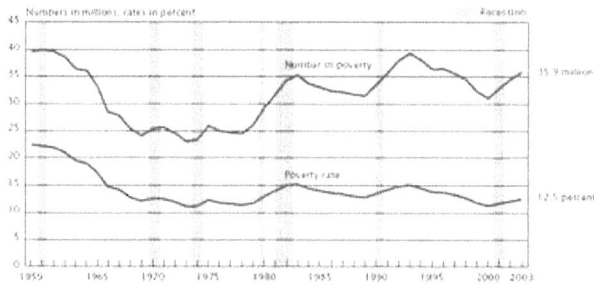

Poverty Thresholds in 2003 by Size of Family and Number of Related Children
Under 18 Years

A surprising characteristic of the United States for many people is that the U.S. has a large proportion of its population that lives in poverty. It is necessary to note that poverty can be measured in a number of ways (see poverty line), but by the standards used by the U.S. Census Bureau (see below), roughly 12.5% of United Statesians live in poverty. That translates into close to 35 million people (source). The discussion of sociological theories relating to stratification below helps explain this economic disparity.

Theories of Stratification

Two classic approaches to social stratification provide interesting insights into this phenemonon, structural-functionalism and social-conflict theories. A third approach, dependency theory, has roots in and extends Marxist thought and conflict theory by applying that approach to the world at a global/international level.

Structural-Functionalism

The structural-functional approach to social stratification asks the same question of social stratification that it does of the other components of society: What function or purpose does stratification serve? Underlying this question is the assumption that stratification serves some purpose because it exists in virtually every society (though it is almost non-existent in hunter-gatherer societies). The resulting answer is often that it must exist in society in order to facilitate stability and equilibrium; some level of hierarchical organization must be necessary in order for complex societies to function. Additionally, the structural-functional approach argues that positions higher in the social hierarchy must be of more functional importance to the society, which is why they result in greater rewards. In other words, according to this perspective, it makes sense for the CEO of a company whose position is more important functioanlly for a company to make more than a janitor working for the company.

There are several obvious problems with this approach to social stratification. First, the answer to the function of stratification of society results in an answer that is guilty of begging the question. The answer only exists because the question is asked the way that it is; it is assumed from the asking of the question that there must be a function, thus, a function is found. The second major problem with this approach is that it assumes social stratification is necessary for the functioning of society. While it may be the case that only hunter-gatherer societies have existed with minimal stratification and no complex societies have developed a purely egalitarian system, it should not be assumed that such a system is impossible. The third significant problem with this approach is that it supports the status quo of existing systems, regardless of how the power of the ruling group is derived (e.g., totalitarianism, dictatorship, oligarchy, etc.). While it may be the case that social stratification facilitates the stability of societies, the structural-functional approach falls short in developing lucid arguments to that end.

Social-Conflict Theory and Marxism

The social-conflict approach to stratification sees social hierarchies, like most other elements of society, as embodying inequality (which is virtually *by definition* in this instance). The conflict theory approach argues that individuals at the top of social hierarchies are there at the expense of people in lower positions. Additionally, people higher up in the hierarchy will use their power to strengthen both the hierarchy and their standing in it.

A particularly clear example of the social-conflict perspective is Marx's early analysis of capitalism. Marx argued that positions in the social hierarchy were directly related to an individuals' relationship to the means of production. Individuals in the upper-class are the owners of the means of production or bourgeoisie. Those who use the means of production to produce goods (or services) and own only their labor power, the proletariat, are members of the lower or working classes.

Because capitalists rise to the top of the social hierarchy on the backs of the proletariat through exploiting their labor power, Marx believed the proletariat would eventually rise up in protest to their exploitation. Marx hoped that the workers of the world would develop a *collective conscience* or universal sense of injustice that would lead them to overthrow the ruling class of capitalists and institute a new socio-economic system, communism.

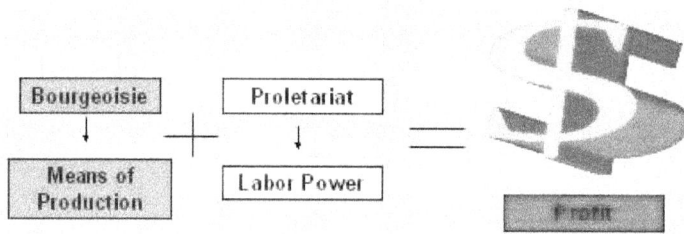

The astute student may be asking why such a revolution did not occur in every capitalist society. Of course, some communist revolutions did occur: the U.S.S.R., China, Cuba, and Vietnam are all examples of countries where communist revolutions took place. But there are a number of non-communist countries that have not experienced revolutions in their economic systems, the U.S. being a prime example. If, as Marx proposed, the exploitation of the proletariat would ultimately lead to the overthrowing of the capitalists at the top of the social hierarchy, one is left asking why this has not happened in the U.S. The answer lies in the concessions made by capitalists to proletariats who joined together as labor unions to fight for worker's rights.

In a truly capitalist society, the only restrictions placed upon capitalists would be the restrictions they place upon themselves. In other words, if a capitalist wanted to have her laborers work 20-hour shifts, in a true capitalist society, there would be no restrictions preventing such practices. The U.S. is not a true capitalist society in this sense. The federal and state governments have instituted legislation limiting the labor practices of corporations and capitalists, including:

- regulated working hours

- minimum wage requirements

- laws against child labor

- mandated working conditions

Many of these concessions have resulted from the efforts of organized labor unions.

To return, then, to the question posed above, revolution has been averted through the gradual transformation of capitalist societies into more socialistic societies. By improving the working conditions and wages of the proletariat, capitalists have been able to prevent the over-throwing of the capitalist system.

Dependency Theory of Global Stratification

Dependency theory is the body of theories that propound a worldview suggesting the wealthy countries of the world need a peripheral group of poorer countries to remain wealthy.

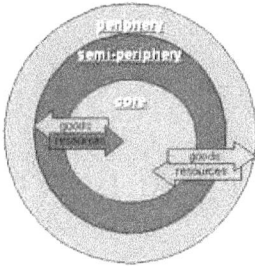

As depicted in the diagram, wealthy nations are seen as the core countries; poorer nations are seen as the peripheral countries (with some countries falling in between). Core countries extract resources from the periphery countries and eventually return those resources as manufactured goods. This works to maintain the superiority of the core countries by stripping the periphery countries of their natural resources and forcing them to buy manufactured goods at high prices - the proceeds going to the people and corporations of the core countries. Thus, poor nations provide natural resources, cheap labour, a destination for obsolete technology, and markets to the wealthy nations. Without the poorer, peripheral nations, the wealthy, core countries could not have the standard of living they enjoy.

The theory contends that core countries actively, but not necessarily consciously, perpetuate a state of dependency through various policies and initiatives. This state of dependency is multifaceted, involving economics, media control, politics, banking and finance, education, sports, and all aspects of human resource development. Any attempt by the dependent nations to resist the influences of dependency will result in economic sanctions and/or military invasion and control. While military invasion is somewhat rare, dependency of the periphery countries on the core countries is strongly enforced by the wealthy nations setting the rules of international trade and commerce.

Another example of the extreme poverty experienced in some parts of the world. Dependency Theory would attribute this poverty to the exploitation of periphery countries by core countries.

The system of dependency was likely created with the industrial revolution and the expansion of European empires around the world due to their superior power and wealth. Some argue that before this expansion exploitation and dependency was internal to countries, with the major economic centres dominating the rest of the country (for example southeast England dominating the British Isles, or the Northeast United States dominating the south and east). Establishing global trade patterns in the nineteenth century allowed this system to spread to a global level. This resulted in the isolation of the wealthy from both the dangers of peasant revolts and rebellions by the poor. Rather than turn on their oppressors as in the American Civil War or in communist revolutions, the poor could no longer reach the wealthy and thus the less developed nations became engulfed in regular civil wars. With the superiority of rich nations established, it is difficult, if not impossible, for poorer countries to move away from this system. This control ensures that all profits in less developed countries are taken by the better developed nations, preventing reinvestment and growth.

Dependency theory first emerged in the 1950s, advocated by Raul Prebisch, whose research found that the wealth of poor nations tended to decrease when the wealth of rich nations increased. Dependency theory became increasingly popular in the 1960s and 1970s as a criticism of standard development theory that seemed to be failing due to the continued widespread poverty of large parts of the world.

Notes

The antonym of *inequality* is, of course, *equality*, but there is debate as to what *equality* should mean. Different definitions include:

- Legal equality

- Equality of opportunity

- Equality of outcome

References

- UNICEF

  This page also draws heavily on the following Wikipedia articles:

- social stratification

- economic inequality

- poverty line

External Links

- Inequality topic at Worldrevolution.org

- An introduction to dependency theory

  See also:

- Positive freedom

- Negative freedom

- Millennium Development Goals from the United Nations

- Caste system

- Social inequality

- Elitism

- Theodor Geiger

- Marxism

- Three-component theory of stratification

Organizations

See http://en.wikipedia.org/wiki/Organisation

Family

This article is about the domestic group. For other uses, see Family (disambiguation).

Image:Family Ouagadougou.jpg A family of Ouagadougou, Burkina Faso in 1997

A **family** is a domestic group of people, or a number of domestic groups linked through descent (demonstrated or stipulated) from a common ancestor, marriage or adoption. Families have some degree of kinship.

In Western culture, a family is defined specifically as a group of people affiliated by blood or by legal ties such as marriage or adoption. Many anthropologists argue that the notion of "blood" must be understood metaphorically; some argue that there are many non-Western societies where family is understood through other concepts rather than "blood."

Article 16(3) of the Universal Declaration of Human Rights says, "The family is the natural and fundamental group unit of society and is entitled to protection by society and the State".

Family cross-culturally

According to sociology and anthropology, the primary function of the family is to reproduce society, either biologically, socially, or both. Thus, one's experience of one's family shifts over time. From the perspective of children, the family is a **family of orientation**: the family serves to locate children socially, and plays a major role in their enculturation and socialization. From the point of view of the parent(s), the family is a **family of procreation** the goal of which is to produce and enculturate and socialize children. However, producing children is not the only function of the family. In societies with a sexual division of labor, marriage, and the resulting relationship between a husband and wife, is necessary for the formation of an economically productive household. In modern societies marriage entails particular rights and privilege that encourage the formation of new families even when there is no intention of having children.

Family is the first and most important component of psychological environment for most children. Since families differ in many respects, so does their influence imprinting upon their children. An old observation says: "If you want to know the future of any society, look on the ways how their children are raised, and you will know the future". This puts a great responsibility on psychologists and sociologists to revise their doctrines from the viewpoint of the proven impact on people and society. Sociologists usually analyse, classify and describe societies and their components, but they refrain from discussing their advantages and disadvantages, and especially from attributing any moral values to them. This seems to be a sound scientific approach, but problems begin when those theories find their way into practice, which oftten happens through the influence of teachers, of the media, and through changes in laws. Doctrines do have practical consequences; it is enough to remind here the tremendous impact of many religions, or the Marx and Engels doctrine which was obscure on its birth, but was determining the lives of more than one billion people a century later; or fascism/Nazism having roots in the socio-darvinism at the beginning of the twentieth century. For this reason it would be desirable for researchers to analyze the actual social results of various doctrines.

The structure of families traditionally hinges on relations between parents and children, between spouses, or both. Consequently, there are three major types of family: matrifocal, consanguineal and conjugal. (Note: these are ideal families. In all societies there are acceptable deviations from the ideal or statistical norm, owing either to incidental circumstances, such as the death of a member of the family, infertility or personal preferences).

A **matrifocal** family consists of a mother and her children. Generally, these children are her biological offspring, although adoption of children is a practice in nearly every society. This kind of family is common where women have the resources to rear their children by themselves, or where men are more mobile than women.

A **consanguineal** family consists of a mother and her children, and other people â€" usually the family of the mother. This kind of family is common where mothers do not have the resources to rear their children on their own, and especially where property is inherited. When important property is owned by men, consanguineal families commonly consist of a husband and wife, their children and other members of the husband's family.

A **conjugal** family consists of one or more mothers and their children, and/or one or more spouses (usually husbands). This kind of family is common where men desire to assert control over children, or where there is a sexual division of labor requiring the participation of both men and women, and where families are relatively mobile.

Family in the West

The preceding types of families are found in a wide variety of settings, and their specific functions and meanings depend largely on their relationship to other social institutions. Sociologists are especially interested in the function and status of these forms in stratified, especially capitalist, societies.

Non-scholars, especially in the United States and Europe, use the term "nuclear family" to refer to conjugal families. Sociologists distinguish between conjugal families that are relatively independent of the kindreds of the parents and of other families in general, and nuclear families which maintain relatively close ties with their kindreds.

Non-scholars, especially in the United States and Europe, also use the term "extended family". This term has two distinct meanings. First, it is used synonymously with consanguinal family. Second, in societies dominated by the conjugal family, it is used to refer to **kindred** (an egocentric network of relatives that extends beyond the domestic group) who do not belong to the conjugal family.

These types refer to ideal or normative structures found in particular societies. In any society there is some variation in the actual composition and conception of families. Much sociological, historical and anthropological research is dedicated to understanding this variation, and changes over time in the family form. Thus, some speak of the **bourgeois family**, a family structure arising out of 16th and 17th century European households, in which the center of the family is a marriage between a man and woman, with strictly defined gender roles. The man typically is responsible for income and support, the woman for home and family matters. In contemporary Europe and the United States, people academic, political and civil sectors have called attention to single-father-headed households, and families headed by same-sex couples, although academics point out that these forms exist in other societies.

Economic role of the family

In traditional society the family is an economic unit. This role has gradually diminished in modern times and in societies like the United States is much smaller except for certain sectors such as agriculture and a few upper class families. In Chinese culture the family as an economic unit still plays a strong if somewhat diminished role.

Kinship terminology

A **kinship terminology** is a specific system of familial relationships. The anthropologist Louis Henry Morgan argued that kinship terminologies reflect different sets of distinctions. For example, most kinship terminologies distinguish between **sexes** (this is the difference between a brother and a sister) and between **generation** (this is the difference between a child and a parent). Moreover, he argued, kinship terminologies distinguish between relatives by **blood** and **marriage** (although recently some anthropologists have argued that many societies define kinship in terms other than "blood").

But Morgan also observed that different languages (and thus, societies) organize these distinctions differently. He thus proposed to describe kin terms and terminologies as either **descriptive** or **classificatory**. "Descriptive" terms refer to only one type of relationship, while "classificatory" terms refer to many types of relationships. Most kinship terminologies include both descriptive and classificatory terms. For example, in Western societies there is only one way to be related to one's brother (brother = parents' son); thus, in Western society, brother is a descriptive term. But there are many ways to be related to one's cousin (cousin = mother's brother's son, mother's sister's son, father's brother's son, father's sister's son, and so on); thus, in Western society, "cousin" is a classificatory term.

Morgan discovered that what may be a descriptive term in one society can be a classificatory term in another society. For example, in some societies there are many different people that one would call "mother" (the woman of whom one was born, as well as her sister and husband's sister, and also one's father's sister). Moreover, some societies do not lump together relatives that the West classifies together (in other words, in some languages there is no word for cousin because mother's sister's children and father's sister's children are referred to in different terms).

Armed with these different terms, Morgan identified six basic patterns of kinship terminologies:

- **Hawaiian**: the most classificatory; only distinguishes between sex and generation.

- **Sudanese**: the most descriptive; no two relatives are referred to by the same term.

- **Eskimo**: has both classificatory and descriptive terms; in addition to sex and generation, also distinguishes between lineal relatives (who are related directly by a line of descent) and collateral relatives (who are related by blood, but not directly in the line of descent). Lineal relatives have highly descriptive terms, collateral relatives have highly classificatory terms.

- **Iroquois**: has both classificatory and descriptive terms; in addition to sex and generation, also distinguishes between siblings of opposite sexes in the parental generation. Siblings of the same sex are considered blood relatives, but siblings of the opposite sex are considered relatives by marriage. Thus, one's mother's sister is also called mother, and one's father's brother is also called father; however, one's mother's brother is called father-in-law, and one's father's sister is called mother-in-law.

- **Crow**: like Iroquois, but further distinguishes between mother's side and father's side. Relatives on the mother's side of the family have more descriptive terms, and relatives on the father's side have more classificatory terms.

- **Omaha**: like Iroquois, but further distinguishes between mother's side and father's side. Relatives on the mother's side of the family have more classificatory terms, and relatives on the father's side have more descriptive terms.

Societies in different parts of the world and using different languages may share the same basic terminology; in such cases it is very easy to translate the kinship terms of one language into another. But it is usually impossible to translate directly the kinship terms of a society that uses one system into the language of a society that uses a different system.

Some languages, such as Chinese, Japanese, and Hungarian, add another dimension to some relations: relative age. There are different words for "older brother" and "younger brother."

Western kinship terminology

Most Western societies employ Eskimo Kinship terminology. This kinship terminology is common in societies based on conjugal (or nuclear) families, where nuclear families must be relatively mobile.

Members of the nuclear family use descriptive kinship terms:

- **Mother**: the female parent

- **Father**: the male parent

- **Son**: the males born of the mother

- **Daughter**: the females born of the mother

- **Brother**: a male born of the same mother

- **Sister**: a female born of the same mother

It is generally assumed that the mother's husband is also the genitor. In some families, a woman may have children with more than one man or a man may have children with more than one woman. Children who share one parent but not another are called "half-brothers" or "half-sisters." Children who do not share parents, but whose parents are married, are called "step-brothers" or "step-sisters." If a person is married to the parent of a child, but is not the parent of the child themselves, then they are the "step-parent" of the child, either the "stepmother" or "stepfather". Children who are adopted into a family are generally called by the same terms as children born into the family.

Typically, societies with conjugal families also favor neolocal residence; thus upon marriage a person separates from the nuclear family of their childhood (family of orientation) and forms a new nuclear family (family of procreation). This practice means that members of one's own nuclear family were once members of another nuclear family, or may one day become members of another nuclear family.

Members of the nuclear families of members of one's own nuclear family may be lineal or collateral. When they are lineal, they are referred to in terms that build on the terms used within the nuclear family:

- **Grandfather**: a parent's father

- **Grandmother**: a parent's mother

- **Grandson**: a child's son

- **Granddaughter**: a child's daughter

When they are collateral, they are referred to in more classificatory terms that do not build on the terms used within the nuclear family:

- **Uncle**: father's brother, father's sister's husband, mother's brother, mother's sister's husband

- **Aunt**: father's sister, father's brother's wife, mother's sister, mother's brother's wife

- **Nephew**: sister's sons, brother's sons

- **Niece**: sister's daughters, brother's daughters

When separated by additional generations (in other words, when one's collateral relatives belong to the same generation as one's grandparents or grandchildren), these terms are modified by the prefix "great".

Most collateral relatives were never members of the nuclear family of the members of one's own nuclear family.

172

- **Cousin**: the most classificatory term; the children of aunts or uncles. Cousins may be further distinguished by degree of collaterality and generation. Two persons of the same generation who share a grandparent are "first cousins" (one degree of collaterality); if they share a great-grandparent they are "second cousins" (two degrees of collaterality) and so on. If the shared ancestor is the grandparent of one individual and the great-grandparent of the other, the individuals are said to be "first cousins once removed" (removed by one generation); if the shared ancestor is the grandparent of one individual and the great-great-grandparent of the other, the individuals are said to be "first cousins twice removed" (removed by two generation), and so on. Similarly, if the shared ancestor is the great-grandparent of one person and the great-great-grandparent of the other, the individuals are said to be "second cousins once removerd."

Distant cousins of an older generation (in other words, one's parents' first cousins) are technically first cousins once removed, but are often classified with "aunts" and "uncles".

Similarly, a person may refer to close friends of one's parents as "aunt" or "uncle," or may refer to close friends as "brother" or "sister". This practice is called **fictive kinship**.

Relationships by marriage, except for wife/husband, are qualified by the term "-in-law". The mother and father of one's spouse are one's mother-in-law and father-in-law; the spouse of one's son or daughter is one's son-in-law or daughter-in-law.

The term "sister-in-law" refers to three essentially different relationships, either the wife of one's brother, of the sister of one's spouse, or the wife of one's spouse's sibling. "Brother-in-law" is similarly ambiguous. There are no special terms for the rest of one's spouse's family.

Specific distinctions vary among Western societies. For instance, in French, the prefix *beau-* or *belle-* is used for both "-in-law" and "step-"; in other words, one's *belle-soeur* could be the sister of one's spouse, the wife of one's sibling, the wife of one's spouse's sibling, or the daughter of one's parent's spouse. In Spanish, each of the roles that English creates with the suffix "-in-law" has a different word (*suegros-* parents-in-law, *yerno-*son-in-law, *nuera-*daughter-in-law, *cuÃ±ados-*siblings-in-law), but there is a suffix *-astro* or *-astra* that is equivalent to "step-".

See also

- Ancestor

- Consanguinity

- Clan

- Complex family

- Dysfunctional family

- Family law

- Family life in literature

- Family name

- Family relationship

- Family as a model for the state

- Genealogy

- Household

- Illegitimacy

- Marriage

- Pedigree collapse

References

- *American Kinship*, David Schneider

  This page is adapted 9 April 2005 from the Wikipedia article, Family.

External links

- *Online Dictionary of the Social Sciences*: http://bitbucket.icaap.org/

- *Cousins*: http://www.tedpack.org/cousins.html

- *The Good Enough Family*: http://samvak.tripod.com/family.html

- *Cousin marriages*: http://www.cousincouples.com/

- *Family Court*: http://www.stephenbaskerville.net/

- *Wiktionary entries for Western kinship terminology providing multilingual translations*

- mother, father, son, daughter, brother, sister

- grandmother grandfather grandson granddaughter

- uncle aunt nephew niece

- cousin

The economy

See http://en.wikipedia.org/wiki/Economics

Religion

⌐Temples in Bali.

Introduction

The **sociology of religion** combines demographic analysis of religious bodies with attempts to understand the different components of religiosity. Also, some sociological studies of religion are ethnographic in nature; they attempt to understand religious behavior from the viewpoint of the adherents of the religion.

It is important to point out at the beginning of this chapter that sociologists study religion not to disprove or normatively evaluate it but rather to understand it. However, and this is a contentious point in the social scientific study of religion, it is also often the case that studying religion from this perspective can challenge people's religious beliefs because the social scientific study of religion provides alternative explanations for many components of religious experience (e.g., the sources of conversion experiences; see Batson, Schoenrade, and Ventis 1993).

Definitions of Religion

The starting point for any study of religion should begin with a definition of the concept. This is particularly important in the study of religion because the definition determines which groups will be included in the analysis. Three general definitions have been proposed, each of which will be discussed briefly. Each definition has its merits and detriments, but what one often finds is that the definition of religion employed by a particular researcher or in the investigation of a particular topic depends on the question being asked.

Sacred vs. Profane

Perhaps the most well known definition of religion is that provided by Emile Durkheim (1995). Durkheim argued that the definition of religion hinged on the distinction between things that are sacred (set apart from daily life) and things that are profane (everyday, mundane elements of society). The sacred elements of social life are what make up religion.

For example, the Torah in Judaism is sacred and treated with reverence and respect. The reverential treatment of the Torah would be contrasted with all sorts of more mundane things like cars or toys, which, for most people, are not considered sacred. Yet, the acute reader will be quick to point out that for some, cars (and even toys) are considered sacred and treated almost as reverentially as the Torah is treated in Judaism. This introduces one of the most significant criticisms of this definition - the typology can include things that are not traditionally understood to be religious (like cars or toys). As a result, the definition is extremely broad and can encompass substantial elements of social life. For instance, while most people in the United States would not consider their nationalism to be religious, they do hold the flag, the nation's capitol, and other national monuments to be sacred. Under this definition, nationalism would be considered religion.

Religion as Existential Questioning

Another common definition of religion among social scientists (particularly social psychologists) views religion as any attempt to answer existential questions (e.g., 'Is there life after death?'; see Batson, Scheonrade, and Ventis 1993). This definition casts religion in a functional light as it is seen as serving a specific purpose in society. As is the case with the sacred/profane typology, this definition is also often critiqued for being broad and overly encompassing. For instance, using this definition, someone who attends religious services weekly but makes no attempt to answer existential questions would not be considered religious. At the other extreme, an atheist who believes that existence ends with physical death, would be considered religious because he/she has attempted to answer a key existential question.

The Greek god Zeus.

Religion as Supernature

The third social scientific definition views religion as the collective beliefs and rituals of a group relating to supernature (Tylor 1976). This view of religion draws a sometimes ambiguous line between beliefs and rituals relating to empirical, definable phenomona and those relating to undefinable or unobservable phenomena, such as spirits, god(s), and angels. This definition is not without its problems as well, as some argue it can also include atheists who have a specific position against the existence of a god (or gods). Yet because the beliefs and rituals are understood to be shared by a group, this definition could be argued to exclude atheists. Despite the problems with this last definition, it does most closely adhere to the traditional (and popular) view of what constitutes a religion.

The Church-Sect Typology

Having defined religion, we now move to one of the most common classification schemes employed in sociology for differentiating between different types of religions. This scheme has its origins in the work of Max Weber, but has seen numerous contributions since then. The basic idea is that there is a continuum along which religions fall, ranging from the protest-like orientation of *sects* to the equilibrium maintaining *churches*. Along this continuum are several additional types, each of which will be discussed in turn. The reader may notice that many of the labels for the types of religion are commonly employed by non-sociologists to refer to religions and tend to be used interchangeably. Sociologists, when speaking technically, will not use these labels interchangeably as they are designations for religions with very specific characteristics.

Before describing these different religions, it is important for the reader to understand that these classifications are a good example of what sociologists refer to as *ideal types*. Ideal types are *pure* examples of the categories. Because there is significant variation in each religion, how closely an individual religion actually adheres to their *ideal type* classification will vary. Even so, the classification scheme is useful as it also outlines a sort of developmental process for religions.

The Church-Sect Continuum

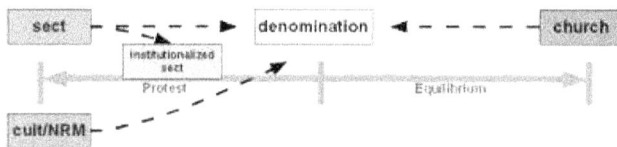

Church and Ecclesia

The first type of religion is the *church*. The *church* classification describes religions that are all-embracing of religious expression in a society. Religions of this type are the guardians of religion for all members of the societies in which they are located and tolerate no religious competition. They also strive to provide an all-encompassing worldview for their adherents and are typically enmeshed with the political and economic structures of society.

Johnstone (1997) provides the following six characteristics of churches:

5.   claim universality, include all members of the society within their ranks, and have a strong tendency to equate 'citizenship' with 'membership

6.   exercise religious monopoloy and try to eliminate religious competition

7.   very closely allied with the state and secular powers - frequently there is overlapping of responsibilities and much mutual reinforcement

8.   extensively organized as a hierarchical bureaucratic institution with a complex division of labor

9.   employ professional, full-time clergy who possess the appropriate credentials of education and formal ordination

10.   almost by definition gain new members through natural reproduction and the socialization of children into the ranks

11.   allow for diversity by creating different groups within the church (e.g., orders of nuns or monks) rather than through the formation of new religions

The classical example of a *church* is the Roman Catholic Church, especially in the past. Today, the Roman Catholic Church has been forced into the denomination category because of religious pluralism or competition among religions. This is especially true of Catholicism in the United States. The change from a *church* to a *denomination* is still underway in many Latin American countries where the majority of citizens remain Catholics.

A slight modification of the *church* type is that of *ecclesia* (von Wiese 1932). Ecclesias include the above characteristics of churches with the exception that they are generally less successful at garnering absolute adherence among all of the members of the society and are not the sole religious body. The state churches of some European countries would fit this type.

Denominations

The *denomination* lies between the church and the sect on the continuum. Denominations come into existence when churches lose their religious monopoly in a society. A denomination is one religion among many. When churches and/or sects become denominations, there are also some changes in their characteristics. Johnstone provides the following eight characteristics of denominations:

4.   similar to churches, but unlike sects, in being on relatively good terms with the state and secular powers and may even attempt to influence government at times

5.   maintain at least tolerant and usually fairly friendly relationships with other denominations in a context of religious pluralism

6.   rely primarily on birth for membership increase, though it will also accept converts; some even actively pursue evangelization

7.   accept the principle of at least modestly changing doctrine and practice and tolerate some theological diversity and dispute

8.   follow a fairly routinized ritual and worship service that explicitly discourages spontaneous emotional expression

9.   train and employ professional clergy who must meet formal requirements for certification

10.   accept less extensive involvement from members than do sects, but more involvement than churches

11.   often draw disproportionately from the middle and upper classes of society

Most of the major religious bodies in the U.S. are denominations (e.g., Baptists, Methodists, Lutherans).

Sects

Sects are newly formed religious groups that form to protest elements of their parent religion (generally a denomination). Their motivation tends to be situated in accusations of apostasy or heresy in the parent denomination; they are often decrying liberal trends in denominational development and advocating a return to *true* religion.

Interestingly, leaders of sectarian movements (i.e., the formation of a new sect) tend to come from a lower socio-economic class than the members of the parent denomination, a component of sect development that is not entirely understood. Most scholars believe that when sect formation does involve social class distinctions they involve an attempt to compensate for deficiencies in lower social status. An often seen result of such factors is the incorporation into the theology of the new sect a distaste for the adornments of the wealthy (e.g., jewelry or other signs of wealth).

Another interesting fact about sects is that after their formation, they can take only three paths - dissolution, institutionalization, or eventual development into a denomination. If the sect withers in membership, it will dissolve. If the membership increases, the sect is forced to adopt the characteristics of denominations in order to maintain order (e.g., bureaucracy, explicit doctrine, etc.). And even if the membership does not grow or grows slowly, norms will develop to govern group activities and behavior. The development of norms results in a decrease in spontaneity, which is often one of the primary attractions of sects. The adoption of denomination-like characteristics can either turn the sect into a full-blown denomination or, if a conscious effort is made to maintain some of the spontaneity and protest components of sects, an *institutionalized sect* can result. Institutionalized sects are halfway between sects and denominations on the continuum of religious development. They have a mixture of sect-like and denomination-like characteristics. Examples include: Hutterites and the Amish.

Most of the well-known denominations of the U.S. existing today originated as sects breaking away from denominations (or Churches, in the case of Lutheranism). Examples include: Methodists, Baptists, and Seventh-day Adventists.

Cults or New Religious Movements

Cults are, like sects, new religious groups. But, unlike sects, they can form without breaking off from another religious group (though they often do). The characteristic that most distinguishes cults from sects is that they are not advocating a return to *pure* religion but rather the embracement of something new or something that has been completely lost or forgotten (e.g., lost scripture or new prophecy). Cults are also more likely to be led by *charismatic leaders* than are other religious groups and the charismatic leaders tend to be the individuals who bring forth the new or lost component that is the focal element of the cult (e.g., The Book of Mormon).

Falun Gong practitioners in London; Falun Gong is a new religious movement.

Cults, like sects, often integrate elements of existing religious theologies, but cults tend to create more esoteric theologies from many sources. Cults emphasize the individual and individual peace. Cults also tend to attract the socially disenchanted or unattached (though this isn't always the case; see Aho 1990 and Barker 1984). Cults tend to be located in urban centers where they can draw upon large populations for membership. Finally, cults tend to be transitory as they often dissolve upon the death or discrediting of their founder and charismatic leader.

Cults, like sects, can develop into denominations. As cults grow, they bureaucratize and develop many of the characteristics of denominations. Some scholars are hesitant to grant cults denominational status because many cults maintain their more esoteric characteristics (e.g., Temple Worship among Mormons). But given their closer semblance to denominations than to the *cult* type, it is more accurate to describe them as denominations. Some denominations in the U.S. that began as cults include: Mormons or The Church of Jesus Christ of Latter-day Saints, Christian Science, and The Nation of Islam.

Finally, it should be noted that there is a push in the social scientific study of religion to begin referring to *cults* as *New Religious Movements* or *NRMs*. The reasoning behind this is because *cult* has made its way into popular language as a derogatory label rather than as a specific type of religious group. Most religious people would do well to remember the social scientific meaning of the word *cult* and, in most cases, realize that three of the major world religions originated as cults, including: Islam, Christianity, and Buddhism.

Theories of Religion

Many of the early sociological theorists (e.g., Marx and Durkheim) proposed theories

181

attempting to explain religion. In addition to these classical approaches to understanding religion, one modern explanation for the continued high levels of religiosity will be proposed along with a social psychological explanation that will attempt to explain the continued attraction of religion. These theories approach religion from slightly different perspectives, trying to explain: (1) the function of religion in society; (2) the role of religion in the life of the individual; and (3) the nature (and origin) of religion.

Structural-Functional

The *Structural-Functional* approach to religion has its roots in Emile Durkheim's work on religion (1912). Durkheim argued that religion is, in a sense, the celebration and even (self-) worship of human society. Given this approach, Durkheim proposed that religion has three major functions in society:

7.   social cohesion - religion helps maintain social solidarity through shared rituals and beliefs

8.   social control - religious based morals and norms help maintain conformity and control in society; religion can also legitimize the political system

9.   providing meaning and purpose - religion can provide answers to existential questions (see the social-psychological approach below)

The primary criticism of the structural-functional approach to religion is that it overlooks religion's dysfunctions. For instance, religion can be used to justify terrorism and violence (Juergensmeyer 2000). Religion has often been the justification of and motivation for war. In one sense, this still fits the structural-functional approach as it provides social cohesion among the members of one party in a conflict (e.g., the social cohesion among the members of a terrorist group is high), but in a broader sense, religion is obviously resulting in conflict, not the resolution of such.

Social-Conflict

The social-conflict approach is rooted in Marx's analysis of capitalism. According to Marx, religion plays a significant role in maintaining the status quo. Marx argued that religion was actually a tool of the bourgeoisie to keep the proletariat content. Marx argued that religion is able to do this by promising rewards in the after-life rather than in this life. It is in this sense that Marx said, "Religion is the sigh of the oppressed creature, the feeling of a heartless world, and the soul of soulless circumstances. It is the opium of the people... The abolition of religion as the illusory happiness of the people is the demand for their real happiness" (Marx 2000:72). What Marx meant is that it would be necessary for the proletariat to throw off religion and its deceit about *other-worldly* rewards in order for the proletariat to rise up against the bourgeoisie and gain control over the means of production so they could realize *this-worldly* rewards. Thus, the social-conflict approach to religion highlights how it functions to maintain social inequality by providing a worldview that justifies oppression.

It should be reiterated here that Marx's approach to sociology was critical in the sense that it advocated change (in contrast to the *knowledge for knowledge's sake* approach). Because criticism of the system in place when he was writing was inherent in Marx's approach, he took a particular stand on the existence of religion, namely, that it should be done away with.

===**Social Constructionist**=== The *social constructionist* approach to religion presents a naturalistic explanation of the origins of religion. Berger (1967) laid a framework for this approach, "Religion is the human enterprise by which a sacred cosmos is established. Put differently, religion is cosmization in a sacred mode. Use of the word sacred in this context refers to a quality of mysterious and awesome power, other than man and yet related to him, which is believed to reside in certain objects of experience" (p. 25). In other words, for the social constructionist, religion is not created by (or for) supernatural beings but rather is the result of societies delineating certain elements of society as sacred. In the social constructionist frame of mind, these elements of society are then objectified in society so they seem to take on an existence of their own. As a result, they can then act back on the individual (e.g., the influence of a religion on the individual).

Another important element of religion discussed by Berger in his outline of the social constructionist approach is the idea of *plausibility structures*. According to Berger,

The reality of the Christian world depends upon the presence of social structures within which this reality is taken for granted and within which successive generations of individuals are socialized in such a way that this world will be real to them. When this plausibility structure loses its intactness or continuity, the Christian world begins to totter and its reality ceases to impose itself as self-evident truth. (p. 46)

In short, plausibility structures are the societal elements that provide the support for a set of beliefs (not necessarily religious), including people, institutions, and the processes by which the beliefs are spread, e.g. socialization. Another important element to consider of plausibility structures is mentioned by Berger, "When an entire society serves as the plausibility structure for a religiously legitimated world, all the important social processes within it serve to confirm and reconfirm the reality of this world" (p. 47). In other words, in certain societies, every component of society functions to reinforce the belief system. A good example of this may be Iran, where everything is structured to reinforce the Islamic faith as *reality*.

Religious Pluralism

Religious pluralism is the belief that one can overcome religious differences between different religions and denominational conflicts within the same religion. For most religious traditions, religious pluralism is essentially based on a non-literal view of one's religious traditions, allowing for respect to be engendered between different traditions on core principles rather than more marginal issues. It is perhaps summarized as an attitude which rejects focus on immaterial differences and instead gives respect to those beliefs held in common.

The existence of religious pluralism depends on the existence of freedom of religion. Freedom of religion is when different religions of a particular region possess the same rights of worship and public expression. Freedom of religion is consequently weakened when one religion is given rights or privileges denied to others, as in certain European countries where Roman Catholicism or regional forms of Protestantism have special status. (For example see the Lateran Treaty and Church of England; also, in Saudi Arabia the public practice of religions other than Islam is forbidden.) Religious freedom has not existed at all in some communist countries where the state restricts or prevents the public expression of religious belief and may even actively persecute individual religions (see for example North Korea).

Religious Pluralism has also been argued to be a factor in the continued existence of religion in the U.S. This theoretical approach (Moore 1994) proposes that because no religion was guaranteed a monopoly in the U.S., religious pluralism led to the conversion of religions in the U.S. into capitalist organizations. As a result, religions are now better understood as capitalist corporations peddling their wares in a highly competitive market than they are as monopolistic Churches like Roman Catholicism was prior to The Reformation (or, some might argue, still is in Latin America) or as small, fervent, protest-like sects are. The result of religious pluralism is, like capitalism generally in the U.S., a *consumer* attitude: people *consume* religion like they do other goods. Because religions are good at marketing themselves as the providers of social psychological compensators (see below), they have been successful.

Social-Psychological

The primary social-psychological reason why religion continues to exist is because it answers existential questions that are difficult, if not impossible, to address scientifically. For instance, science cannot address the question of what happens when someone dies other than to provide a biological explanation (i.e., the body's cells eventually die due to lack of nutrition, the body then decomposes, etc.). Science is also unable to address the question of a *higher* purpose in life other than simply to reproduce. Finally, science cannot disprove or prove the existence of a higher being. Each of these existential components are discussed below in greater detail.

Studies have found that fear is a factor in religious conversion. Altemeyer and Hunsberger (1997), in their book *Amazing Conversions*, note that one of the primary motivations for people to seek religion was fear of the the unknown; specifically, fear of the after-life and what it portends. While fear likely does not motivate all religious people, it certainly is a factor for some. Religion can provide a *non-falsifiable* answer to the question of what happens after people die. Such answers can provide comfort for individuals who want to know what will happen when they die.

Religion providing a purpose in life was also a motivation found by Altemeyer and Hunsberger (1997) in their analysis of religious converts. Batson et. al. (1993) and Spilka, Hunsberger, Gorsuch, and Hood (2003) also point to this factor as an explanation for the continued interest in religiosity. Interestingly, Diener (1999), in his research on subjective well-being (SWB) notes that one of the keys to high SWB (a.k.a. happiness) is a goal or purpose in life. However, he introduces a caveat that is particularly telling for religious individuals â€" for the most positive impact on SWB, goals should be difficult but attainable. *Difficult but attainable* is a good description of salvation for religious people. People have to work toward salvation, but they believe it can be achieved. Thus, religion can provide a goal and purpose in life for people who believe they need one.

Belief in God is attributable to a combination of the above factors (i.e., God's existence alleviates fear of death and provides meaning), but is also informed by a discussion of socialization. The biggest predictor of adult religiosity is parental religiosity; if a person's parents were religious when she was a child, she is likely to be religious when she grows up. Children are socialized into religion by their parents and their peers and, as a result, they tend to stay in religions. Alternatively, children raised in secular homes tend not to convert to religion. This is the underlying premise of Altemeyer and Hunsberger's (1997) main thesis â€" they found some interesting cases where just the opposite seemed to happen; secular people converted to religion and religious people became secular. Despite these rare exceptions, the process of socialization is certainly a significant factor in the continued existence of religion.

Combined, these three social-psychological components explain, with the help of religious pluralism, the continued high levels of religiosity in the U.S. People are afraid of things they do not understand (death), they feel they need a purpose in life to be happy (a.k.a. SWB), and they are socialized into religion and believing in God by parents.

World Religions and Religious History

If one were to ask any sociologist of religion which are the *world* religions, they would likely give the standard answer that there are five world religions:

- Christianity

- Hinduism

- Islam

- Buddhism

- Judaism

Traditionally, these have been considered *world* religions due to their size and/or influence on society. A detailed description of these religions is beyond the scope of this chapter and the interested reader is encouraged to follow the above links for more information.

A Jewish synagogue.

One note is, however, in order concerning these religious groups. The classification of these groups as *world* religions is, like all classifications, artificial. Considering the remarkable dissimilarity between these five religious bodies, that they are grouped together at all is remarkable. Three are *religions of the book* and can be practiced somewhat distinctly from oneâ€(tm)s primary cultural identity (e.g., being an American and Episcopalian), while two are better understood as synonymous with culture (Buddhism and Hinduism). Additionally, the religions of the book have numerous branches, some so dissimilar that there is more contention within the world religions than between them (e.g., Mormons vs. fundamentalist Christians, Catholics vs. Episcopalians). Finally, while four of these religious groups are very populous, Judaism is not. In short, classification as a world religion seems a little arbitrary. Even so, most people should make an effort to familiarize themselves with these religious groups to facilitate understanding.

Religion and Other Social Factors

Religion and Gender

Batson et. al. (1993) provide a clear summary of the differences in religiosity between men and women:

There is considerable evidence that women are more likely to be interested and involved in religion than men. Women rate their religious beliefs as important more than do men, and they are more likely to report having had a religious or mystical experience... More women than men report having attended religious services in the past week (46% compared with 33%); more women hold membership in a church or synagogue (74% compared with 63%); and more women report watching religious programs (53% compared with 44%). Women are more likely than men to read the Bible at least monthly (56% compared with 41%) and to report having "a great deal of confidence" in organized religion (62% compared with 52%)... Among Christian denominations, as one moves away from the established, traditional churches (e.g., Catholic, Eastern Orthodox, Episcopal) toward newer, less traditional ones (e.g., Assembly of God, Pentecostal) the proportion of women members relative to men increases... In sum, although the differences are not always large, they are remarkably consistent: Women appear to be more religious-than-men. (p. 33)

One explanation for the greater involvement of women in religion is socialization. Batson et. al. (1993:37) discuss the idea that women may be socialized into roles in which religion is more highly emphasized than it is in men's roles.

Religion and Race

Batson et. al. (1993:38) provide a clear summary of differences in religiosity by race (limited presently to just blacks and whites). They include five distinctions in their discussion. If you are black in the U.S., you are more likely to:

4.   attend religious services

5.   hold traditional religious beliefs

6.   feel strongly about your religious beliefs

7.   report having had religious experiences

8.   consider religion to be important in your life - both when you were growing up and as an adult

Batson et. al. (1993) attribute the differences in religiosity between blacks and whites to the role religious institutions have played among blacks. Religion has been one of the primary resources blacks have drawn upon since their arrival in the U.S. Religion has provided a sense of community and support for blacks and was also extremely influential in the Civil Rights Movement (see Morris 1984). As a result, religion has a more prominent role in the day-to-day lives of blacks.

Religion and Class

Socioeconomic status (SES) or class tends to be associated more with how religion is practiced rather than degree of religiosity (i.e., very religious vs. not very religious). Members of lower classes tend to associate with more fundamentalist religions and sect-like groups. Members of the middle class tend to belong to more formal churches. "In the United States, Presbyterians and Episcopalians tend to be above average in SES; Methodists and Lutherans about average; and Baptists and members of Protestant fundamentalist sects below average" (Batson et. al. 1993:38-39).

Religion and Education

An important study published in 1997 by Johnson draws a particularly clear picture of the relationship between religion and education. Johnson found a dichotomization of religiosity as a result of college education. Those who make it through college with their religious beliefs intact tend to be more devout than those who do not attend college to begin with yet remain religious. On the other side, those who don't make it through college with their religious beliefs intact end up far less orthodox and are more likely to disavow religion altogether. The relationship between education and religiosity is a dichotomization â€" college education strengthens both religiosity and irreligiosity, it just depends on where you end up. Johnson's finding is particularly insightful in light of the social psychological theory of cognitive dissonance, which argues that religious people will (at least initially) reinforce their beliefs in light of disconfirming evidence.

Religion and Health

According to Batson et. al. (1993:240-290), the relationship between religion and mental health is highly nuanced. In order to understand this nuanced relationship, it is necessary to clarify the different types of religiosity Batson et. al. are studying. Batson et. al. distinguish between three types of religiosity. These types or orientations stem from the work of Gordon Allport who distinguished two types of religiosity and provided their corresponding labels: intrinsic and extrinsic religiosity. Extrinsic religiosity refers to people who use religion as a means to an end (e.g., social contacts). Intrinsic religiosity refers to people who see religion as the end (e.g., religion is the answer to life's questions). Batson et. al. add a third â€" quest religiosity. Quest religiosity refers to the religious seeker who constantly asks questions and may not believe there are any clear answers to them.

If one does not take into consideration the different types of religiosity (i.e., extrinsic, intrinsic, and quest), religion tends to be associated with poorer mental health (p. 240). Specifically, Batson et. al. find a negative relationship between religion and three components of mental health, "personal competence and control, self-acceptance or self-actualization, and open-mindedness and flexibility" (p. 240).

However, if one does take into consideration the different types of religiosity, then intrinsic and quest oriented individuals tend to see mental health benefits from their religious involvement. Extrinsically-oriented individuals, on the other hand, find that their religious involvement results in a negative influence on their mental health (p. 289).

The Future of Religion

Despite the claims of many classical theorists and sociologists, religion continues to play a vital role in the lives of individuals. In America, for example, church attendance has remained relatively stable in the past 40 years. In Africa and South America, the emergence of Christianity has occurred at a startling rate. While Africa could claim roughly 10 million Christians in 1900, recent estimates put that number closer to 200 million. The rise of Islam as a major world religion, especially its newfound influence in the West, is another significant development. In light of these developments, sociologists have been forced to reconsider the early proclamations of the demise of religion. In addition to discussing secularization and how the theory has been modified due to the continued existence of religion, religious fundamentalism is briefly touched upon as it is playing a significant role in society today.

Secularization

Secularization is a varied term with multiple definitions and levels of meaning. It should also be noted that in addition to multiple definitions, secularization is both a *theory* and a *process*. By theory, it is meant that some scholars (e.g. Marx, Freud, Weber, Durkheim) believed that as society modernized it would also see a decline in levels of religiosity. This understanding of classical secularization theory is currently being refined and modified (see discussion below). The 'process' component of secularization would refer to how the theory is actualized. It is in this sense that secularization has multiple definitions. The most common meaning is in reference to the decline of levels of religiosity in society, but this is a broad and diffuse meaning that should be clarified by referring to one of the more specific meanings outlined below.

Sommerville (1998) outlined six (6) uses of the term *secularization* in the scientific literature. The first five are more along the lines of *definitions* while the sixth application of the term is more of a 'clarification of use' issue:

4.   When discussing social structures, secularization can refer to differentiation. Differentiation (or specialization) is a reference to the increasing division of labor and occupational specialization in society. While some might consider this a foray into social *progress*, few would argue that modern societies are less differentiated than more primitive, tribal societies (following the work of Gerhard Emmanuel Lenski).

5.   When discussing institutions, secularization can refer to the transformation of an institution that had once been considered religious in character into something not thought of as religious. A good example of this type of secularization (and differentiation, for that matter) is the transition of Harvard University from a predominantly religious institution into a secular institution (with a divinity school now housing the religious element illustrating differentiation).

6.   When discussing activities, secularization refers to the transfer of activities from institutions of a religious nature to others without that character. While the trend toward government assistance in social welfare seems to be reversing in recent years, for much of the 20th century activities that had been in the religious domain (e.g. soup kitchens) were slowly moving into the secular (or a-religious) realm, often that of government.

7.   When discussing mentalities, secularization can refer to the transition from *ultimate* concerns to *proximate* concerns. This is the most common understanding and usage of the term at the individual level and refers specifically to personal religious decline or movement toward a secular lifestyle.

8.   When discussing populations, secularization can refer to a societal decline in levels of

religiosity (as opposed to the individual-level secularization of definition four). It should be noted that this understanding of secularization is distinct from definition one (1) in that it refers specifically to religious decline rather than societal differentiation. A clear example of this definition of secularization would be the declining religious affiliations in much of modern Europe.

9.   When discussing religion generally, secularization can only be used unambiguously when referring to religion in a generic sense. For example, to argue that Christianity is 'secularizing' is not clear unless one specifies exactly which elements of which version of Christianity are being discussed. What's more, depending on the venue of the discussion, these elements of Christianity may not be recognized by other 'Christian' groups as elements of their version of Christianity. Thus, if you are interested in discussing religious decline within a specific denomination or religion, you need to specify which elements of that specific group you believe are declining, as Christianity is too variably defined to allow for generalizations for a specific denomination.

Current Issues in the Study of Secularization

At present, secularization (as understood in definition five above) is being debated in the sociology of religion. Some scholars (e.g., Rodney Stark) have argued that levels of religiosity are not declining (though their argument tends to be limited to the U.S., an admitted anomaly in the developed world). As there appears to be some merit to this position, other scholars (e.g., Mark Chaves) have countered by introducing the idea of neo-secularization, which broadens the definition of individual level religious decline by arguing that secularization can also refer to the decline of religious authority. In other words, rather than using a-religious apostates as the solitary measure of a population's secularity, neo-secularization theory argues that individuals are increasingly looking outside of religion for authoritative positions on different topics. Neo-secularizationists would argue that religion is no longer the authority on issues like whether to use birth control and would therefore argue that while religious affiliation may not be declining in the U.S. (a debate still taking place), religion's authority is declining and secularization is taking place.

Religious Fundamentalism

Fundamentalism describes a movement to return to what is considered the defining or founding principles of a religion. It has especially come to refer to any religious enclave that intentionally resists identification with the larger religious group in which it originally arose, on the basis that fundamental principles upon which the larger religious group is supposedly founded have become corrupt or displaced by alternative principles hostile to its identity. A full analysis of what constitutes religious fundamentalism is beyond the scope of this chapter. However, the interested reader is encouraged to explore this topic further by reading the Wikipedia article on fundamentalism.

The destruction of the World Trade Centers in 2001 was inspired by fundamentalist religion.

Religious fundamentalism is of great importance to sociologists because of its increasingly prominent role in social life, especially politics. Kenneth Wald (2003) points out how religious fundamentalism can be detrimental to politics, specifically a democratic system. The fundamentalist approach to politics can hurt a democratic system because of fundamentalists' unwillingness to compromise. Religious fundamentalists tend to take the view that 'God said it, so it will have to be this way.' Because anything short of Godâ€(tm)s will is unacceptable, religious fundamentalists don't allow for a middle ground - which is a vital element of the democratic process.

What the future of religious fundamentalism holds for human society is unknown, but because of the impact of this particular religious approach on society today, religious fundamentalism warrants continued study.

Notes

Need sections:

- religious conversion

- religion and politics

- religion and violence (terrorism)

References

- Batson, C. Daniel, Schoenrade, Patricia, and Ventis, W. Larry. 1993. Religion and the Individual: A Social-Psychological Perspective. Oxford: Oxford University Press. ISBN 0195062094

- Berger, Peter L. 1967, 1990 edition. The Sacred Canopy: Elements of a Sociological Theory. Doubleday. ASIN B0006BQVHY

- Chaves, Mark. 1994. "Secularization As Declining Religious Authority." Social Forces 72(3):749-74.

- Diener, E.; Suh, E. M.; Lucas, R. E., and Smith, H. L. 1999. Subjective Well-Being: Three Decades of Progress. Psychological Bulletin. 125(2).

- Durkheim, Emile. 1995. Elementary Forms of the Religious Life. Free Press. ISBN 0029079373

- Johnson, Daniel Carson. Formal Education vs. Religious Belief: Soliciting New Evidence with Multinomial Logit Modeling. Journal for the Scientific Study of Religion. 1997; 36:231-246.

- Johnstone, Ronald L. 1997. Religion in Society: A Sociology of Religion. Fifth Edition. Upper Saddle River, NJ: Prentice Hall. ISBN 0131254367

- Juergensmeyer, Mark. 2000. Terror in the Mind of God. University of California Press. ISBN 0520240111

- Marx, Karl; McLellan, David. 2000. Karl Marx: Selected Writings. .Oxford University Press. ISBN 0198782659.

- Moore, R. Laurence. 1994. Selling God. Oxford University Press. ISBN 0195098382

- Morris, Aldon D. 1984. The Origins of the Civil Rights Movement. New York: The Free Press. ISBN 0029221307

- Sommerville, C. J. 1998. "Secular Society Religious Population: Our Tacit Rules for Using the Term 'Secularization'." Journal for the Scientific Study of Religion 37 (2):249-53.

- Spilka, B.; Hunsberger, B.; Gorsuch, R.; Hood, R.W. Jr. 2003. The Psychology of Religion. The Guilford Press. ISBN 1572309016.

- Stark, Rodney, Laurence R. Iannaccone, Monica Turci, and Marco Zecchi. 2002. "How Much Has Europe Been Secularized?" Inchiesta 32(136):99-112.

- Tylor, Edward Burnett. 1976. Primitive culture: Researches into the development of mythology, philosophy, religion, language, art, and custom. Gordon Press. ISBN 087968464X

- von Wiese, Leopold. 1932. Systematic sociology. Chapman and Hall.

- Wald, Kenneth D. 2003. Religion and Politics in the United States. Fourth ed. New York: Rowman & Littlefield Publishers, Inc.. ISBN 0742518418

This chapter also draws heavily on the following Wikipedia articles:

- sociology of religion
- religion
- development of religion

- secularization
- fundamentalism
- religious pluralism

External Links

- American Religion Data Archive
- Hadden: Religion and the Quest for Meaning and Order
- A test of the Stark-Bainbridge theory of affiliation with cults and sects
- Adherents.com

Politics

See http://en.wikipedia.org/wiki/Politics

Government

See http://en.wikipedia.org/wiki/Government

Media

See http://en.wikipedia.org/wiki/Mass_media

Education

Education is a <u>social science</u> that <u>encompasses</u> <u>teaching</u> and <u>learning</u> specific <u>skills</u>. Practicing teachers in the field of education use a variety of methods and materials in their instruction to impart a curriculum. There has been a plethora of literature in the field of education that addresses these areas. Such literature addresses the facets of teaching practices to include instructional strategies, behavior management, environmental control, motivational strategies, and technological resources. However, the single most important factor in any teacher's effectiveness is the interaction style and personality of the teacher, for the quality of their relationships with the students provides the impetus for inspiration. The best teachers are able to translate good <u>judgment</u>, experience, and <u>wisdom</u> into the art of communication that students find compelling. It is their compassion for varied human qualities, passion, and the creativity of potential that assists teachers to invigorate students to higher expectations of themselves and society at large. The goal of education is the growth of students so that they become productive citizens of a <u>dynamic</u>, everchanging, society. Fundamentally, the imparting of <u>culture</u> from generation to generation (see <u>socialisation</u>)promotes a greater awareness and responsiveness through social maturity to the needs of an increasingly diversified society.

Overview

It is widely accepted that the process of education begins at birth and continues throughout life. Some believe that education begins even earlier than this, as evidenced by some parents' playing music or reading to the baby in the womb in the hope it will influence the child's development.

The word 'education' is often used to refer solely to formal education (see below). However, it covers a range of experiences, from formal learning to the building of understanding through day to day experiences. Ultimatley, all that we experience serves as a form of education.

Individuals can receive informal education from a variety of sources. <u>Family</u> members and <u>society</u> have a strong influence on the informal education of the individual.

Origins of the Word "Education"

The word "education" is derived from the <u>Latin</u> *educare* meaning "leading out" or "leading forth". This reveals one of the theories behind the function of education - of developing innate abilities and expanding horizons.

Formal Education

Formal education occurs when society or a group or an individual sets up a <u>curriculum</u> to educate people, usually the young. Formal education can become systematic and thorough. Formal education systems can be used to promote ideals or values as well as knowledge and this can sometimes lead to abuse of the system.

Life-long or adult education has become widespread in many countries. However, 'education' is still seen by many as something aimed at children, and adult education is often branded as 'adult learning' or 'lifelong learning'.

Adult education takes on many forms from formal class-based learning to self-directed learning. Lending libraries provide inexpensive informal access to books and other self-instructional materials. Many adults have also taken advantage of the rise in computer ownership and internet access to further their informal education.

Technology and Education

Technology has become an increasingly influential factor in education. Computers and associated technology are being widely used in developed countries to both complement established education practices and develop new ways of learning such as online education (a type of distance education). While technology clearly offers powerful learning tools that can engage students, research has provided no evidence to date that technology actually improves student learning.

History of education

In 1994 Dieter Lenzen, president of the Freie Universität Berlin, said education began either millions of years ago or at the end of 1770. (The first chair of pedagogy was founded at the end of the 1770s at the University of Halle, Germany.) This quote by Lenzen includes the idea that education as a science cannot be separated from the educational traditions that existed before.

Education was the natural response of early civilizations to the struggle of surving and thriving as a culture, requiring adults to train the young of their society in the knowledge and skills they would need to master and eventually pass on. The evolution of culture, and human beings as a species, has depended on this practice of transmittining knowledge. In pre-literate societies this was achieved orally, story-telling from one generation to the next. As oral langauage developed into witten symbols and letters, the depth and breadth of knowledge that could be preserved and passed increased exponentially.

As cultures began to extend their knowledge beyond the basic skills of communicating, trading, gathereing food, religious practices, etc., the beginnings of formal education, schooling, eventually followed. There is evidence that schooling in this sense was already in place in Egypt between 3000 and 500BC.

Basic education today is considered those skills that are necessary to function in society.

Challenges in education

The goal of education is the transference of ideas and skills from one person to another, or from one person to a group. Current education issues include which teaching method(s) are most effective, how to determine what knowledge should be taught, which knowledge is most relevant, and how well the pupil will retain incoming knowledge. Educators such as George Counts and Paulo Freire identified education as an inherently political process with inherently political outcomes. The challenge of identifying *whose* ideas are transferred and what goals they serve has always stood in the face of formal and informal education.

In addition to the "Three R's", reading, writing, and arithmetic, Western primary and secondary schools attempt to teach the basic knowledge of history, geography, mathematics (usually including calculus and algebra), physics, chemistry and sometimes politics, in the hope that students will retain and use this knowledge as they age or that the skills acquired will be transferrable. The current education system measures competency with tests and assignments and then assigns each student a corresponding grade. The grades usually come in the form of either a letter grade or a percentage, which are intended to represent the amount of all material presented in class that the student understood.

Educational progressives or advocates of unschooling often believe that grades do not necessarily reveal the strengths and weaknesses of a student, and that there is an unfortunate lack of youth voice in the educative process. Some feel the current grading system risks lowering students' self-confidence, as students may receive poor marks due to factors outside their control. Such factors include poverty, child abuse, and prejudiced or incompetent teachers.

By contrast, many advocates of a more traditional or "back to basics" approach believe that the direction of reform needs to be quite the opposite. Students are not sufficiently inspired or challenged to achieve success because of the dumbing down of the curriculum and the replacement of the "canon" with inferior material. Their view of self-confidence is that it arises not from removing hurdles such as grading, but by making them fair and encouraging students to gain pride from knowing they can jump over these hurdles.

On the one hand, Albert Einstein, one of the most famous physicists of our time, credited with helping us understand the universe better, was not a model school student. He was uninterested in what was being taught, and he did not attend classes all the time. However, his gifts eventually shone through and added to the sum of human knowledge. On the other hand, for millenia those who have been challenged and well-educated in traditional schools have risen to great success and to a lifelong love of learning because their minds were made better and more powerful, as well as because of their mastery of a wide range of skills.

There are a number of highly controversial issues in education. Should some knowledge be forgotten? What should be taught, are we better off knowing how to build nuclear bombs, or is it best to let such knowledge be forgotten?

In developing countries

In developing countries, the number and seriousness of the problems faced is naturally greater. People are sometimes unaware of the importance of education, and there is economic pressure from those parents who prioritize their children's making money in the short term over any long-term benefits of education. Recent studies on child labor and poverty have suggested, however, that when poor families reach a certain economic threshold where families are able to provide for their basic needs, parents return their children to school. This has been found to be true, once the threshold has been breached, even if the potential economic value of the children's work has increased since their return to school. Teachers are often paid less than other similar professions.

A lack of good universities, and a low acceptance rate for good universities is evident in countries with a relatively high population density. In some countries there are uniform, overstructured, inflexible centralized programs from a central agency that regulates all aspects of education.

- Due to globalization, increased pressure on students in curricular activities

- Removal of a certain percentage of students for improvisation of academics (usually practised in schools, after 10th grade)

India however is starting to develop technologies that will skip land based phone and internet lines. Instead, they have launched a special education satellite that can reach more of the country at a greatly reduced cost. There is also an initiative started by AMD and other corporations to develop the $100 dollar computer which should be ready by 2006. This computer will be sold in units of 1 million, and will be assembled in the country where the computer will be used. This apperas to be a different computer to that developed by MIt, with the same price tag, believed to be powered by clockwork and a generator. This will enable poorer countries to give their children a digital education and to close the digital divide across the world.

In Africa, NEPAD has launched an "e-school programme" to provide all 600,000 primary and high schools with computer equipment, learning materials and internet access within 10 years.

Parental involvement

Parental involvement is an essential aspect of a child's educational development. Early and consistent parental involvement in the child's life is critical such as reading to children at an early age, teaching patterns, interpersonal communication skills, exposing them to diverse cultures and the community around them, educating them on a healthy lifestyle, etc. The socialization and academic education of a child are aided by the involvement of the student, parent(s), teachers, and others in the community and extended family.

References

- This page is adapated 4 December 2005 from the Wikipedia article, Education.

197

Health and medicine

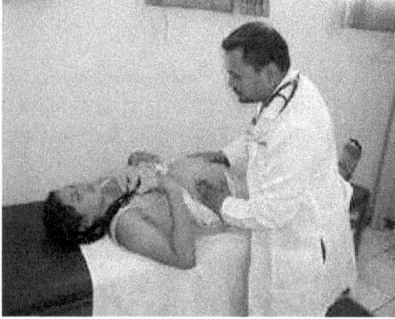
A doctor conducting a pre-natal examination of a patient in El Salvador.

Introduction

The World Health Organization (WHO) defines **health** as "a state of complete physical, mental and social well-being, and does not consist only of the absence of disease or infirmity" (source) Though this is a useful and accurate definition, some would consider it idealistic and non-realistic because using the WHO definition classifies 70-95% of people as unhealthy. This definition also overlooks the fact that several factors influence both the definition of health and standards of health.

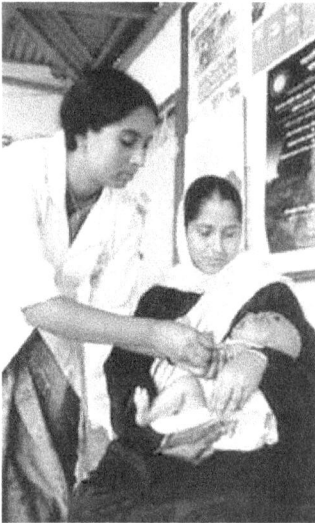
Immunizations from various diseases have improved health worldwide.

What it means to be healthy can vary from culture to culture and is often connected with advances in technology. In some cultures, larger body sizes are seen as a sign of healthiness as it indicates an individual has a preponderance of food. In other cultures, largess is more closely associated with unhealthy lifestyles (e.g., lack of exercise, poor eating habits, etc.). Advances in technology have also expanded the idea of what it means to be healthy. What are understood today to be healthy practices were not emphasized prior to clear understandings of disease and the contributions of lifestyles to health.

Health care (or **healthcare**) is an industry associated with the the prevention, treatment, and management of illness along with the promotion of mental and physical well-being through the services offered by the medical and allied health professions. Healthcare is one of the world's largest and fastest-growing industries, consuming over 10 percent of gross domestic product of most developed nations. In 2000, health care costs paid to hospitals, doctors, diagnostic laboratories, pharmacies, medical device manufacturers and other components of the health care system, consumed an estimated 14 percent of the gross national product of the United States, the largest of any country in the world. For the G8 countries (eight of the most developed countries in the world) the average is about nine percent.

The sociology of health and medicine is concerned with the distribution of healthcare services globally, in particular inequalities in healthcare, and how conceptions of health have changed over time.

The Evolution of Health Care and Medicine

All human societies have beliefs that provide explanations for, and responses to, childbirth, death, and disease. Throughout the world, illness has often been attributed to witchcraft, demons, or the will of the gods, ideas that retain some power within certain cultures and communities (see faith healing). However, the rise of scientific medicine in the past two centuries has altered or replaced many historic health practices.

Folk Medicine

Folk medicine refers collectively to procedures traditionally used for treatment of illness and injury, aid to childbirth, and maintenance of wellness. It is a body of knowledge distinct from modern, *scientific medicine* but may coexist in the same culture. It is usually unwritten and transmitted orally until someone *collects* it. Within a given culture, elements of folk medicine may be diffusely known by many adults or may be gathered and applied by those in a specific role of healer, shaman, midwife, witch, or dealer in herbs. Elements in a specific culture are not necessarily integrated into a coherent system and may be contradictory. Folk medicine is sometimes associated with quackery when practiced as theatrics or otherwise practiced fraudulently, yet it may also preserve important knowledge and cultural tradition from the past.

Herbal medicine is an aspect of folk medicine that involves the use of gathered plant parts to make teas, poultices, or powders that purportedly effect cures. Many effective treatments adopted by physicians over the centuries were derived from plants (i.e. aspirin), and botany was an important part of the *materia medica* of professional medical training before the 20th century.

Increasing attention is being paid to the folk medicine of indigenous peoples of remote areas of the world in hope of finding new pharmaceuticals. Of special concern is the extinction of many species by the clearing of formerly wild rainforests. Such activity may lead to the loss of species of plants that could provide aids to modern medicine. Attitudes toward this type of knowledge gathering and plant preservation vary and political conflicts have increasingly arisen over *ownership* of the plants, land, and knowledge in several parts of the world.

Alternative Medicine

Alternative medicine describes methods and practices used in place of, or in addition to, conventional medical treatments. The precise scope of alternative medicine is a matter of some debate and depends to a great extent on the definition of *conventional medicine*. Positions on the distinction between the two include those who reject the safety and efficacy of the other, and a number of positions in between.

The debate on alternative medicine is also complicated by the diversity of treatments that are categorized as *alternative*. These include practices that incorporate spiritual, metaphysical, or religious underpinnings; non-European medical traditions; newly developed approaches to healing; and a number of others. Proponents of one class of alternative medicine may reject the others while much of alternative medicine is rejected by conventional medicine.

Many in the scientific community label all healthcare practices that have not undergone scientific testing (i.e., peer-reviewed, controlled studies) as alternative medicine. Yet, the boundary between alternative and mainstream medicine has changed over time. Some methods once considered alternative have later been adopted by conventional medicine, when confirmed by controlled studies. Many very old conventional medical practices are now seen as alternative medicine, as modern controlled studies have shown that certain treatments were not actually effective. Supporters of alternative methods suggest that much of what is currently called alternative medicine will be similarly assimilated by the mainstream in the future.

Criticisms of alternative medicine

Due to the wide range of therapies that are considered *alternative*, few criticisms apply to all of them. Criticisms directed at specific branches of alternative medicine range from the fairly minor (e.g., conventional treament is believed to be more effective in a particular area) to incompatibility with the known laws of physics. Some of the criticisms of alternative medicine include:

- Lack of proper testing. Despite the large number of studies regarding alternative therapies, critics contend that there are no statistics on exactly how many of these studies were controlled, double-blind peer-reviewed experiments or how many produced results supporting alternative medicine or parts thereof. They contend that many forms of alternative medicine are rejected by conventional medicine because the efficacy of the treatments has not been demonstrated through double-blind randomized controlled trials. Where alternative methods provide temporary symptomatic relief, this has been explained as being due to the placebo effect, or to natural healing, or to the cyclic nature of some illnesses. Richard Dawkins, professor of the

Public Understanding of Science at Oxford University, defines alternative medicine as "that set of practices that cannot be tested, refuse to be tested or consistently fail tests" (see Diamond 2003).

- Not proven to be an alternative. Some doctors and scientists feel that the term *alternative medicine* is misleading, as these treatments have not been proven to be an effective alternative to regulated conventional medicine.

- Safety issues. Some *alternative* practices have caused deaths indirectly when patients have used alternatives in attempts to treat such conditions as appendicitis and failed. Proponents of alternative medicine say that people should be free to choose whatever method of healthcare they want. Critics agree that people should be free to choose, but when choosing, people must be certain that whatever method they choose will be safe and effective. People who choose alternative medicine may think they are choosing a safe, effective medicine, while they may only be getting quack remedies. This issue is particularly important in the treatment of children and individuals whose capacity to evaluate the treatment is impaired.

- Delay in seeking conventional medical treatment.There is a concern that patients may delay seeking conventional medicine that could be more effective, while they undergo alternative therapies, potentially resulting in harm.

- Poor diagnosis. Medical doctors hold that alternative medical practitioners sometimes fail to correctly diagnose illnesses and therefore do not provide safe therapies. William T. Jarvis contends in a web article "How Quackery Harms Cancer Patients" that "Dubious therapies can cause death, serious injury, unnecessary suffering, and disfigurement" and gives an example of how an unlicenced naturopath caused severe disfigurement of a patient (source).

- Issues of regulation. In countries where healthcare is state-funded or funded by medical insurance, alternative therapies are often not covered, and must be paid for by the patient. Further, in some countries, some branches of alternative medicine are not properly regulated. As a result, there is no governmental control on who practices alternative medicine and no real way of knowing what training or expertise they possess. In the United States, herbal remedies, vitamins, and supplements are not regulated by the Food and Drug Administration (FDA). This means that companies are not required to prove that these supplements are either effective or safe. The failure to regulate supplements has lead to serious problems, including some deaths. Such problems did ultimately lead the FDA to ban the sale of ephedra, an herbal supplement implicated in several deaths (source).

- Testing and studies. The scientific community argues that many studies carried out by alternative medicine promoters are flawed, as they often use testimonials and hearsay as evidence, leaving the results open to observer bias. They argue that the only way to counter observer bias is to run a double-blind experiment in which neither the patient nor the practitioner knows whether the real treatment is being given or if a placebo has been administered. This research should then be reviewed by peers to determine the validity of the research methodology. Testimonials are particularly disturbing in this regard because, by chance alone, some people may see some improvement in the ailment for which they are being treated and will proceed to testify that the method helped them when the method was not the true cause of improvement (see here for more on this topic).

- Lack of funding. Some argue that less research is carried out on alternative medicine because many alternative medicine techniques cannot be patented; as a result there is little financial incentive to study them. Conventional pharmaceutical research, by contrast, can be very lucrative. However, funding for research into alternative medicine has increased. Increasing the funding for research of alternative medicine techniques is the explicit purpose of the National Center for Complementary and Alternative Medicine (NCCAM). NCCAM and its predecessor, the Office of Alternative Medicine, have spent more than $200 million on such research since 1991 (source).

Modern Medicine

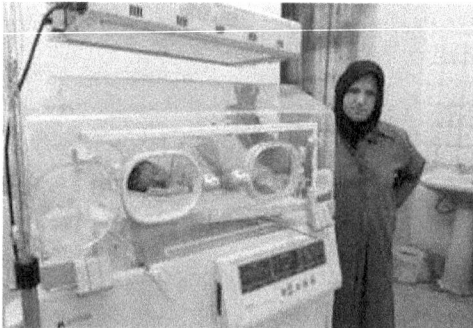
⊡Modern medicine has substantially improved quality of life around the world.

The more generally accepted view of healthcare is that improvements result from advancements in medical science. The medical model focuses on the eradication of illness through diagnosis and effective treatment. In contrast the social model of healthcare places emphasis on changes that can be made in society and in people's own lifestyles to make the population healthier. It defines illness from the point of view of the individual's functioning within society rather than by monitoring for changes in biological or physiological signs.

Modern, *western* medicine has proven uniquely effective and widespread compared with all other medical forms, but has fallen far short of what once seemed a realistic goal of conquering all disease and bringing health to even the poorest of nations. Modern medicine is notably secular, indifferent to ideas of the supernatural or the spirit, and concentrating on the body to determine causes and cures - an emphasis that has provoked something of a backlash in recent years. Backlashes notwithstanding, modern, *western* medicine is clearly the most effective contributor to the health of humans in the world today.

Health Disparities

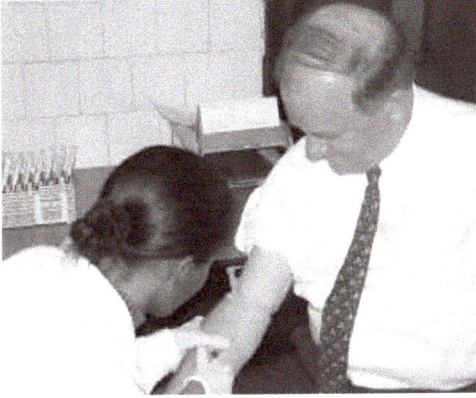

In an effort to dispel the stigma associated with HIV/AIDS testig in Ethiopia, Randall Tobias, U.S. Global AIDS Coordinator, was publicly tested.

While technology has advanced the practice of medicine and generally improved health, not all people have the same access to health care or the same quality of health care. According to the Health Resources and Services Administration of the U.S., *health disparities* are the "population-specific differences in the presence of disease, health outcomes, or access to health care" (source). Of particular interest to sociologists are the differences in health and quality of health care across racial, socioeconomic, and ethnic groups.

In the United States, health disparities are well documented in minority populations such as African Americans, Native Americans, Asian Americans, and Hispanics. When compared to whites, these minority groups have higher incidents of chronic diseases, higher mortality, and poorer health outcomes. Among the disease-specific examples of racial and ethnic disparities in the United States is the cancer incidence rate among African Americans/blacks, which is 10 percent higher than among whites. In addition, adult blacks and Hispanics have approximately twice the risk as whites of developing diabetes. Minorities also have higher rates of cardiovascular disease, HIV/AIDS, and infant mortality than whites.

Figure 11.4. Age- sex-adjusted percent of persons of all ages who assessed their health as excellent or very good, by race/ethnicity: United States, 2004

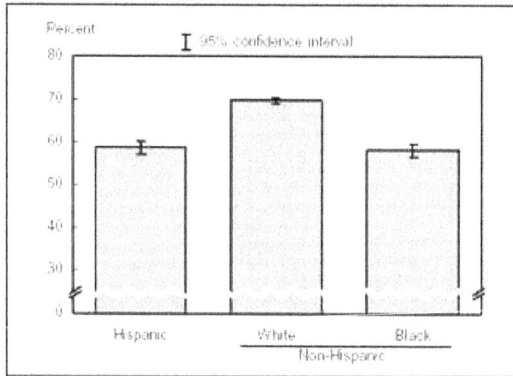

Causes of Health Disparities

There is debate about what causes health disparities between ethnic and racial groups. However, it is generally accepted that disparities can result from three main areas:

- From the differences in socioeconomic and environmental characteristics of different ethnic and racial groups. For instance, blacks and hispanics tend to live in poorer neighborhoods that are near to industrial areas and are older than new suburban subdivisions. Industrial pollutants and lead-paint, common in older homes, can both lead to increased incidents of disease.

- From the barriers certain racial and ethnic groups encounter when trying to enter into the health care delivery system.

- From the quality of health care different ethnic and racial groups receive.

Most attention on the issue has been given to the health outcomes that result from differences in access to medical care among groups and the quality of care different groups receive. Reasons for disparities in access to health care are many, but can include the following:

- Lack of insurance coverage. Without health insurance, patients are more likely to postpone medical care, more likely to go without needed medical care, and more likely to go without prescription medicines. Minority groups in the United States lack insurance coverage at higher rates than whites.

204

Figure 1.3. Age- sex-adjusted percent of persons of all ages without health insurance coverage, by race/ethnicity: United States, 2004

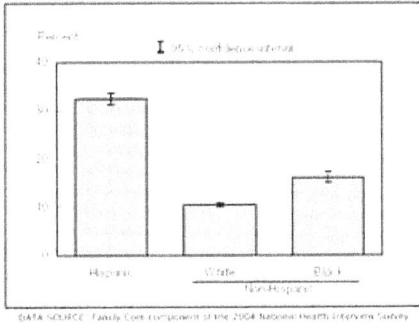

DATA SOURCE: Family Core component of the 2004 National Health Interview Survey

- Lack of a regular source of care. Without access to a regular source of care, patients have greater difficulty obtaining care, fewer doctor visits, and more difficulty obtaining prescription drugs. Compared to whites, minority groups in the United States are less likely to have a doctor they go to on a regular basis and are more likely to use emergency rooms and free or reduced rate, government subsidized clinics as their regular source of care.

- Lack of financial resources. Although the lack of financial resources is a barrier to health care access for many Americans, the impact on access appears to be greater for minority populations.

- Structural barriers. Structural barriers to health care include poor transportation, an inability to schedule appointments quickly or during convenient hours, and excessive time spent in the waiting room, all of which affect a person's ability and willingness to obtain needed care.

- The health financing system. The Institute of Medicine in the United States says fragmentation of the U.S. health care delivery and financing system is a barrier to accessing care. Racial and ethnic minorities are more likely to be enrolled in health insurance plans which place limits on covered services and offer a limited number of health care providers.

- Scarcity of providers. In inner cities, rural areas, and communities with high concentrations of minority populations, access to medical care can be limited due to the scarcity of primary care practitioners, specialists, and diagnostic facilities. In addition more private practices are putting limits on the number of medicaid and medicare patients that they will accept because these programs reimburse at a much lower percentage than private insurers. Finding physicians who accept Medicaid and Medicare is becoming increasingly difficult.

- Linguistic barriers. Language differences restrict access to medical care for minorities in the United States who are not English-proficient.

- Low Health literacy. This is where patients have problems obtaining, processing, and understanding basic health information. For example, patients with a poor understanding of good health may not know when it is necessary to seek care for certain symptoms. Similarly,

205

they may not understand the medical jargon that is used by health professionals and, consequently, are unable to accurately follow medical instructions. While problems with health literacy are not limited to minority groups, the problem can be more pronounced in these groups than in whites due to socioeconomic and educational factors.

- Lack of diversity in the health care workforce. Cultural differences between predominantly white health care providers and minority patients is also often cited as a barrier to health care. Only 4% of physicians in the United States are African American; Hispanics represent just 5%. These percentages are much lower than these groups' respective proportions of the United States population.

- Provider discrimination. This is where health care providers either unconsciously or consciously treat certain racial and ethnic patients differently than they treat their white patients. Some research suggests that minorities are less likely than whites to receive a kidney transplant once on dialysis or to receive pain medication for bone fractures. Critics question this research and say further studies are needed to determine how doctors and patients make their treatment decisions. Others argue that certain diseases cluster by ethnicity and that clinical decision making does not always reflect these differences.

Paying for Medical Care

As noted in the previous section, disparities in health care are often related to an individual's or a group's ability to pay for health care. This section discusses the costs of healthcare and the different approaches to health care that have been taken by governments around the world

Health Insurance

Health insurance is a type of insurance whereby the insurer pays the medical costs of the insured if the insured becomes sick due to covered causes or accidents. The insurer may be a private organization or a government agency. According to the 2005 United States Census Bureau, approximately 85% of Americans have health insurance. Approximately 60% obtain health insurance through their place of employment or as individuals and various government agencies provide health insurance to 25% of Americans.

Figure 1.2. Percent of persons under age 65 years without health insurance
coverage, by age group and sex: United States, 2004

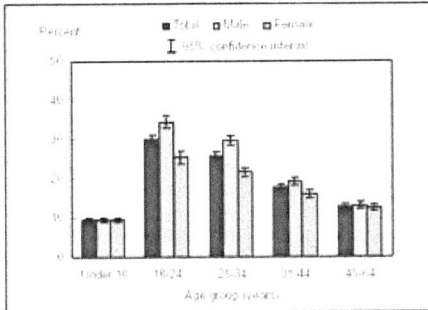

Figure 1.2. Percent of persons under age 65 years without health insurance
coverage, by age group and sex: United States, 2004

DATA SOURCE: Family Core component of the 2004 National Health Interview Survey.

While the rising cost of health care is debated, some contributing causes are accepted. Ageing populations require more health care as a result of increased life expectancy. Advances in medical technology have arguably driven up the prices of procedures, especially cutting edge and experimental procedures. Poor health choices also increase health care costs by increasing the incident of disease and disability. Preventable health issues are related to:

- insufficient exercise

- unhealthy food choices

- excessive alcohol consumption

- smoking

- obesity (more on this below)

Figure 3.3. Age- sex-adjusted percent of persons of all ages who failed to
obtain needed medical care due to cost at some time during the past 12
months, by race/ethnicity: United States, 2004

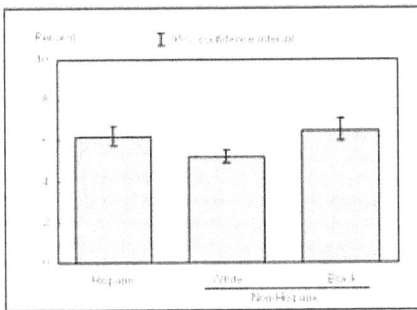

NOTES: The analysis excluded 316 persons (0.2%) with unknown success in obtaining needed medical care. Estimates are age- and sex-adjusted to the 2000 projected U.S. standard population using three age groups: under 18 years, 18-64 years, and 65 years and over.

DATA SOURCE: Family Core component of the 2004 National Health Interview Survey.

207

In theory, people could lower health insurance prices by exercising, eating healthy food, and avoiding addictive substances that are damaging to the body. Healthier lifestyles protect the body from disease, and with fewer diseases, there would be fewer health care related expenses.

Another element of high health care costs is related to the private management of healthcare by large corporations. While this is discussed in greater detail below, it is worth noting that corporate profits have also played a role in increased health care premiums.

Private Insurance and Free-Market Health Care

Two types of health insurance have developed in modern society: private health insurance (or free-market) models and publicly funded health insurance models. The benefits and drawbacks of each of these models is discussed in this and the following section.

Private insurance refers to health insurance provided by a non-governmental organization, usually a privately owned or publically traded corporation. Private insurance as the primary provider of health care in a developed nation is really only found in the United States. It is important to note that while the United States is the most private of any system, there is a substantial public component. Of every dollar spent on health care in the United States, 44 cents comes from some level of government. In addition, government also increases private sector costs by imposing licensing and regulatory barriers to entry into both the practice of medicine and the drug trade within America. Private practitioners also face inflated costs through the government's use of protectionist measures against foreign companies, to uphold the intellectual property rights of the U.S. pharmaceutical industry.

Advocates of the private model argue that this approach to health care has the following benefits:

- Some economists argue that the free market is better able to allocate discretionary spending where consumers value it the most. There is variation among individuals about how much they value peace of mind and a lower risk of death. For example, while a public-funded system (see below) might decide to pay for a pap smear only once every five years if the patient was not positive for the human papilloma virus based on cost efficiency, in a private system a consumer can choose to be screened more often and enjoy the luxury of greater peace of mind and marginally reduced risk. When evaluating the pool of current medical spending available to fund cost effective care for the uninsured, this discretionary spending might be moved to non-medical luxury goods. Also, since current private plans are not very good at limiting spending to cost effective procedures and schedules, those consumers exploiting this will view the transition to a public system as a reduction in their compensation or benefits, and will question whether a society that will allow them to buy a better car or a European vacation, but not better health care, is truly free.

- Advocates also point to the remarkable advances in medical technology that have accompanied the private insurance/free-market approach to health care. When health care is privately funded, the opportunity for making large amounts of money is an attractive proposition for researchers in medical technology and pharmaceuticals. Thus, the private insurance system, while it may not provide adequate care for everyone (see the criticisms below), does provide cutting edge technology for those who have who can afford it.

- Advocates also argue that private industry is more efficient than government, which can be quite susceptible to bloat and bureaucracy. However, as is discussed below, this is not always true.

Despite these possible benefits, the private insurance approach is not without its drawbacks. Following are some of the more common criticisms of the private health insurance approach to health care:

- As noted above, private insurance can be a boon to those who can afford the cutting edge technology. But the flipside to this boon is that the United States, the only mostly-private health delivery system in a developed country, is below average among developed nations by almost every health measure, including: infant mortality, life expectancy, and cancer survival rates.

- Another significant criticism of the private system is that it ends up being more costly than publicly funded systems. In 2001 the United States government spent $4,887 per person on health care. That is more than double the rate of any other G8 country, except Japan which spends close to $2,627 per capita annually. Surprisingly, the United States also spends a greater fraction of its national budget on health than such nations as Canada, Germany, France, or Japan. This is particularly surprising considering private insurers are supposed to cover the majority of health care costs.

- Most experts believe that significant market failure occurs in health markets, thereby leading free market insurance models to operate inefficiently. The consumers of health care are vastly less knowledgeable than the medical professionals they buy it from. An individual is especially less likely to make rational choices about his/her own health care in a case of emergency. The extreme importance of health matters to the consumer adds to the problem of the information gap. This gives the medical profession the ability to set rates that are well above free market value. The need to ensure competence and qualifications among medical professionals also means that they are inevitably closely controlled by professional associations that can exert monopolistic control over prices. Monopolies are made even more likely by the sheer variety of specialists and the importance of geographic proximity. Patients in most markets have no more than one or two heart specialists or brain surgeons to choose from, making competition for patients between such experts very limited.

- In theory when a government sets billing rates it can negotiate with the professional societies with equal heft and knowledge, reaching a total cost that is closer to the ideal than an unregulated market. In private insurance systems, each insurance company is responsible for negotiating its own salaries. A possible result of this approach is the higher pay in doctors' salaries. Doctors' salaries do tend to be much lower in public systems. For instance, doctors' salaries in the United States are twice those in Canada.

- The private insurance or free-market approach also fails to provide an efficient delivery for health care because prevention is such an essential component, but one that most people misjudge. Screening for diseases such as cancer saves both lives and money, but there is a tendency within the general population to not correctly assess their risk of disease and thus to not have regular check ups. Many people are only willing to pay a doctor when they are sick, even though this care may be far more expensive than regular preventative care would have been. The one exception is when extensive publicity, such as that for mammograms, is undertaken. Making regular appointments cheaper, or even free (as is done in public systems), has been shown to reduce both rates of illness and costs of health care. Conversely, placing the cost of a visit to a general practitioner too low will lead to excessive visits wasting both a patient's and a doctor's time. Thus while some experts believe free doctor visits produce ideal results, most believe that forcing people to pay some fraction of the cost of an appointment is better.

- When a claim is made, particularly for a sizeable amount, the use of paperwork and bureaucracy can allow insurance companies to avoid payment of the claim or, at a minimum, greatly delay it. Some people simply give up pursuing their claims with their insurance provider. This is a cost-cutting technique employed by some companies; fighting claims legally is actually less expensive in some instances than paying the claims outright.

- Insurance companies usually do not announce their health insurance premiums more than one year in advance. This means that, if one becomes ill, he or she may find that the premiums have greatly increased. This largely defeats the purpose of having insurance in the eyes of many. However, this is not a concern in many group health plans because there are often laws that prevent companies from charging a single individual in the plan more than others who are enrolled in the same insurance plan.

- Health insurance is often only widely available at a reasonable cost through an employer-sponsored group plan. This means that unemployed individuals and self-employed individuals are at an extreme disadvantage and will have to pay for more for their health care.

- Experimental treatments are generally not covered. This practice is especially criticized by those who have already tried, and not benefited from, all *standard* medical treatments. Because insurance companies can avoid paying claims for experimental procedures, this has lead some insurers to claim that procedures are still *experimental* well after they have become standard medical practice. This phenomenon was especially prevalent among private insurance companies after organ transplants, particularly kidney transplants, first became standard medical practice, due to the tremendous costs associated with this procedure and other organ transplantation. This approach to avoiding paying premiums can also undermine medical advances.

- Health Maintenance Organizations or (HMO) types of health insurance are often criticized for excessive cost-cutting policies that include accountants or other administrators making medical decisions for customers. Rather than allowing such decisions to be made by health care professionals who know which procedures or treatments are necessary, these health plan administrators are dictating medical practice through their refusal to cover claims.

- As the health care recipient is not directly involved in payment of health care services and products, they are less likely to scrutinize or negotiate the costs of the health care they receive. To care providers (health care professionals, not the insurers), insured care recipients are viewed as customers with relatively limitless financial resources who do not consider the prices of services. To address this concern, many insurers have implemented a program of bill review in which insured individuals are allowed to challenge items on a bill (particularly an inpatient hospital bill) as being for goods or services *not received*. If a challenge is proven accurate, insured individuals are awarded with a percentage of the amount that the insurer would have otherwise paid for this disputed item or service.

Concerns about health insurance are prevalent in the United States. A June 2005 survey of a random national sample by the Kaiser Family Foundation found that twice as many United Statesians are more worried about rising health care costs than losing their job or being the victim of a terrorist attack (source).

Publicly Funded Health Care

An alternative to private health insurance and the free-market approach to health care is publicly funded health care. Publicly funded medicine is health care that is paid wholly or mostly by public funds (i.e., taxes). Publicly funded medicine is often referred to as *socialized medicine* by its opponents, whereas supporters of this approach tend to use the terms *universal healthcare*, *single payer healthcare*, or *National Health Services*. It is seen as a key part of a welfare state.

This approach to health care is the most common and popular among developed (and developing) nations around the world today. The majority of developed nations have publicly funded health systems that cover the great majority of the population. For some examples, see the British National Health Service, medicare Canada and medicare Australia.

Even among countries that have publicly funded medicine, different countries have different approaches to the funding and provision of medical services. Some areas of difference are whether the system will be funded from general government revenues (e.g. Italy, Canada) or through a government social security system (France, Japan, Germany) on a separate budget and funded with special separate taxes. Another difference is how much of the cost of care will be paid for by government or social security system, in Canada all hospital care is paid for by the government while in Japan patients must pay 10 to 30% of the cost of a hospital stay. What will be covered by the public system is also important; for instance, the Belgian government pays the bulk of the fees for dental and eye care, while the Australian government covers neither.

The United States has been virtually alone among developed nations in not maintaining a publicly-funded health-care system since South Africa adopted a publicly-funded system after toppling its apartheid regime. However, a few states in the U.S. have taken serious steps toward achieving this goal, most notably Minnesota. Other states, while not attempting to insure all of their residents strictly speaking, cover large numbers of people by reimbursing hospitals and other health-care providers using what is generally characterized as a charity care scheme, which often includes levies.

Publicly funded medicine may be administered and provided by the government, but in some systems that is not an obligation: there exist systems where medicine is publicly funded, yet most health providers are private entities. The organization providing public health insurance is not necessarily a public administration, and its budget may be isolated from the main state budget. Likewise, some systems do not necessarily provide universal healthcare, nor restrict coverage to public health facilities.

Proponents of publicly funded medicine cite several advantages over private insurance or free-market approaches to health care:

- Publicly funded approaches provide universal access to health care to all citizens, resulting in equality in matters of life and death.

- Publicly funded health care reduces contractual paperwork.

- Publicly funded health care facilitates the creation of uniform standards of care.

- It is also the case that publicly funded systems result in a reduction in the percentage of societal resources devoted to medical care; meaning public systems cost less than private systems.

Publicly funded health care is not without its criticisms. Some purported disadvantages of the public system include:

- Some critics argue there is a greater likelihood of lower quality health care than privately funded systems. However, because of the universal accessibility of health care, this claim is generally not true.

- Another criticism of publicly funded health care is that there is less motivation for medical innovation and invention and less motivation for society's most skilled people to become doctors, because of the lower amount of monetary compensation.

- Price no longer influences the allocation of resources, thus removing a natural self-corrective mechanism for avoiding waste and inefficiency (though the redundancy of the private system - competing insurers - often results in more inefficiency than a single, public system).

- Health care workers' pay is often not related to quality or speed of care. Thus very long waits can occur before care is received.

- Because publicly funded medicine is a form of socialism, many of the general concerns about socialism can be applied to this approach.

- People are afraid that they can't choose their own doctor. The state chooses for them. This also tends to be an over-exaggerated and ill-founded concern as there is some degree of freedom in choosing medical practitioners in public systems.

Parallel Public/Private Systems

Almost every country that has a publicly funded health care system also has a parallel private system, generally catering to the wealthy. While the goal of public systems is to provide equal service, the egalitarianism tends to be closer to *partial egalitarianism*. Every nation either has parallel private providers or its citizens are free to travel to a nation that does, so there is effectively a two-tier healthcare system that reduces the equality of service. Since private providers are typically better paid, those medical professionals motivated by remunerative concerns migrate to the private sector while the private hospitals also get newer and better equipment and facilities. A number of countries such as Australia attempt to solve the problem of unequal care by insisting that doctors divide their time between public and private systems.

Proponents of these parallel private systems argue that they are necessary to provide flexibility to the system and are a way to increase funding for the health care system as a whole by charging the wealthy more. Opponents believe that they are allowed to exist mainly because politicians and their friends are wealthy and would prefer better care. They also argue that all citizens should have access to high quality healthcare. The only country not to have any form of parallel private system for basic health care is Canada. However, wealthy Canadians can and travel to the United States for care.

Also, in some cases, doctors are so well paid in both systems that prestige is often more important to them than remuneration. This is very much the case in the United Kingdom where private medicine is seen as less prestigious than public medicine by much of the population. As a result, the best doctors tend to spend the majority of their time working for the public system, even though they may also do some work for private healthcare providers. The British in particular tend to use private healthcare to avoid waiting lists rather than because they believe that they will receive better care from it.

Difficulties of analysis

Cost-benefit analysis of healthcare is extremely difficult to do accurately, or to separate from emotional entanglement. For instance, prevention of smoking or obesity is presented as having the potential to save the costs of treating illnesses arising from those choices. Yet, if those illnesses are fatal or life shortening, they may reduce the eventual cost to the system of treating that person through the rest of their life, and it is possible that they will die of an illness every bit as expensive to treat as the ones they avoided by a healthy lifestyle.

This has to be balanced against the loss of taxation or insurance revenue that might come should a person have a longer productive (i.e. working and tax or insurance-paying) life. The cost-benefit analysis will be very different depending on whether you adopt a whole-life accounting, or consider each month as debits and credits on an insurance system. In a system financed by taxation, the greatest cost benefit comes from preserving the working life of those who are likely to pay the most tax in the future, i.e. the young and rich.

Few politicians would dare to present the big picture of costs in this way, because they would be condemned as callous. Nevertheless, behind the scenes, a responsible government must be performing cost analysis in order to balance its budget; it is not likely, however, to take the most purely cost effective route. It may choose to provide the *best* health care according to some other model, but the cost of this still must be estimated and funded, and there is no uncontroversial definition of *best*.

In producing a definition of quality of healthcare there is an implication that quality can be measured. In fact, the effectiveness of healthcare is extremely difficult to measure, not only because of medical uncertainty, but because of intangible quantities like *quality of life*. This is likely to lead to systems that measure *only* what is easy to measure (such as length of life, waiting times or infection rates). As a result the importance of treating chronic, but non-fatal, conditions, or of providing the best care for the terminally ill may be reduced. Thus, it is possible for personal satisfaction with the system to go down, while metrics go up.

Behavior and Environmental Influences on Health

The following sections explore some of the ways behaviors and environment can impact human health.

Smoking

The Centers for Disease Control and Prevention describes tobacco use as "the single most important preventable risk to human health in developed countries and an important cause of premature death worldwide" (source). A person's increased risk of contracting disease is directly proportional to the length of time that a person continues to smoke as well as the amount smoked. However, if someone stops smoking the risks of developing diseases steadily decline, although gradually, as the damage to their body is repaired.

The main health risks from tobacco smoking pertain to diseases of the cardiovascular system, in particular smoking is a major risk factor for: myocardial infarction (heart attack); diseases of the respiratory tract, such as Chronic Obstructive Pulmonary Disease (COPD) and emphysema; and cancer, particularly lung cancer and cancers of the larynx and tongue. Prior to World War I, lung cancer was considered to be a rare disease, one most physicians would never see during their career. With the postwar rise in popularity of cigarette smoking came a virtual epidemic of lung cancer.

Alcohol

Alcoholism is a dependency on alcohol characterized by craving (a strong need to drink), loss of control (being unable to stop drinking despite a desire to do so), physical dependence and withdrawal symptoms, and tolerance (increasing difficulty of becoming drunk).

Although acceptance of the *American Disease Model* is not without controversy, the American Medical Association, the American Psychiatric Association, the American Hospital Association, the American Public Health Association, the National Association of Social Workers, the World Health Organization, and the American College of Physicians have all classified alcoholism as a disease.

In a 1992 JAMA article, the Joint Committee of the National Council on Alcoholism and Drug Dependence and the American Society of Addiction Medicine published this definition for alcoholism: "Alcoholism is a primary chronic disease with genetic, psychosocial, and environmental factors influencing its development and manifestations. The disease is often progressive and fatal. It is characterized by impaired control over drinking, preoccupation with the drug alcohol, use of alcohol despite adverse consequences, and distortions in thinking, mostly denial. Each of these symptoms may be continuous or periodic."

Symptoms of a person's dependence on alcohol may include, but are not limited to, a feeling of necessity in regards to consumption of alcohol, or an inability to resist alcohol if offered. Though these symptoms often arise from a physical dependence on the substance, it is not uncommon for individuals, especially teenagers and adolescents between the ages of fifteen and twenty, to rely on alcohol as a means of social interaction. If a person cannot refuse alcohol in the presence of others, insists on drinking alcohol excessively for fear of alienation and neglect, or feels they cannot socially interact with others unless under the influence then this person is considered socially dependent on the substance. These traits can be noticed in individuals who relocate (such as students attending a new university) whereby an individual with no past history of alcohol consumption begins to consume alcohol in order to associate and relate to others. Social dependence, though not physically threatening in early stages, can lead to physical dependence if the person cannot control their urges and more so their reasons for drinking.

The causes for alcohol abuse and dependence cannot be easily explained, but the long-standing, unscientific prejudice that alcoholism is the result of moral or ethical weakness on the part of the sufferer has been largely altered. Recent polls show that 90% of Americans currently believe that alcoholism is, in fact, a disease (source?). Of the two thirds of the North American population who consume alcohol, 10% are alcoholics and 6% consume more than half of all alcohol. Stereotypes of alcoholics are often found in fiction and popular culture. In modern times, the recovery movement has led to more realistic portraits of alcoholics and their problems.

The social problems arising from alcoholism can include loss of employment, financial problems, marital conflict and divorce, convictions for crimes such as drunk driving or public disorder, loss of accommodation, and loss of respect from others who may see the problem as self-inflicted and easily avoided. Exhaustive studies, including those by author Wayne Kritsberg, show that alcoholism affects not only the addicted but can profoundly impact the family members around them. Children of alcoholics can be affected even after they are grown. This condition is usually referred to as *The Adult Children of Alcoholics Syndrome*. Al-Anon, a group modelled after Alcoholics Anonymous, offers aid to friends and family members of alcoholics.

Moderate Drinking

Of course, not everyone who consumes alcohol is an alcoholic or is at danger of becoming an alcoholic. In fact, there is some debate as to whether there are some benefits derived from moderate consumption of alcohol. The controversy over moderate drinking is an ongoing debate about the claimed benefit or harm to human health from moderate consumption of alcoholic beverages. Moderate consumption typically means the consumption of 1 to 3 drinks of an alcoholic beverage a day; the number varies with age and gender. There is wide consensus that over-drinking is harmful: alcohol damages human cells and organs such as the brain, liver and kidney.

Many studies show that consumers of up to 3 drinks a day have a 10% to 40% lower risk of coronary heart disease than those who abstain. Rimm *et al.* (1999) predict a 24.7% decrease in the risk of coronary heart disease based upon 30g alcohol/day.

Critics of moderate drinking claim that any benefits are far outweighed by the possible consequences of over consumption and that these benefits can be had by less risky means. Scientists also note that studies supporting the benefits of moderate drinking do not control for other factors, such as lifestyle differences between moderate drinkers and nondrinkers. There is evidence that moderate drinkers are more affluent than nondrinkers and as such lead lifestyles that are more conducive to good health in general.

Research on the effects of moderate drinking is in its early stages. No long term studies have been done and control groups would be difficult to establish because of the many variables. Given the current state of the research, an editorial concludes in the December 1997 issue of the *Journal of the Royal Society of Medicine* that the recommendation to be a moderate drinker is "not only meaningless but also irresponsible" given that the many obvious health hazards of alcohol outweigh "the benefits of alcohol [which] are small and ill-understood" particularly when so many other cardiovascular treatments are available.

Effects of fetal alcohol exposure

Fetal alcohol exposure is regarded by researchers as the leading known cause of mental and physical birth defects, surpassing both spina bifida and Down syndrome, producing more severe abnormalities than heroin, cocaine, or marijuana, and is the most common preventable cause of birth defects in the United States (source).

It can cause mental retardation, facial deformities, stunted physical and emotional development, behavioral problems, memory deficiencies, attention deficits, impulsiveness, an inability to reason from cause to effect; a failure to comprehend the concept of time; and an inability to tell reality from fantasy. Secondary disabilities develop over time because of problems fitting into the environment.

Researchers believe that the risk is highest early in the pregnancy, but there are risks throughout because the fetus' brain develops throughout the entire pregnancy. No amount of alcohol, during any trimester, is absolutely safe.

Obesity

Obesity is a condition in which the natural energy reserve of humans, which is stored in fat tissue, is expanded far beyond usual levels to the point where it impairs health. While cultural and scientific definitions of obesity are subject to change, it is accepted that excessive body weight predisposes to various forms of disease, particularly cardiovascular disease.

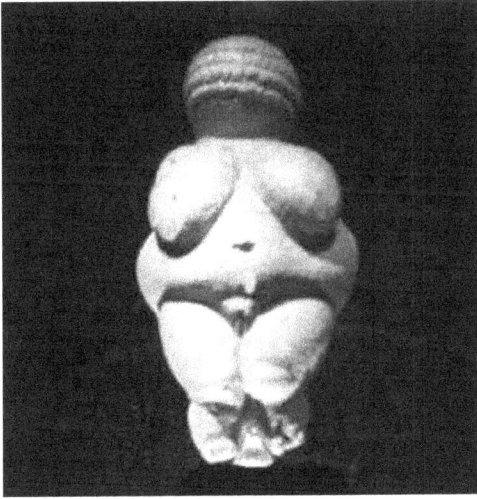
Venus of Willendorf

There is continuous debate over obesity, at several levels. The scientific evidence informing these debates is more contradictory than most simple arguments assume. Statistics demonstrating correlations are typically misinterpreted in public discussion as demonstrating causation, a fallacy known as the spurious relationship.

In several human cultures, obesity is (or has been) associated with attractiveness, strength, and fertility. Some of the earliest known cultural artifacts, known as Venuses, are pocket-sized statuettes representing an obese female figure. Although their cultural significance is unrecorded, their widespread use throughout pre-historic Mediterranean and European cultures suggests a central role for the obese female form in magical rituals and implies cultural approval of (and perhaps reverence for) this body form.

Obesity functions as a symbol of wealth and success in cultures prone to food scarcity. Well into the early modern period in European cultures, it still served this role. Contemporary cultures which approve of obesity, to a greater degree than European and Western cultures, include African, Arabic, Indian, and Pacific Island cultures. In Western cultures, obesity has come to be seen more as a medical condition than as a social statement.

Figure 6.3. Age-adjusted prevalence of obesity among adults aged 20 years and over, by sex and race/ethnicity: United States, 2004

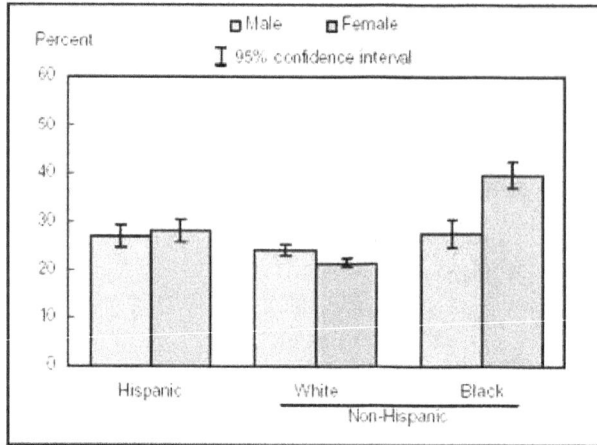

NOTES: Obesity is defined as a Body Mass Index (BMI) of 30 kg/m² or more. The measure is based on self-reported height and weight. The analyses excluded 1521 people (5.0%) with unknown height or weight. Estimates are age-adjusted to the 2000 projected U.S. standard population using five age groups: 20-24 years, 25-34 years, 35-44 years, 45-64 years, and 65 years and over.

DATA SOURCE: Sample Adult Core component of the 2004 National Health Interview Survey.

Various stereotypes of obese people have found their way into expressions of popular culture. A common stereotype is the obese character who has a warm and dependable personality, presumedly in compensation for social exclusion, but equally common is the obese vicious bully. Gluttony and obesity are commonly depicted together in works of fiction. It can be argued that depiction in popular culture adds to and maintains commonly perceived stereotypes, in turn harming the self esteem of obese people. A charge of prejudice and/or discrimination on the basis of appearance could be leveled against these depictions.

Causes of Obesity

Conventional wisdom holds that obesity is caused by over-indulgence in fatty or sugary foods, portrayed as either a failure of will power or a species of addiction. Various specialists strongly oppose this view. For example, Professor Thomas Sanders, the director of the Nutrition, Food & Health Research Centre at King's College London, emphasises the need for balance between activity and consumption:

In trials, there is no evidence suggesting that reducing fat intake has an effect on obesity. As long as your expenditure equals what you eat, you won't put on weight, regardless of how high the fat content is in your diet (The Times, London, 10 March 2004).

Obesity is generally a result of a combination of factors:

- Genetic predisposition

218

- Energy-rich <u>diet</u>

- Limited exercise and sedentary lifestyle

- <u>Weight cycling</u>, caused by repeated attempts to lose weight by dieting

- Underlying illness

- Certain <u>eating disorders</u>

  Some eating disorders can lead to obesity, especially <u>binge eating disorder</u> (BED). As the name indicates, patients with this disorder are prone to overeat, often in binges. A proposed mechanism is that the eating serves to reduce anxiety, and some parallels with substance abuse can be drawn. An important additional factor is that BED patients often lack the ability to recognize hunger and satisfaction, something that is normally learned in childhood. <u>Learning theory</u> suggests that early childhood conceptions may lead to an association between food and a calm mental state.

  While it is often quite obvious why a certain individual gets fat, it is far more difficult to understand why the average weight of certain societies have recently been growing. While genetic causes are central to who is obese, they cannot explain why one culture grows fatter than another.

Figure 1. Prevalence of overweight among children and adolescents ages 6-19 years

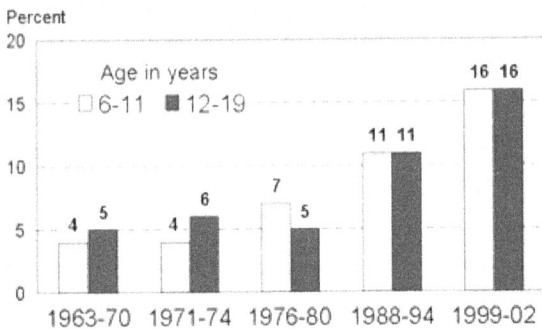

NOTE: Excludes pregnant women starting with 1971-74. Pregnancy status not available for 1963-65 and 1966-70. Data for 1963-65 are for children 6-11 years of age, data for 1966-70 are for adolescents 12-17 years of age, not 12-19 years. SOURCE: CDC/NCHS, NHES and NHANES

Increase in Overweight among US Children and Adolescents.

Although there is no definitive explanation for the recent epidemic of obesity, the <u>evolutionary</u> hypothesis comes closest to providing some understanding of this phenomenon. In times when food was scarce, the ability to take advantage of rare periods of abundance and use such abundance by storing energy efficiently was undoubtedly an evolutionary advantage. This is precisely the opposite of what is required in a sedentary society, where high-energy food is available in abundant quantities in the context of decreased exercise. Although many people may have a genetic propensity towards obesity, it is only with the reduction in physical activity and a move towards high-calorie diets of modern society that it has become so widespread.

The obesity epidemic is most notable in the United States. In the years from just after the Second World War until 1960 the average person's weight increased, but few were obese. In 1960 almost the entire population was well fed, but not overweight. In the two and a half decades since 1980 the growth in the rate of obesity has accelerated markedly and is increasingly becoming a public health concern. There are a number of theories as to the cause of this change since 1980. Most believe it is a combination of various factors:

- Obese people appear to be less active in general than lean people, and not just because of their obesity. A controlled increase in calorie intake of lean people did not make them less active, nor, correspondingly, when obese people lost weight did they become more active. Weight change does not affect activity levels, but the converse seems to be the case (Levine 2005).

- Another important contributor to the current obesity concern is the much lower relative cost of foodstuffs: agricultural subsidies in the United States and Europe have led to lower food prices for consumers than at any other point in history.

- Marketing may also play a role. In the early 1980s the Reagan administration lifted most regulations for advertising to children. As a result, the number of commercials seen by the average child increased greatly, and a large proportion of these were for fast food and candy (source?).

- Changes in the price of gasoline may also have had an effect, as unlike during the 1970s it is now affordable in the United States to drive everywhere, curtailing both foot traffic and the riding of bikes. An indication of the reliance on cars in the U.S. is the increasing number of areas that are built without sidewalks and parks.

- Increases in the service sector of the economy have resulted in a greater percentage of the population spending most of their workday behind a desk or computer.

- A social cause that is believed by many to play a role is the increasing number of *two income households* where one parent no longer remains home to look after the house. This increases the number of restaurant and take-out meals.

- Urban sprawl may also contribute to the increase in obesity rates, possibly due to less walking and less time for cooking (Lopez 2004).

- Since 1980 both sit-in and fast food restaurants have seen dramatic growth in terms of the number of outlets and customers served. Low food costs and intense competition for market share led to increased portion sizes. For example, McDonalds' french fries portions rose from 200 calories in 1960 to over 600 calories today.

- Increasing affluence itself may be a cause or contributing factor since obesity tends to flourish as a disease of affluence in countries which are developing and becoming westernised (for more information on this factor, see here). This is supported by the observation of a dip in American GDP after 1990, the year of the Gulf War, followed by an exponential increase. U.S. obesity statistics followed the same pattern, offset by two years (source).

Some obesity co-factors are resistant to the theory that the *epidemic* is a new phenomenon. In particular, a class co-factor consistently appears across many studies. Comparing net worth with BMI scores, a 2004 study (Zagorsky 2004) found obese American subjects approximately half as wealthy as thin ones. When income differentials were factored out, the inequity persisted: thin subjects were inheriting more wealth than fat ones. Another study finds women who married into a higher status were thinner than women who married into lower status.

Policy Responses to Obesity

On top of controversies about the causes of obesity, and about its precise health implications, come policy controversies about the correct policy approach to obesity. The main debate is between *personal responsibility* advocates, who resist regulatory attempts to intervene in citizen's private dietary habits, and *public interest* advocates, who promote regulations on the same public health grounds as the restrictions applied to tobacco products. In the U.S., a recent bout in this controversy involves the so-called Cheeseburger Bill, an attempt to indemnify food industry businesses from frivolous law suits by obese clients.

On July 16, 2004, the U.S. Department of Health and Human Services officially classified obesity as a disease. Speaking to a Senate committee, Tommy Thompson, the Secretary of Health and Human Services, stated that Medicare would cover obesity-related health problems. However, reimbursement would not be given if a treatment was not proven to be effective.

References

- Levine JA, Lanningham-Foster LM, McCrady SK, Krizan AC, Olson LR, Kane PH, Jensen MD, Clark MM. *Interindividual variation in posture allocation: possible role in human obesity*. Science 2005;307:584-6. PMID 15681386.

- Lopez R. *Urban sprawl and risk for being overweight or obese*. Am J Publ Health 2004;94:1574-9. PMID 15333317.

- Rimm et al, 1999 (missing reference)

- December 1997 issue of the JOURNAL OF THE ROYAL SOCIETY OF MEDICINE [90(12):651

- Diamond 2003 (missing reference)

This chapter also draws heavily on the following Wikipedia articles:

- obesity

- folk medicine

- alternative medicine

- health insurance

- smoking

- alcoholism

External links

- International health statistics comparison

- International Health Statistics: What the Numbers Mean for the United States - 1994

- Joint CDC/StatsCan comparison on the two health care systems - 2004 (pdf)

- Fetal Alcohol Syndrome Diagnostic & Prevention Network (FAS DPN)

- Well.com FAS Fact Sheet

- FAQ on FAS from National Organization on Fetal Alcohol Syndrome

- Dr Sterling Clarren's keynote address on FASD, Prairie Northern Conference on Fetal Alcohol Syndrome, Yukon 2002

- Moderate alcohol intake and lower risk of coronary heart disease: meta-analysis of effects on lipids and haemostatic factors

- National Center on Minority Health and Health Disparities

- Understanding Health Disparities

- Initiative to Eliminate Racial and Ethnic Disparities in Health United States government minority health initiative

- Health Disparities Collaborative

- American Public Health Association. "Eliminating Health Disparities: Toolkit" (2004)

- Obesity, BMI and Calorie assessment Calculators

- Body Mass Index Calculator

- Obesity advice / FAQs

- International Task Force on Obesity

- Childhood Obesity

- Argument that the concern for obesity is overwrought

- BMJ Article on Obesity and Public policy

- Economics of Obesity

- *The Worldwide Obesity Epidemic* by Frank Sacks MD

Collective behaviour

Introduction

Collective behavior refers to the action or behavior of people in groups or crowds where, due to physical proximity and properties of the group, individual behavior deviates from normal, tending toward unpredictable and potentially explosive behavior. Collective behavior does not reflect existing social structure (e.g., laws, conventions, and institutions) but emerges in a *spontaneous* way. The category excludes conforming events, such as religious rituals and conversation at the dinner table, and also deviant events, such as crime or the exercise of bad manners. Examples of collective behavior episodes might include: religious revivals, panics in burning theatres, outbreaks of swastika painting on synagogues, a change in popular preferences in toothpaste, the Russian Revolution, and a sudden widespread interest in body piercing. Mother =fat Collective behavior differs from *group* behavior in three ways:

6.   collective behavior involves limited social interaction; groups tend to remain together longer than do collectivities

7.   collective behavior has no clear social boundaries; anyone can be a member of the collective while group membership is usually more discriminating

8.   collective behavior generates weak and unconventional norms; groups tend to have stronger and more conventional norms

The term collective behavior was first used by Robert E. Park, and employed definitively by Herbert Blumer. The claim that this set of seemingly diverse episodes constitutes a single field of inquiry is, of course, a theoretical assertion - one with which not all sociologists will concur. But numerous classic articles testify to the viability of the definition and field of inquiry (see Blumer 1951, Smelser 1963, and Turner and Killian 1987).

Collective behavior can be differentiated into several categories, each with its own properties. These are discussed in turn below.

Crowds

A *crowd* is a gathering of people who share a purpose or intent and influence one another. Crowds are a common occurrence in modern life. Most sporting events, concerts, and other performances result in the gathering of crowds. Blumer (1951) differentiated four types of crowds:

- casual - loose collection of people with no real interaction (e.g, people at the mall)

- conventional - deliberately planned meeting (e.g., community meeting organized by political leaders)

- expressive - depicts a crowd at an emotionally charged event (e.g., a political rally or soccer game in Europe or Latin America)

- acting - a crowd intent on accomplishing something (e.g., fans rushing a stage during or after a concert)

When crowd behavior is directed toward a specific, violent end, the result is a mob. Mobs tend to be highly emotional. Examples of mob violence include the lynchings of the Southern U.S. during the 19th and 20th centuries. Violent crowd behavior without a specific goal is a riot. Because riots do not have a specific end, it is assumed that their intention is to express general dissatisfaction.

Panic

Panic is a sudden terror which dominates thinking and often affects groups of people. Panics typically occur in disaster situations, such as during a fire, and may endanger the overall health of the affected group. Architects and city planners try to accommodate the symptoms of panic, such as herd behavior, during design and planning, often using simulations to determine the best way to lead people to a safe exit.

Confrontation between protestors and riot police during a Belizian riot, 2005.

Theories of Crowd Behavior

Contagion Theory

Originally proposed by Gustave LeBon (1896), *contagion theory* proposes that crowds exert a hypnotic influence on their members. The hypnotic influence, combined with the anonymity of belonging to a large group of people, results in irrational, emotionally charged behavior. Or, as the name implies, the frenzy of the crowd is somehow *contagious*, like a disease, and the contagion feeds upon itself, growing with time. This also implies that the behavior of a crowd is an emergent property of the people coming together and not a property of the people themselves.

There are several problems with LeBon's theory. First, contagion theory presents members of crowds as irrational. Much crowd behavior, however, is actually the result of rational fear (e.g., being trapped in a burning theater) or a rational sense of injustice (e.g., the Cincinnati race riots). Second, crowd behavior is often instigated by and guided by individuals. That the crowd seems to take on a life of its own is certainly true, but the influence of the individual should not be overlooked.

It is also worth noting that LeBon's book is from the perspective of a frightened aristocrat. He interprets the crowd episodes of the French Revolution as irrational reversions to animal emotion, which he sees as characteristic of crowds in general. Blumer sees crowds as emotional, but as capable of any emotion, not only the negative ones of anger and fear.

Convergence Theory

Convergence theory argues that the behavior of a crowd is not an emergent property of the crowd but is a result of like-minded individuals coming together. In other words, if a crowd becomes violent (a mob or riot), convergence theory would argue that this is not because the crowd encouraged violence but rather because people who wanted to become violent came together in the crowd.

The primary criticism of convergence theory is that there is a tendency for people to do things in a crowd that they would not do on their own. Crowds have an anonymizing effect on people, leading them to engage in sometimes outlandish behavior. Thus, while some crowds may result from like-minded individuals coming together to act collectively (e.g., political rally), some crowds actually spur individuals into behavior that they would otherwise not engage in.

Emergent-Norm Theory

Emergent-Norm Theory combines the above two theories, arguing that it is a combination of like-minded individuals, anonymity, and shared emotion that leads to crowd behavior. This theory takes a symbolic interactionist approach to understanding crowd behavior. It argues that people come together with specific expectations and norms, but in the interactions that follow the development of the crowd, new expectations and norms can emerge, allowing for behavior that normally would not take place.

Diffuse Crowds

Collective behavior can also refer to behavior that is diffuse or dispersed over large distances. Not all collective behavior has to occur in the immediate vicinity of others (local crowds). This is especially true with the advent of mass media, which allows for the rapid distribution of information around the world.

Mass Hysteria

Hysteria is a diagnostic label applied to a state of mind, one of unmanageable fear or emotional excesses. People who are "hysterical" often lose self-control due to the overwhelming fear.

The term also occurs in the phrase *mass hysteria* to describe mass public near-panic reactions. It is commonly applied to the waves of popular medical problems that *everyone gets* in response to news articles, such as the yuppy flu of the late 1980s. A similar usage refers to any sort of *public wave* phenomenon, and has been used to describe the periodic widespread reappearance and public interest in UFO reports, crop circles, and similar examples.

Hysteria is often associated with movements like the Salem Witch Trials, the Red Scare, McCarthyism, and Satanic ritual abuse, where it is better understood through the related sociological term of *moral panic*.

Moral Panic

A *moral panic* is a mass movement based on the perception that some individual or group, frequently a minority group or a subculture, is dangerously deviant and poses a menace to society. These panics are generally fuelled by media coverage of social issues (although semi-spontaneous moral panics do occur), and often include a large element of mass hysteria. A moral panic is specifically framed in terms of morality, and usually expressed as outrage rather than unadulterated fear. Though not always, very often moral panics revolve around issues of sex and sexuality. A widely circulated and new-seeming urban legend is frequently involved. These panics can sometimes lead to mob violence. The term was coined by Stanley Cohen in 1972 to describe media coverage of Mods and Rockers in the United Kingdom in the 1960s.

Image:Heavinsteven.jpg Image from the Garbage Pail Kids fad.

Recent moral panics in the UK have included the ongoing tabloid newspaper campaign against pedophiles, which led to the assault and persecution of a pediatrician by an angry, if semi-literate, mob in August 2000, and that surrounding the murder of James Bulger in Liverpool, England in 1993. (See this page for examples of moral panic.)

Fads

A fad, also known as a craze, refers to a fashion that becomes popular in a culture (or subcultures) relatively quickly, remains popular, often for a rather brief period, then loses popularity dramatically. (See this page for a list of fads.)

Research Examples

Berk (1974) uses *game theory* to suggest that even a panic in a burning theater can reflect rational calculation: If members of the audience decide that it is more rational to run to the exits than to walk, the result may look like an animal-like stampede without in fact being irrational. In a series of empirical studies of assemblies of people, McPhail (1991) argues that such assemblies vary along a number of dimensions, and that traditional stereotypes of emotionality and unanimity often do not describe what happens.

Notes

References

- Berk, Richard. 1974. Collective Behavior. W. C. Brown Co. ISBN 0697075257

- Blumer, Herbert. 1951. Collective Behavior. In Lee, Alfred McClung, Ed., Principles of Sociology. Second Edition. Barnes and Noble. ASIN B0007I3ODA

- LeBon, Gustave. 1896. The Crowd: A Study of the Popular Mind. Dover Publications ISBN 0486419568

- McPhail, Clark. 1991. The Myth of the Madding Crowd. .Aldine. ISBN 0202303756

- Smelser, Neil J.. 1963. Theory of Collective Behavior. Free Press. ISBN 0029293901

- Turner, Ralph H. and Killian, Lewis M.. 1987. Collective Behavior. Third Edition. Prentice Hall College Division. ISBN 0131406825

This chapter draws heavily on the following Wikipedia articles:

- collective behavior

- fad

- panic

- hysteria

External Links

Social movements

Introduction

Social movements are any broad social alliances of people who are connected through their shared interest in blocking or affecting social change. Social movements do not have to be formally organized. Multiple alliances may work separately for common causes and still be considered a social movement.

A distinction is drawn between social movements and *social movement organizations* (SMOs). A social movement organization is a formally organized component of a social movement. But an SMO may only make up a part of a particular social movement. For instance, PETA (People for the Ethical Treatment of Animals) advocates for vegan lifestyles along with its other aims. But PETA is not the only group to advocate for vegan diets and lifestyles; there are numerous other groups actively engaged toward this end (see vegan and Maurer 2002). Thus, the social movement may be a push toward veganism (an effort with numerous motivations; see Maurer 2002) and PETA is an SMO working within the broader social movement.

Modern social movements became possible through the wider dissemination of literature and increased mobility of labor due to the industrialization of societies. Organised social structures like modern day armies, political societies, and popular movements required freedom of expression, education and relative economic independence.

Giddens (1985) has identified four areas in which social movements operate in modern societies:

9. democratic movements that work for political rights

10. labor movements that work for control of the workplace

11. ecological movements that are concerned with the environment

12. peace movements that work toward, well, peace

It is also interesting to note that social movements can spawn counter movements. For instance, the women's movement of the 1960s and 1970s resulted in a number of counter movements that attempted to block the goals of the women's movement, many of which were reform movements within conservative religions (see Chaves 1997).

Types of Social Movements

Aberle (1966) described four types of social movements based upon two characteristics: (1) who is the movement attempting to change and (2) how much change is being advocated. Social movements can be aimed at change on an individual level (e.g., AA) or change on a broader, group or even societal level (e.g., anti-globalization). Social movements can also advocate for minor changes (e.g., tougher restrictions on drunk driving; see MADD) or radical

229

changes (e.g., prohibition).

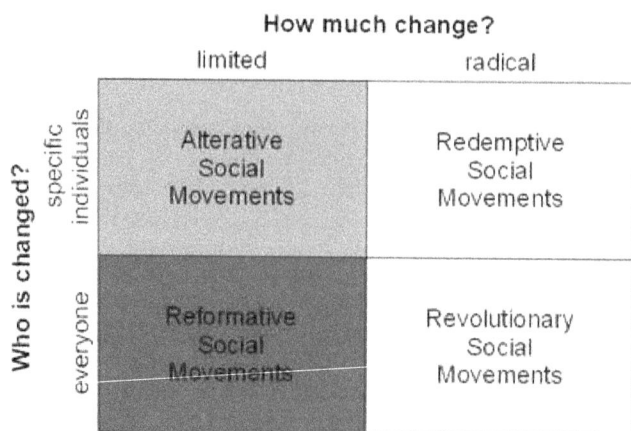

How much change?

	limited	radical
specific individuals	Alterative Social Movements	Redemptive Social Movements
everyone	Reformative Social Movements	Revolutionary Social Movements

Who is changed?

Based on Aberle (1966)

Stages in Social Movements

Blumer (1969), Mauss (1975), and Tilly (1978) have described different stages social movements often pass through. Movements emerge for a variety of reasons (see the theories below), coalesce, and generally bureaucratize. At that point, they can take a number of paths, including: finding some form of movement success, failure, co-optation of leaders, repression by larger groups (e.g., government), or even the establishment of the movement within the mainstream.

Whether these paths will result in movement decline or not varies from movement to movement. In fact, one of the difficulties in studying social movements is that movement success is often ill-defined because movement goals can change. For instance, MoveOn.org, a website founded in the late 1990s, was originally developed to encourage national politicians to move past the Clinton impeachment proceedings (see here). Since that time, the group has developed into a major player in national politics in the U.S. and developed into a Political Action Committee or PAC. In this instance, the movement may or may not have attained its original goal - encouraging the censure of Clinton and moving on to more pressing issues - but the goals of the SMO have changed. This makes the actual stages the movement has passed through difficult to discern.

Stages of Social Movements

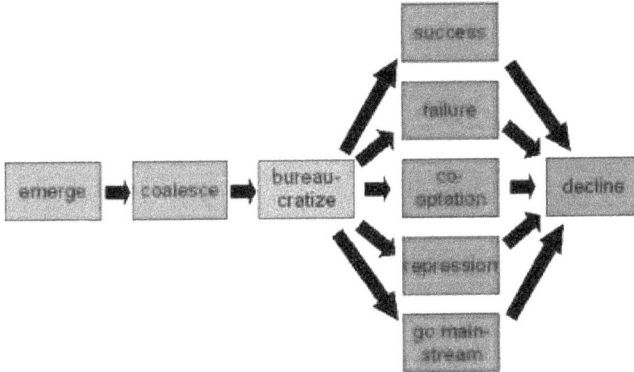

Adapted from Blumer (1969), Mauss (1975), and Tilly (1978)

Social Movement Theories

A variety of theories have attempted to explain how social movements develop. Some of the better-known approaches are outlined below.

Deprivation Theory

Deprivation Theory argues that social movements have their foundations among people who feel deprived of some good(s) or resource(s). According to this approach, individuals who are lacking some good, service, or comfort are more likely to organize a social movement to improve (or defend) their conditions (Morrison 1978).

There are two significant problems with this theory. First, since most people feel deprived at one level or another almost all the time, the theory has a hard time explaining why the groups that form social movements do when other people are also deprived. Second, the reasoning behind this theory is circular - often the only evidence for deprivation is the social movement. If deprivation is claimed to be the cause but the only evidence for such is the movement, the reasoning is circular (Jenkins and Perrow 1977).

Mass-Society Theory

Mass-Society Theory argues that social movements are made up of individuals in large societies who feel insignificant or socially detached. Social movements, according to this theory, provide a sense of empowerment and belonging that the movement members would otherwise not have (Kornhauser 1959).

Very little support has been found for this theory. Aho (1990), in his study of Idaho Christian Patriotism, did not find that members of that movement were more likely to have been socially

231

detached. In fact, the key to joining the movement was having a friend or associate who was a member of the movement.

Structural-Strain Theory

Structural-Strain Theory proposes six factors that encourage social movement development (Smelser 1962):

8. structural conduciveness - people come to believe their society has problems

9. structural strain - people experience deprivation

10. growth and spread of a solution - a solution to the problems people are experiencing is proposed and spreads

11. precipitating factors - discontent usually requires a catalyst (often a specific event) to turn it into a social movement

12. lack of social control - the entity that is to be changed must be at least somewhat open to the change; if the social movement is quickly and powerfully repressed, it may never materialize

13. mobilization - this is the actual organizing and active component of the movement; people do what needs to be done

This theory is also subject to circular reasoning as it incorporates, at least in part, deprivation theory and relies upon it, and social/structural strain for the underlying motivation of social movement activism. However, social movement activism is, like in the case of deprivation theory, often the only indication that there was strain or deprivation.

Resource-Mobilization Theory

Resource-Mobilization Theory emphasizes the importance of resources in social movement development and success. Resources are understood here to include: knowledge, money, media, labor, solidarity, legitimacy, and internal and external support from power elite. The theory argues that social movements develop when individuals with grievances are able to mobilize sufficient resources to take action. The emphasis on resources offers an explanation why some discontented/deprived individuals are able to organize while others are not.

Some of the assumptions of the theory include:

• there will always be grounds for protest in modern, politically pluralistic societies because there is constant discontent (i.e., grievances or deprivation); this de-emphasizes the importance of these factors as it makes them ubiquitous

• actors are rational; they weigh the costs and benefits from movement participation

• members are recruited through networks; commitment is maintained by building a collective identity and continuing to nurture interpersonal relationships

- movement organization is contingent upon the aggregation of resources

- social movement organizations require resources and continuity of leadership

- social movement entrepreneurs and protest organizations are the catalysts which transform collective discontent into social movements; social movement organizations form the *backbone* of social movements

- the form of the resources shapes the activities of the movement (e.g., access to a TV station will result in the extensive use TV media)

- movements develop in contingent *opportunity structures* that influence their efforts to mobilize; as each movement's response to the opportunity structures depends on the movement's organization and resources, there is no clear pattern of movement development nor are specific movement techniques or methods universal

Critics of this theory argue that there is too much of an emphasize on resources, especially financial resources. Some movements are effective without an influx of money and are more dependent upon the movement members for time and labor (e.g., the civil rights movement in the U.S.).

Political Process Theory

Political Process Theory is similar to resource mobilization in many regards, but tends to emphasize a different component of social structure that is important for social movement development: political opportunities. Political process theory argues that there are three vital components for movement formation: insurgent consciousness, organizational strength, and political opportunities.

Insurgent consciousness refers back to the ideas of deprivation and grievances. The idea is that certain members of society feel like they are being mistreated or that somehow the system is unjust. The insurgent consciousness is the collective sense of injustice that movement members (or potential movement members) feel and serves as the motivation for movement organization.

Photo taken at the 2005 U.S. Presidential inauguration protest.

233

Organizational strength falls inline with resource-mobilization theory, arguing that in order for a social movement to organize it must have strong leadership and sufficient resources.

Political opportunity refers to the receptivity or vulnerability of the existing political system to challenge. This vulnerability can be the result of any of the following (or a combination thereof):

- growth of political pluralism

- decline in effectiveness of repression

- elite disunity; the leading factions are internally fragmented

- a broadening of access to institutional participation in political processes

- support of organized opposition by elites

One of the advantages of the political process theory is that it addresses the issue of timing or emergence of social movements. Some groups may have the insurgent consciousness and resources to mobilize, but because political opportunities are closed, they will not have any success. The theory, then, argues that all three of these components are important.

Critics of the political process theory and resource-mobilization theory point out that neither theory discusses movement culture to any great degree. This has presented culture theorists an opportunity to expound on the importance of culture.

One advance on the political process theory is the *political mediation model,* which outlines the way in which the political context facing movement actors intersects with the strategic choices that movements make. An additional strength of this model is that it can look at the outcomes of social movements not only in terms of success or failure but also in terms of consequences (whether intentional or unintentional, positive or negative) and in terms of collective benefits.

Culture Theory

Culture theory builds upon both the political process and resource-mobilization theories but extends them in two ways. First, it emphasizes the importance of movement culture. Second, it attempts to address the *free-rider problem*.

Both resource-mobilization theory and political process theory include a sense of injustice in their approaches. Culture theory brings this sense of injustice to the forefront of movement creation by arguing that, in order for social movements to successfully mobilize individuals, they must develop an *injustice frame*. An injustice frame is a collection of ideas and symbols that illustrate both how significant the problem is as well as what the movement can do to alleviate it.

In emphasizing the injustice frame, culture theory also addresses the free-rider problem. The free-rider problem refers to the idea that people will not be motivated to participate in a social movement that will use up their personal resources (e.g., time, money, etc.) if they can still receive the benefits without participating. In other words, if person X knows that movement Y is working to improve environmental conditions in his neighborhood, he is presented with a choice: join or not join the movement. If he believes the movement will succeed without him, he can avoid participation in the movement, save his resources, and still reap the benefits - this is *free-riding*. A significant problem for social movement theory has been to explain why people join movements if they believe the movement can/will succeed without their contribution. Culture theory argues that, in conjunction with social networks being an important contact tool, the injustice frame will provide the motivation for people to contribute to the movement.

Examples of Social Movements

- civil rights movement in the United States

- environmental movement

- green movement

- gay rights movement

- labor movement

- anti-globalization movement

- vegetarian movement

Notes

Additional Topics may include:

- Joining Movements

References

- Aberle, David F. 1966. The Peyote Religion among the Navaho. Chicago: Aldine. ISBN 0806123826

- Aho, James Alfred. 1990. Politics of Righteousness: Idaho Christian Patriotism. Washington: University of Washington Press. ISBN 0295969970

- Blumer, Herbert G. 1969. "Collective Behavior." In Alfred McClung Lee, ed., Principles of Sociology. Third Edition. New York: Barnes and Noble Books, pp. 65-121.

- Chaves, Mark. 1997. Ordaining Women: Culture and Conflict in Religious Organizations. Cambridge: Harvard University Press. ISBN 0674641469

- Giddens, Anthony. 1985. The Nation-State and Violence. Cambridge, England: Polity Press.

ISBN 0520060393

- Jenkins, J. Craig and Perrow, Charles. 1977. Insurgency of the Powerless Farm Worker Movements (1946-1972). American Sociological Review. 42(2):249-268.

- Kornhauser, William. 1959. The Politics of Mass Society. New York: Free Press. ISBN 0029176204

- Maurer, Donna. 2002. Vegetarianism: Movement or Moment? Philadelphia: Temple University Press. ISBN 156639936X

- Mauss, Armand L. 1975. Social Problems of Social Movements. Philadelphia: Lippincott.

- Morrison, Denton E. 1978. "Some Notes toward Theory on Relative Deprivation, Social Movements, and Social Change." In Louis E. Genevie, ed., Collective Behavior and Social Movements. Itasca, Ill.: Peacock. pp. 202-209.

- Smelser, Neil J. 1962. Theory of Collective Behavior. New York: Free Press. ISBN 0029293901

- Tilly, Charles. 1978. From Mobilization to Revolution. Reading, Massachusetts: Addison-Wesley, 1978.

This page draws heavily on the following Wikipedia articles:

- social movement

External Links

Human ecology

Human ecology

4.   Rural

5.   Urban

For now, read the Wikipedia articles:

- urban sociology

- rural sociology

- ecology

License

GNU Free Documentation License

Version 1.2, November 2002

0. PREAMBLE

The purpose of this License is to make a manual, textbook, or other functional and useful document "free" in the sense of freedom: to assure everyone the effective freedom to copy and redistribute it, with or without modifying it, either commercially or noncommercially. Secondarily, this License preserves for the author and publisher a way to get credit for their work, while not being considered responsible for modifications made by others.

This License is a kind of "copyleft", which means that derivative works of the document must themselves be free in the same sense. It complements the GNU General Public License, which is a copyleft license designed for free software.

We have designed this License in order to use it for manuals for free software, because free software needs free documentation: a free program should come with manuals providing the same freedoms that the software does. But this License is not limited to software manuals; it can be used for any textual work, regardless of subject matter or whether it is published as a printed book. We recommend this License principally for works whose purpose is instruction or reference.

1. APPLICABILITY AND DEFINITIONS

This License applies to any manual or other work, in any medium, that contains a notice placed by the copyright holder saying it can be distributed under the terms of this License. Such a notice grants a world-wide, royalty-free license, unlimited in duration, to use that work under the conditions stated herein. The "Document", below, refers to any such manual or work. Any member of the public is a licensee, and is addressed as "you". You accept the license if you copy, modify or distribute the work in a way requiring permission under copyright law.

A "Modified Version" of the Document means any work containing the Document or a portion of it, either copied verbatim, or with modifications and/or translated into another language.

A "Secondary Section" is a named appendix or a front-matter section of the Document that deals exclusively with the relationship of the publishers or authors of the Document to the Document's overall subject (or to related matters) and contains nothing that could fall directly within that overall subject. (Thus, if the Document is in part a textbook of mathematics, a Secondary Section may not explain any mathematics.) The relationship could be a matter of historical connection with the subject or with related matters, or of legal, commercial, philosophical, ethical or political position regarding them.

The "Invariant Sections" are certain Secondary Sections whose titles are designated, as being those of Invariant Sections, in the notice that says that the Document is released under this License. If a section does not fit the above definition of Secondary then it is not allowed to be designated as Invariant. The Document may contain zero Invariant Sections. If the Document does not identify any Invariant Sections then there are none.

The "Cover Texts" are certain short passages of text that are listed, as Front-Cover Texts or Back-Cover Texts, in the notice that says that the Document is released under this License. A Front-Cover Text may be at most 5 words, and a Back-Cover Text may be at most 25 words.

A "Transparent" copy of the Document means a machine-readable copy, represented in a format whose specification is available to the general public, that is suitable for revising the document straightforwardly with generic text editors or (for images composed of pixels) generic paint programs or (for drawings) some widely available drawing editor, and that is suitable for input to text formatters or for automatic translation to a variety of formats suitable for input to text formatters. A copy made in an otherwise Transparent file format whose markup, or absence of markup, has been arranged to thwart or discourage subsequent modification by readers is not Transparent. An image format is not Transparent if used for any substantial amount of text. A copy that is not "Transparent" is called "Opaque".

Examples of suitable formats for Transparent copies include plain ASCII without markup, Texinfo input format, LaTeX input format, SGML or XML using a publicly available DTD, and standard-conforming simple HTML, PostScript or PDF designed for human modification. Examples of transparent image formats include PNG, XCF and JPG. Opaque formats include proprietary formats that can be read and edited only by proprietary word processors, SGML or XML for which the DTD and/or processing tools are not generally available, and the machine-generated HTML, PostScript or PDF produced by some word processors for output purposes only.

The "Title Page" means, for a printed book, the title page itself, plus such following pages as are needed to hold, legibly, the material this License requires to appear in the title page. For works in formats which do not have any title page as such, "Title Page" means the text near the most prominent appearance of the work's title, preceding the beginning of the body of the text.

A section "Entitled XYZ" means a named subunit of the Document whose title either is precisely XYZ or contains XYZ in parentheses following text that translates XYZ in another language. (Here XYZ stands for a specific section name mentioned below, such as "Acknowledgements", "Dedications", "Endorsements", or "History".) To "Preserve the Title" of such a section when you modify the Document means that it remains a section "Entitled XYZ" according to this definition.

The Document may include Warranty Disclaimers next to the notice which states that this License applies to the Document. These Warranty Disclaimers are considered to be included by reference in this License, but only as regards disclaiming warranties: any other implication that these Warranty Disclaimers may have is void and has no effect on the meaning of this License.

2. VERBATIM COPYING

You may copy and distribute the Document in any medium, either commercially or noncommercially, provided that this License, the copyright notices, and the license notice saying this License applies to the Document are reproduced in all copies, and that you add no other conditions whatsoever to those of this License. You may not use technical measures to obstruct or control the reading or further copying of the copies you make or distribute. However, you may accept compensation in exchange for copies. If you distribute a large enough number of copies you must also follow the conditions in section 3.

You may also lend copies, under the same conditions stated above, and you may publicly display copies.

3. COPYING IN QUANTITY

If you publish printed copies (or copies in media that commonly have printed covers) of the Document, numbering more than 100, and the Document's license notice requires Cover Texts, you must enclose the copies in covers that carry, clearly and legibly, all these Cover Texts: Front-Cover Texts on the front cover, and Back-Cover Texts on the back cover. Both covers must also clearly and legibly identify you as the publisher of these copies. The front cover must present the full title with all words of the title equally prominent and visible. You may add other material on the covers in addition. Copying with changes limited to the covers, as long as they preserve the title of the Document and satisfy these conditions, can be treated as verbatim copying in other respects.

If the required texts for either cover are too voluminous to fit legibly, you should put the first ones listed (as many as fit reasonably) on the actual cover, and continue the rest onto adjacent pages.

If you publish or distribute Opaque copies of the Document numbering more than 100, you must either include a machine-readable Transparent copy along with each Opaque copy, or state in or with each Opaque copy a computer-network location from which the general network-using public has access to download using public-standard network protocols a complete Transparent copy of the Document, free of added material. If you use the latter option, you must take reasonably prudent steps, when you begin distribution of Opaque copies in quantity, to ensure that this Transparent copy will remain thus accessible at the stated location until at least one year after the last time you distribute an Opaque copy (directly or through your agents or retailers) of that edition to the public.

It is requested, but not required, that you contact the authors of the Document well before redistributing any large number of copies, to give them a chance to provide you with an updated version of the Document.

4. MODIFICATIONS

You may copy and distribute a Modified Version of the Document under the conditions of sections 2 and 3 above, provided that you release the Modified Version under precisely this License, with the Modified Version filling the role of the Document, thus licensing distribution and modification of the Modified Version to whoever possesses a copy of it. In addition, you must do these things in the Modified Version:

A. Use in the Title Page (and on the covers, if any) a title distinct from that of the Document, and from those of previous versions (which should, if there were any, be listed in the History section of the Document). You may use the same title as a previous version if the original publisher of that version gives permission.

B. List on the Title Page, as authors, one or more persons or entities responsible for authorship of the modifications in the Modified Version, together with at least five of the principal authors of the Document (all of its principal authors, if it has fewer than five), unless they release you from this requirement.

C. State on the Title page the name of the publisher of the Modified Version, as the publisher.

D. Preserve all the copyright notices of the Document.

E. Add an appropriate copyright notice for your modifications adjacent to the other copyright notices.

F. Include, immediately after the copyright notices, a license notice giving the public permission to use the Modified Version under the terms of this License, in the form shown in the Addendum below.

G. Preserve in that license notice the full lists of Invariant Sections and required Cover Texts given in the Document's license notice.

H. Include an unaltered copy of this License.

I. Preserve the section Entitled "History", Preserve its Title, and add to it an item stating at least the title, year, new authors, and publisher of the Modified Version as given on the Title Page. If there is no section Entitled "History" in the Document, create one stating the title, year, authors, and publisher of the Document as given on its Title Page, then add an item describing the Modified Version as stated in the previous sentence.

J. Preserve the network location, if any, given in the Document for public access to a Transparent copy of the Document, and likewise the network locations given in the Document for previous versions it was based on. These may be placed in the "History" section. You may omit a network location for a work that was published at least four years before the Document itself, or if the original publisher of the version it refers to gives permission.

K. For any section Entitled "Acknowledgements" or "Dedications", Preserve the Title of the section, and preserve in the section all the substance and tone of each of the contributor acknowledgements and/or dedications given therein.

L. Preserve all the Invariant Sections of the Document, unaltered in their text and in their titles. Section numbers or the equivalent are not considered part of the section titles.

M. Delete any section Entitled "Endorsements". Such a section may not be included in the Modified Version.

N. Do not retitle any existing section to be Entitled "Endorsements" or to conflict in title with any Invariant Section.

O. Preserve any Warranty Disclaimers.

If the Modified Version includes new front-matter sections or appendices that qualify as Secondary Sections and contain no material copied from the Document, you may at your option designate some or all of these sections as invariant. To do this, add their titles to the list of Invariant Sections in the Modified Version's license notice. These titles must be distinct from any other section titles.

You may add a section Entitled "Endorsements", provided it contains nothing but endorsements of your Modified Version by various parties-- for example, statements of peer review or that the text has been approved by an organization as the authoritative definition of a standard.

You may add a passage of up to five words as a Front-Cover Text, and a passage of up to 25 words as a Back-Cover Text, to the end of the list of Cover Texts in the Modified Version. Only one passage of Front-Cover Text and one of Back-Cover Text may be added by (or through arrangements made by) any one entity. If the Document already includes a cover text for the same cover, previously added by you or by arrangement made by the same entity you are acting on behalf of, you may not add another; but you may replace the old one, on explicit permission from the previous publisher that added the old one.

The author(s) and publisher(s) of the Document do not by this License give permission to use their names for publicity for or to assert or imply endorsement of any Modified Version.

5. COMBINING DOCUMENTS

You may combine the Document with other documents released under this License, under the terms defined in section 4 above for modified versions, provided that you include in the combination all of the Invariant Sections of all of the original documents, unmodified, and list them all as Invariant Sections of your combined work in its license notice, and that you preserve all their Warranty Disclaimers.

The combined work need only contain one copy of this License, and multiple identical Invariant Sections may be replaced with a single copy. If there are multiple Invariant Sections with the same name but different contents, make the title of each such section unique by adding at the end of it, in parentheses, the name of the original author or publisher of that section if known, or else a unique number. Make the same adjustment to the section titles in the list of Invariant Sections in the license notice of the combined work.

In the combination, you must combine any sections Entitled "History" in the various original documents, forming one section Entitled "History"; likewise combine any sections Entitled "Acknowledgements", and any sections Entitled "Dedications". You must delete all sections Entitled "Endorsements."

6. COLLECTIONS OF DOCUMENTS

You may make a collection consisting of the Document and other documents released under this License, and replace the individual copies of this License in the various documents with a single copy that is included in the collection, provided that you follow the rules of this License for verbatim copying of each of the documents in all other respects.

You may extract a single document from such a collection, and distribute it individually under this License, provided you insert a copy of this License into the extracted document, and follow this License in all other respects regarding verbatim copying of that document.

7. AGGREGATION WITH INDEPENDENT WORKS

A compilation of the Document or its derivatives with other separate and independent documents or works, in or on a volume of a storage or distribution medium, is called an "aggregate" if the copyright resulting from the compilation is not used to limit the legal rights of the compilation's users beyond what the individual works permit. When the Document is included in an aggregate, this License does not apply to the other works in the aggregate which are not themselves derivative works of the Document.

If the Cover Text requirement of section 3 is applicable to these copies of the Document, then if the Document is less than one half of the entire aggregate, the Document's Cover Texts may be placed on covers that bracket the Document within the aggregate, or the electronic equivalent of covers if the Document is in electronic form. Otherwise they must appear on printed covers that bracket the whole aggregate.

8. TRANSLATION

Translation is considered a kind of modification, so you may distribute translations of the Document under the terms of section 4. Replacing Invariant Sections with translations requires special permission from their copyright holders, but you may include translations of some or all Invariant Sections in addition to the original versions of these Invariant Sections. You may include a translation of this License, and all the license notices in the Document, and any Warranty Disclaimers, provided that you also include the original English version of this License and the original versions of those notices and disclaimers. In case of a disagreement between the translation and the original version of this License or a notice or disclaimer, the original version will prevail.

If a section in the Document is Entitled "Acknowledgements", "Dedications", or "History", the requirement (section 4) to Preserve its Title (section 1) will typically require changing the actual title.

9. TERMINATION

You may not copy, modify, sublicense, or distribute the Document except as expressly provided for under this License. Any other attempt to copy, modify, sublicense or distribute the Document is void, and will automatically terminate your rights under this License. However, parties who have received copies, or rights, from you under this License will not have their licenses terminated so long as such parties remain in full compliance.

10. FUTURE REVISIONS OF THIS LICENSE

The Free Software Foundation may publish new, revised versions of the GNU Free Documentation License from time to time. Such new versions will be similar in spirit to the present version, but may differ in detail to address new problems or concerns. See http://www.gnu.org/copyleft/.

Each version of the License is given a distinguishing version number. If the Document specifies that a particular numbered version of this License "or any later version" applies to it, you have the option of following the terms and conditions either of that specified version or of any later version that has been published (not as a draft) by the Free Software Foundation. If the Document does not specify a version number of this License, you may choose any version ever published (not as a draft) by the Free Software Foundation

External links

- GNU Free Documentation License (Wikipedia article on the license)

- Official GNU FDL webpage

www.ingramcontent.com/pod-product-compliance
Lightning Source LLC
Chambersburg PA
CBHW080608270326
41928CB00016B/2971